8.50

Date Due		
APR 1 1963		
APR 2 1963		
APR 6 1963		
4 PM		
JAN 24 1966		
NOXXXX 1970 X		
XXXXX 1970		
DEC 10 1970		
X FEB 25 1971		
PRINTED	IN U. S. A.	

8.50

A History of the Ancient Southwest

Mummy Cave, Canyon del Muerto

A HISTORY OF THE

ANCIENT SOUTHWEST

BY HAROLD STERLING GLADWIN

THE BOND WHEELWRIGHT COMPANY, PORTLAND, MAINE, 1957

Acknowledgments

A NUMBER OF the illustrations in this book have been reproduced from various publications, and my thanks are due to the several authors and publishers who have given me permission to make use of their material.

I wish to express my appreciation to the Museum of the American Indian, Heye Foundation, for illustrations and quotations from their series of *Indian Notes;* to the School of American Research for designs from the *Cameron Creek Village* by Wesley Bradfield; to *Arizona Highways* for the illustration of Kinishba; to the Arizona State Museum for quotations, diagrams and illustrations from their *Social Science Bulletins;* to Dr. Ralph L. Beals for quotations and designs from *Archaeological Studies in Northeast Arizona;* to Dr. Harold S. Colton for quotations and plans from publications of the Museum of Northern Arizona; to Harcourt Brace and Company for a quotation from Dr. A. L. Kroeber's *Anthropology;* to the Smithsonian Institution for many quotations and diagrams from the Bulletins and Annual Reports of the Bureau of American Ethnology; to the Southwestern Monuments Association for the illustration of Tuzigoot and permission to photograph ornaments now in the Museum at the Casa Grande National Monument; and, finally, to Dr. J. O. Brew, Director of the Peabody Museum, for permission to quote from the Museum's publications and for his unfailing cooperation and assistance.

In addition to the gratitude that I owe to my friends for their kindnesses and courtesies, I wish particularly to acknowledge my indebtedness to Mrs. Thea Wheelwright for many constructive suggestions and her expert care in seeing this book through the press.

Contents

Illustrations

ILLUSTRATIONS

Introduction

In these days when our world is resounding to the crash of empires and echoing to the thunder of feet of Common Men on the march; when our scientists are predicting dire results from uncontrollable chain reactions, but continue to forge bigger chains and devise more powerful reactions; when our philosophers are lined up along the wailing wall, warning us of inflation, deflation, excess of population, and deficiency of resources, it is a relief to realize that there are some people in this same world who have lived their lives and managed their affairs very well without ever having heard of any of these things.

These people are the Indians who lived and died in the Southwest—that section of North America which covers southwestern Colorado, southern Utah, Arizona, New Mexico, northwestern Chihuahua, northeastern Sonora, and sometimes western Texas and southern California, or an over-all spread of approximately half a million square miles. Within this great area, for a period of ten thousand years or more, there were no problems of overpopulation or exhausted resources, no empires, no flags, bands, parades, or national anthems. Our reconstruction of what happened must be based on such uninspired rubbish as broken fragments of pottery, discarded stone tools, ruined houses, and a few skulls that are often decayed. This is the stuff that constitutes archaeology and, if you do not already know, you will find in the dictionary that an archaeologist is a "student of antiquities," which I take to mean that anyone with a well-developed bump of curiosity who decides to study antiquities thereupon becomes an archaeologist, and strange though it may seem, this is exactly what has often happened. In the Southwest we have had men who started their careers as doctors, lawyers, bankers, brokers, and just plain pick-and-shovel men, but who have spent the best years of their lives digging up dead Indians. Fortunately for us, the Indians have been dead for a long time and cannot protest at the mistakes we make, but I should not be surprised if some of the disturbed burials we find may be the results of the poor devils turning over in their graves.

This brings up the question of how one should go about the study of antiquities so that these inanimate and usually uninteresting objects can be used to identify the various peoples who made them; to find out where they came from; how, when, and where they lived and died; and, finally, what happened to them. Lacking any sort of written records, it sounds like a rather tall order, particularly as it is often difficult to reach agreement on the interpretation of tangible evidence in trying to reconstruct the intangible history of a people. A problem of fundamental importance is posed, for example, when two widely separated groups of people are found to have shared the same knowledge or gadget and one must decide whether such duplications are to be explained as sudden simultaneous independent inventions, or if it is more reasonable to suppose that one group has learned or borrowed from the other. Stated thus, there is some danger of oversimplifying a difficult question, as there are often many factors which may need to be considered. As a general rule, however, it seems to me that when such duplications occur one should begin by suspecting that one group has gained its knowledge from the other, even though the contact or method of diffusion may not be immediately apparent.

A few years ago, a well-known archaeologist came to Santa Barbara to give a lecture on his work in Mexico. Before he began, he had gone to Woolworth's and bought a plain yellow plate, and as he started to talk, he surprised everyone when he smashed the plate by throwing it down. The fragments slid all over the floor. He then went on to explain that these sherds would be swept up by the janitor, mixed with other rubbish, and in due course, thrown on the city dump. In a thousand years or so, a group of archaeologists might run an exploratory trench through the dump—just as archaeologists today cut trenches through ancient rubbish mounds—whereupon they would find the sort of pottery which once was made and used by the people of Santa Barbara. Then, by identifying other articles in the same stratum of the dump, they would be able to establish a definite step in the local cultural development. It was very dramatic and convincing, and I am sure it must have left a lasting impression on the audience. I happened to be sitting near the speaker, however, and when he smashed the plate a large fragment hit my foot. I picked it up and chuckled to myself when I turned it over and found "Made in Japan" printed on the bottom.

Smashing the plate provided an excellent illustration for the explanation of a step in what is known as stratigraphy—meaning simply a recording of successive deposits or layers—but from my point of view, it was an even better illustration of how knowledge and things become widely distributed by communication, imitation, purchase, barter, and theft. I strongly suspect that when and if some archaeologists in the future should cut a cross section through our city dump and should discover the pieces of that yellow plate, they would also find odds and ends from the far corners of the earth, but I know of nothing which might be found in such rubbish that could definitely be said to have originated in Santa Barbara. If, by chance, they should run into a cache of modern perfume bottles, I hope my ghost may be flitting somewhere near by, as it would be great fun to listen to their arguments as to whether such labels as "Danger," "Menace," and "Tabu" should be interpreted as meaning that the bottles had once contained poisons or explosives. It is reasonably certain that no one will guess them to have been love philtres.

As far as the Southwest is concerned, an immense amount of work has been done and countless monographs have been published, but these have usually been confined to single operations and are therefore disconnected and often so technical as to make very tiresome reading even for specialists. The time has come, I think, when someone should try to bring all of this information together and see what it looks like when removed from the classroom and the workshop. In starting such an undertaking, however, it is necessary to post the warning that when one considers the Southwest as a whole one soon runs into a number of interlocking developments which cannot be reconciled with current doctrines and which must be approached from entirely new angles. It is at such a time that one is made to realize that many of the things which have been regarded as established facts are actually nothing more than plausible theories which have gained their authority from frequent repetition, and that many of the old familiar beliefs and classifications have been based on evidence which often was either negative or selective.

To meet the demands which are imposed when one regards the Southwest from an over-all point of view, some new ideas have been advanced in this book which may seem very radical to those who have been brought up on more conventional creeds. It may also be said that I have taken a good many liberties with the work which others have done. This admittedly would be true, and as justification, I can only say that regardless of the care which is taken to obtain sound objective evidence in the field and in the workroom, the interpretation of this evidence, in the last analysis, must depend upon the subjective opinions of the person who makes use of it. Granted a certain amount of commonsense, and using reasonable care, it is a fairly simple matter to dig a ruin, identify the pottery, date some tree-rings, and end up with a report that you have excavated, say, a Chaco site of the tenth century. As more evidence accumulates and your interest broadens, it is not too difficult to take a number of sites from various sections of the Southwest and string them together into several series of successive stages, as has been done in the early chapters of this book. This, however, is very different from the next step where one takes this tangible but impersonal evidence and tries to reconstruct the intangible but personal ways in which people ran their lives, leaving no written records behind them. For those who depend upon the printed word to bring the past to life, it may seem futile to make such an attempt, but to this an archaeologist might reply that written records are often unreliable, if not actually misleading, because of the personal, national, or racial prejudices of the author. In addition, I think it is also true that many, if not most, of the written accounts of ancient civilizations give a somewhat false impression because of too great emphasis on the magnificence of their palaces, monuments, and temples, or the pomp and circumstance of their ruling classes, but not enough about the shapers of stone, the hewers of wood, and the drawers of water, who actually did the work.

In the Southwest there was nothing of this kind. Here one speaks of cultures, not of civilizations. There were kivas, but no temples; rubbish mounds, but no pyramids; pit-houses and pueblos, but no palaces; workers, but no slaves. Nevertheless, the Southwest affords an opportunity of following the activities of various peoples as they adjusted themselves to one another and to the changing conditions of their surroundings over a period of two thousand years. Any individual who attempts to reconstruct the history of these peoples must begin by acknowledging the value of the work which others have done, but he must also admit that he cannot always be governed by their opinions, and in some cases, it may even become necessary to suggest changes in ideas which have been sanctioned by general acceptance. What follows is merely one man's attempt to fit the pieces of the puzzle together.

I

Gila Pueblo

EVERY YEAR there are thousands of people who drive across the desert plateaux of the Southwest, fascinated by its varied beauty and forbidding wastes, amazed by the spectacular ruins of the cliff-dwellings and great pueblos. But they seldom realize that if they should turn off the highway to follow the dirt roads through the reservations of the present-day Indians, they would be as apt as not to drive over someone's home which had been abandoned a thousand years ago. It might be nothing more than a scarcely perceptible mound on the level floor of the desert, perhaps with a few scattered bits of pottery, such as the potsherds with which Job scraped his hide many years ago. If they should stop near by, however, to picnic or to pitch their camp for the night, they would be in danger of being inoculated with the virus of archaeology, for which I know no cure.

That is what happened to us in 1924, and for the next four years we roamed over the Southwest looking for ruins, large and small, photographing them, collecting sherds, and bringing them home in paper bags—an operation which has since come to be known as an archaeological survey. By the autumn of 1928, so much material had accumulated that we realized something would have to be done about it, and a solution was found when our wanderings took us to the neighborhood of Globe, in central Arizona. Here, in September, we came across a very considerable mound of rocks and dirt in Six Shooter Canyon, on the west bank of Pinal Creek. Although it is not usually regarded as an asset in real

Gila Pueblo, in the foothills of the Pinal Mountains

estate, the feature which was partly responsible for our decision to buy the ruin was the character of the pottery on its surface. This was a red ware with a black-on-white decoration which was little known to archaeologists. No one had any idea where it had come from. So, having found a ruin which appeared to have once been a factory for this kind of pottery, we decided that we had found what we had been looking for.

The ruin belonged to a Mrs. Charles Healey who had burrowed into the mound with a whisk broom and a small coal shovel. She had excavated four rooms and what she lacked in knowledge she made up in enthusiasm. One room of her house had been turned into a museum, and on entering, one was greeted by two grinning skulls, with adobe noses, mounted on dress forms to which Mr. Healey had contributed two old army overcoats and his Shriner's fezzes. One wall of the room was festooned with stone axes, hoes, and handstones attached to a length of chicken wire; the other was shelved and here Mrs. Healey had arranged her pottery—and I say *her* advisedly. The first polychrome bowl which she had found was encased in a tight-fitting crocheted cover, painted brown and

Gila Pueblo: The restoration follows the outlines of the old rooms.

varnished, which gave the impression of a deeply indented corrugated exterior. A slipper-shaped jar later turned out to be the nest of a cactus wren. A small round jar was Mrs. Healey's own independent invention, made of Portland cement, covered with canvas, painted brown and varnished, and finished off with a fillet-rim of adhesive tape. And, finally, some fairly large polychrome jars had been completely covered with gold paint in order to show what might have been accomplished if the old people had known about the gold that could be panned in the arroyo west of the Pueblo.

Unfortunately, her efforts were entirely wasted on us, for we were more interested in the polychrome in its original state than in Mrs. Healey's attempts to gild these lilies. Later, after experimenting with various solvents without success, we found that soaking in water and scraping gave the best results, but it did not endear the old lady to us when we had to break the ice in the tubs before starting to scrape her embellishments off the pots.

As soon as we reached an agreement with the Healeys we pitched our tents and began the excavation of the ruin, in October, 1928. As each room was cleared, we rebuilt the walls with rocks and mortar, and in order to retain as much of the character of the original building as possible, we used local Mexican stonemasons who had to trust to their eyes, without the help of level, square, or plumb line. We followed the outlines of the old walls, except for the pottery halls and library which had to be shelved, and when two or three rooms were found to be superimposed, we built two or three stories accordingly. As the restoration progressed, we moved in. First, our secretary, Edith Sangster—without whom we would never have been able to master the problems which arose in evolving a new approach to the study of archaeology. Next, our catalogues and files which she had typed in a tent, with time out to thaw her fingers over an oil stove. Then came storage of material and finally, ourselves. We named our ruin Gila Pueblo, and as Gila is pronounced Heela, this pleased everyone, particularly the Healeys who always referred to it as Healey Pueblo.

BY 1935 the reconstruction of Gila Pueblo was finished, and we had a place for everything, and everything was in its place. The Texas Room was bulging at the seams with the rocks and stones which Sayles had collected and which, he assured us, represented the cream of Texan archaeology. Nevertheless, while stone industries are of absorbing interest to some men, for us pottery is the one product of a people's culture which best reflects their changing fashions. It is indestructible and provides a yardstick by means of which other things can be arranged in their proper order.

When describing the work at Gila Pueblo, the place to begin is the Workroom which was the center of all our activities—surveys, excavations, and speculations—a hive which was constantly humming with the ideas and arguments of archaeologists from all over the world.

To us, our survey ranked first in importance, and from the time the dirt-encrusted sherds were picked up from the ground, they went through an elaborate process, finally emerging as the dictionary of an ancient language of which there is no other written record. The dusty bags of sherds were brought in from near and far and stacked in rows on shelves in the sherd laundry which was an annex of the Workroom. Each bag was marked in the field with its site number in accordance with our map of western North America which covered one of the walls in the North Hall of the Pueblo. This map was divided into quadrangles, covering one degree of latitude and longitude, most of which have been given names such as Kaibab and Wingate. On this map, each such quadrangle was divided into sixteen rectangles of equal size, covering an area of about fourteen by seventeen miles, and sites were then numbered consecutively as found within each rectangle. According to this system, the tenth ruin which we found in the eighth rectangle of the Wingate quadrangle simply became Wingate: 8:10. This automatically placed the site in a certain section of the Southwest, but of even more importance, the alphabetical listing of quadrangles and

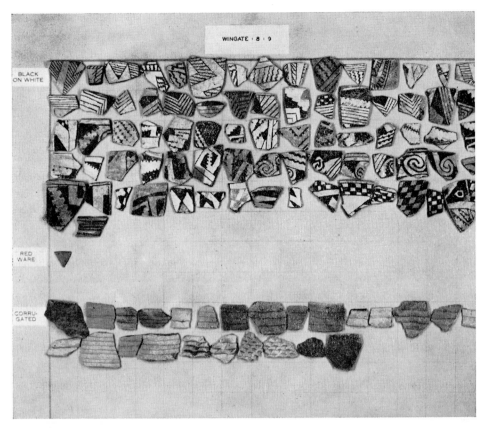

A Sherd-board
The 9th ruin in the 8th rectangle of the Wingate Quadrangle

the numbering of rectangles and sites greatly simplified our filing and cataloguing systems.

As soon as a site was found and given a name it became a part of Gila Pueblo. A Detail Sheet was filled out, describing its location, size, condition, and surroundings; a collection of sherds was made; and a photograph was usually taken. Upon arrival at the Pueblo, the sherds started down an assembly line in wire trays, in which they were soaked in hot water, steeped in acid, scrubbed, rinsed, and finally spread out in wire-bottomed drawers to dry. When thoroughly dry, the sherds were sorted into their various classes; their percentages were figured and listed; sheets of beaverboard, 24 x 30 inches, were ruled into two-inch squares; appropriate labels were stencilled; and when the sherds had been glued down, our sherd-boards served as the leaves of a book which represented the essence of Southwestern archaeology. In addition, we who had worked with them had gained a much better knowledge of the people who had made the original pots than many years of academic work could have given us.

DURING THE WINTER of 1935 the Pueblo was seething. Sayles had returned from his survey of Chihuahua after removing a very considerable part of the state and sending it up to Gila Pueblo. Haury had finished two seasons' work in the San Francisco and Mimbres valleys, and our archaeological storage was knee-deep with chunks of lava of assorted sizes and a ton or more of sherds waiting to be transmuted into pearls of wisdom. On top of all else, we had started the excavation of Snaketown in September, and trucks and people were shuttling back and forth between camp and the Pueblo—all loaded to capacity, the trucks with sacks and cartons of sherds, the people with ideas and problems. Most of the week was spent in catching up with the week-ends when the men came up from Snaketown, bringing smashed pottery which needed to be sorted out and restored. Breakfast was no sooner over than everyone—family, guests, and staff—made a beeline to the Workroom. Men and women who never before had stood up to a washtub, blossomed out in smocks or rubber aprons to spend hours scrubbing sherds, or were late for meals while they searched through trays to find fragments of the pot they were mending. The peak of excitement was reached when Sayles found a demolished storeroom at Snaketown in which fifty-two large jars had been arranged in rows and stacked one above another. The room was 12 x 18 feet and when the roof had crashed the jars were smashed and the floor was covered with plain and decorated sherds to a depth of a foot or more. Sayles marked off the floor into blocks, 3 feet square, lettered along the top and numbered down the side, and after packing the sherds of each block separately, sent them up to the Pueblo to be washed, sorted, and mended. It was equivalent to taking fifty jigsaw puzzles and mixing them all together, but out of the mass of sherds, we succeeded in recovering twenty-six decorated and six plain jars, each so large that the sherds covered a ping-pong table when laid out before being cemented together.

When one had ransacked all the trays and had incited to riot by taking likely looking sherds from other tables, the real fun began. First, two sherds were stuck together with a cellulose cement, held in place with small clamps, laundry clips, or adhesive tape, and balanced in a box filled with sand. Then pairs were fitted to pairs (before the cement had set so as to be sure to get the true curve of the pot), and so on, until the pieces grew to be too large to balance in sand and extra hands were needed. At this stage, while one person held up the neck of a thirty-gallon jar and someone else steadied the bottom, a third could fill in the sides while everyone held their breath and twisted their tongues into knots. Then a broad trunkstrap, provided with a turnbuckle, was fitted and gradually tightened around the greatest circumference, and everyone was warned to keep hands off. Finally, when the cement had thoroughly dried, the pot was turned over to Gladys Sayles who, with plaster, paint, and an extraordinary ability, filled in the missing pieces and gave us a pot which was as good as new. It was a fascinating job and many's the time when, reading in our rooms after a long day, our minds have met without a word being said and we have sneaked quietly down to the Workroom to stick together a few sherds—only to find that others had had the same idea. I think it would please the old girls who originally made the pots if they could realize how much we liked their work and the trouble we took to do justice to their craftsmanship.

MENDING AND RESTORING POTS was always popular, as one could see the finished result of one's work, but to learn about the people who made the pots which were being mended, we held daily meetings known as Sherd Classes.

A Sherd Class consisted of taking about fifty sherd-boards from some one section of the Southwest, say the eleventh rectangle of the Wingate quadrangle. These boards were stacked upright on a table, one in front of another, in the pottery hall which contained the collections from the Wingate district. Then our staff and any visitors who chose to attend discussed the status of each site, and in spite of free-for-all argument—or perhaps because of it—there was never any permanent disagreement. This, I think, was undoubtedly due to the fact that the method we employed in judging a site was simple and direct.

This method was based on the belief that all peoples in the development of their culture have passed through a series of successive steps, or what we have called *phases*, regardless of whether the rate was fast or slow or the trend up or down. In our survey of the Southwest, the recognition of such phases has usually been simplified by finding site after site showing the same types of pottery and architecture, and it is hardly necessary to add that the more monotonous the repetition, the more valid the phase.

Having identified a phase, one can then go on to say that since the development of culture was a continuous process, it should be possible to connect a series of consecutive phases in the same line of evolution into what we call a *branch*, such as the Chaco Branch, which is synonymous with what is otherwise known as the Chaco Culture.

From this it can be seen that, granted some knowledge of Southwestern pottery, there was little about which to disagree. As each site was ticked off, it was recorded as belonging in a certain phase of a certain branch. When all of the sites within a rectangle had been thus identified, the percentages of the various phases and branches therein were shown as the colored segments of a small disc which was then fixed to the large map in the North Hall. On this map, each branch was represented by a certain color, and as there were very few rectangles in the Southwest which were not covered by discs, one could tell at a glance where various peoples had concentrated and whether they were stay-puts or gadabouts.

It was the constant mulling over of problems of this kind which often resulted in sudden enlightenment as to the status of types of pottery which formerly had not been placed. Up to 1935, for example, the decorated pottery in the valley of the Rio Puerco had generally been regarded as "stuff" that was of interest only to pot-hunters. But when we tackled the survey of the Puerco district in our Sherd Classes, Edith Sangster protested that anything which came up as regularly as did some of the pottery from these sites could not be shrugged off as "stuff" simply because no one knew anything about it. She was perfectly right, and it was as a direct result of her protest that we extended our survey of the Puerco in the summer of 1935, selected White Mound Village for excavation in 1936, and opened up an entirely new aspect of early times in the Southwest.

This procedure of undertaking the excavation of a ruin only after a survey had been made was our invariable practice at Gila Pueblo. A survey was the only method known to us of placing a people and their culture in their proper setting, and it was therefore an essential first step in approaching any archaeological problem. I often wish that we had kept track of the miles we have travelled, for since 1924, we or the people who have worked with us have covered a good deal of the country lying between the Pacific Coast and the Mississippi. We have ranged as far north as Montana and as far south as Zacatecas, and from our wanderings we have brought back the descriptions, the sherds, the stone chips and tools, wood and charcoal for dating, and often the photographs, from about ten thousand sites—small, middling, and large. From beginning to end, our purpose has been the same—to obtain a background against which we could draw the boundaries, trace the movements and developments, and eventually attempt to reconstruct the history of the peoples who have lived in this vast and varied land.

The Land and Its People

ALTHOUGH THE SOUTHWEST is littered with ruins, one of its greatest charms is its emptiness. There is a profound sense of peace in the great reaches of open country and the silence and solitude of its canyons. The sky and the weather are so important a part of the Southwest that it is easy to understand how the people who have lived there have been governed by the march of the seasons and the cycles of sun and moon and stars.

An archaeologist in the Southwest has not only the fascinating jobs of treasure hunter and detective to lure him, but in addition a land of incomparable beauty in which to live and work. It is a land of infinite variety, the climate and color of the northern country offering greater attractions than the dust and heat of the southern deserts. On the white headlands of Mesa Verde snow and rainfall are heavy, and the mesas are covered with forests of fir, pine, pinyon, and juniper. About one hundred airline miles to the west lies Monument Valley with its towering red sandstone cliffs. Then south through Marsh Pass, between Black and Skeleton mesas, is Tuba City, where the land is bare and eroded and there is no ground cover. Still farther south are the Painted Desert and the barren wastes of the Little Colorado Basin, turning gradually to gently rolling country bounded by belts of juniper, until the Mogollon Rim is reached at the southern border of the Colorado Plateau. From Seligman in the northwest to the mountains of the Upper Gila in southwestern New Mexico, the sheer escarpment of the Mogollon

Antelope House in Canyon del Muerto

Rim stretches diagonally across central Arizona as a formidable barrier. From its crest, at seven thousand feet or more, the land falls away through broken forested country to the drainage of the Gila and the desert of southern Arizona.

Across this broad stage with its mountains and forests, plateaux and deserts, its cloudbursts and droughts, piercing cold and burning heat, its far horizons and glowing sunsets, various peoples played their parts and have provided us with a vivid drama of human history. For everyone who travels west across the deserts and plateaux of New Mexico and Arizona, the modern descendants of the earlier settlers are to be found on every hand—around Sante Fe, at Acoma, Zuni, the Hopi Villages, or in the desert near Phoenix. But to know these people at their best, you must project your mind back about nine hundred years into the past when they were reaching the peak of their development, to those days before there was a Santa Fe Railroad and its Harvey Houses, or a Highway 66; when there were no trading posts or Indian Agencies, no tourists, no Spaniards, no horses, cattle, or sheep, no clocks, and no money.

At A.D. 1050, the great pueblos in Chaco Canyon, in northwestern New Mexico, were thriving communities. People were living in apartment houses of several hundred rooms, four and five stories high; the men skilled masons and weavers; the women experts in the making of pottery and baskets.

Pueblo Bonito: Chaco Canyon

Cliff Palace: Mesa Verde

In the eleventh and twelfth centuries, the people on Mesa Verde, in south-western Colorado, were developing their arts and crafts in the shelter of their great cliff-dwellings, built in the recesses of the canyon walls.

In Tsegi Canyon and the Province of Tusayan, from the Utah line south to the Verde Valley, were people of another tribe who made and did things which, while similar in some respects, were stamped with their own individuality.

Near Zuni, in the Province of Cibola in western New Mexico, was still another tribe with colonies reaching eastward past Acoma and Laguna to the upper Rio Grande Valley.

To the south, below the Mogollon Rim, were the ancestors of the modern Papago and Pima tribes, who wrested their living from the mountains and deserts of southern Arizona, and who also contributed in some degree to the progress of the various Pueblo peoples on the Plateau, to the north.

In surroundings where white men often have a good deal of difficulty in making both ends meet, these various Southwestern tribes not only succeeded in maintaining themselves but also developed cultures which rank favorably with other native American civilizations and in most cases have outlasted them. When we visit the Tanoan Pueblos of today near Santa Fe, or the Shoshonean Hopi in their villages north of Winslow, we are apt to lose sight of the fact that their architecture, pottery, and other arts, their costumes, dances, and ceremonies, their language and their physique, are all direct heritages from those remote ancestors who long ago drifted into the Southwest and decided to stay there.

We know these people best in their modern setting, and to reconstruct their history we would ordinarily work down from the present into the past. We can do this, however, only as far back as the nineteenth century. Then we run into difficulties since all of the cliff-dwellings and most of the great pueblos had been abandoned before A.D. 1500. A few, such as Oraibi, Zuni, and Acoma, survived the Spanish invasion and remain to this day as living monuments to the life of another era. However, beyond stimulating the imagination and affording an example of an unbelievably picturesque and archaic way of life, they add little to the sum of archaeological knowledge. Unfortunately for the student of history, the modern Pueblos do not seem to be capable of providing any information as to their earlier background. They show no interest in their point of origin or how they came to be what and where they are, and they object strenuously to any poking around in their past if it involves digging up their relatives or taking their pueblos apart to see how they were built.

Acoma: a pueblo which has been continuously occupied since before the days of the Spanish invasion.

Another reason for our lack of knowledge covering the last four hundred years is that the so-called "historic" period of the Pueblos is an almost complete blank as far as information from the Spaniards about the native peoples and their cultures is concerned. The best known of the early Spanish accounts is Castañeda's *Narrative of the Coronado Expedition in* A.D. *1540.* It seems, however, that after spending over two years exploring the Southwest, while Spanish dreams of wealth evaporated into thin air, Castañeda was more concerned in trying to

A Pima and his round house, Snaketown, Arizona

forget the discomforts and disappointments of his trip than in writing an account of the endless days tramping through the blinding heat of the desert. Whatever the cause—and being encased in a cocoon of leather and steel armor during two summers in the Southwest would be enough to quench most men's initiative— Castañeda waited for twenty years before buckling down to the job of writing his descriptions of the country and the events which had occurred. As a result, it is now impossible even to trace the route which was followed by the expedition because of the difficulty of identifying actual localities with Castañeda's recollection of landmarks after such a lapse of time.

Whether a day will ever come when a reliable history of the Southwest can be written by working down from the present into the past is a question that is open to a good deal of doubt. As things stand at present, there can be no doubt that our best course is to work up from the past to the present. This is not as difficult as it sounds, since from the point of view of an archaeologist, the bones and stones and pottery he digs up are often more dependable as evidence than the narratives of individuals which are sometimes colored by sentiment or personal prejudices. In addition, we now have an immense amount of evidence which has been gathered over the years. From the geologists we have learned of the changes on the earth's surface which affected the movements of men. From the palaeontologists we have reports as to the animals of another era which hunted and were hunted by the early discoverers of North America—thousands of years before Leif Ericsson or Christopher Columbus discovered these discoverers. Above all we have a mass of reports on the patient delving of hundreds of archaeologists from various museums and universities. Most of this evidence has come from ruins on the Plateau, and of this the greater part has been obtained from the large pueblos and cliff-dwellings which were occupied in the eleventh, twelfth, and thirteenth centuries. During recent years we have learned more about what happened below the Mogollon Rim, and this has helped to an understanding of much that formerly was incomprehensible. To us, however, the thread on which all of these facts are strung is the survey which has recorded a great number of the small and early sites which often are indicated by nothing more than a depression, a low mound, or a few scattered sherds. It has been the survey which has made it possible to bring together all of the separate accounts of excavations in various areas and so to attempt to write a continuous history of development and dispersion throughout the whole of the Southwest.

III

As It Was in the Beginning

WHEN WE SET OUT on an adventure of writing a tale of this kind we can begin by saying that there are some questions which can be answered with a fair degree of certainty, but we must also admit that there are some problems which cannot now and probably never will be solved to our complete satisfaction. On the positive side we can say with assurance that men did not originate in the Americas, since there are no signs of the subhuman prologue, such as have been found in Asia and Africa, nor is there any evidence of the fossil remains of such early human types as those which have turned up in Java, China, Europe, and Africa. So it is reasonably certain that men reached North America from somewhere outside its borders, and it is generally believed that they came over from Asia in a series of migrations. Beyond this, and contrary to the common belief, the earliest Americans were not Mongoloid but actually were members of the so-called Australoid family which, in the old, old days, roamed over most of the earth. The hallmarks of this family were their beetling brow-ridges, receding foreheads, broad noses, and protruding muzzles—a combination of features which was characteristic of some of the oldest fossil skulls in southeastern Asia, China, and Europe, and has come down into more recent times in India, Australia, North and South America, without as much change as we would expect, considering the great distances and the length of time that separate the ancient and modern. In North America, people who were related in greater or less degree to this Australoid family were once distributed from the coast of southern California eastward to central Texas. You can form a fairly good idea of what the early settlers in the Southwest may have looked like if you can conjure up a sort of composite portrait of a Dravidian Untouchable, a Hairy Ainu, and an Australian Blackfellow—all of whom were also good Australoids.

In addition to any physical likeness that may have been shared, it also looks as if these early Southwesterners made, used, and did many of the same things as their Australian cousins. As weapons, they both used spears with blunt wooden tips for stunning or stone points for piercing, spear-throwers, bone daggers, and curved wooden throwing-clubs or boomerangs. They both twirled bull-roarers, and they both practiced strange ways of mutilating themselves, such as scarifying their hides, knocking out teeth, and lopping off finger joints—activities which wherever and whenever found would seem to indicate the presence of an Australoid in person since these are scarcely the sort of things which friends or acquaintances would be apt to copy. It is a far cry from Australia to the Southwest and the connections are rather roundabout, so that our first inclination is to dismiss as absurd any suggestion that early settlers in the Southwest

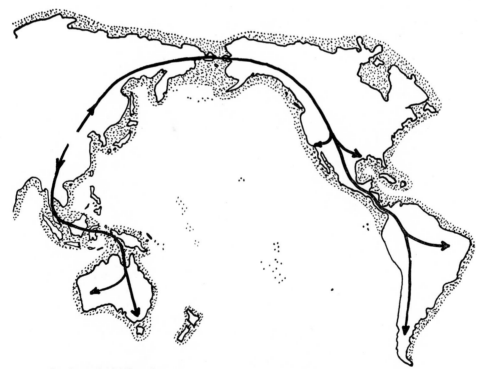

The Australoid Migrations
The Australoids moved down into Australia and across to North America at a time when many islands and continents were joined owing to the lowering of sea level during the last Ice Age. The stippled areas indicate an approximate outline of the coasts which were exposed at the peak of the glaciation.

and the native Australians were originally derived from the same source. A little calm reflection, however, will reveal that the idea is not at all absurd. If, for example, it be granted that men did not originate in the Americas, it would be reasonable to suppose that they came over here from Asia. It is even more certain that men did not evolve from the marsupials in Australia and that the Blackfellows also began their careers on the mainland of Asia. With American and Australian Australoids both spreading out from eastern Asia, and so many physical and cultural resemblances between them, the most plausible explanation seems to be that the early migrants to America and Australia had both originally been distilled out of the same eastern Asiatic brew. Not only is this a reasonable possibility, but it also seems likely that one reason why the Australoids were so widely scattered throughout Europe, Asia, Oceania, and over into the Americas is that they did most of their wandering at a time when many islands and some of the continents were joined due to the lowering of the level of the sea. This occurred during the Pleistocene, or Ice Age, when a large amount of our planet's moisture was impounded in the form of glaciers and ice-sheets, and as a result, the sea level is said to have been lowered some 300 feet or more, exposing land bridges where today there is only open water. The importance of this to our immediate problem is that during the Pleistocene there must have been a number of different occasions when the Bering Isthmus was exposed and it became possible for men and animals to pass dry-shod back and forth between Siberia and Alaska.

When these events took place is a subject for speculation which can best be left to the geologists and geophysicists who are still grappling with the problem—and with each other. When and if they ever reach agreement it will be time for us to make the necessary adjustments, but we are now chiefly concerned with the kinds of people who reached the Southwest, the things they brought with them, and the order of their arrival.

The earliest periods belong to the Stone Age and are rather hazy, since to most people stone tools are the least interesting of all of man's handiwork, being usually crude, often heavy, and sometimes difficult to distinguish from pebbles or boulders that have been banged around in a stream. From a purely archaeological point of view, stone industries are hard to judge, owing to the slowness of change over long periods of time, as the idea seems to have been general in the old days that what was good enough for my grandfather-one-thousand-times-removed is good enough for me. As a result it is usually difficult, if not impossible, to tell the difference between a milling stone which was used to grind seeds at 5,000 B.C. and one which was in use as recently as one hundred years ago. As far as most of us are concerned—

> A handstone by the river's brim
> A sandstone handstone was to him
> And it was nothing more.

From a more philosophical point of view, we should give due credit to our forefathers' ability to make good use of stones, since it gave them an advantage over other animals which were bigger, stronger, or faster than they, and it is probably just as well for the human race that no other animal can pitch a five-ounce rock over a plate 17 inches wide for a call of three strikes. So, even though they may not interest those of us who are accustomed to measuring progress by more sensitive standards, let us grant that stone tools played an important part in helping our ancestors to crack each other's skulls and in protecting them from other beasts of prey.

At a conservative estimate, men have been using stone tools for well over one hundred thousand years, and some anthropologists would set the date back to five hundred thousand years or more. The development of such tools was very slow and uneven, and it is said that in the early stages men went along for thousands of years without changing so simple a thing as a pear-shaped hand axe. As Kroeber wrote in his *Anthropology:* "It may be said with approximate accuracy that the long Chellean period possessed only the one tool; that this is the first definitely shaped tool known to have been made by human hands; and that it is therefore the concrete evidence of the first stage of that long development which we call civilization." He then went on to add that twenty thousand of these axes had been found at St. Acheul in the valley of the Somme—but whether this means that twenty thousand Acheulians each had his own axe or a smaller number had one for each day of the week has not yet been settled.

Although these axes are useless to us as time-markers, they are important in having been the first stone tools to be worked to a definite shape by percussion-flaking—that is to say, by striking off flakes from a nodule of flint, leaving a core of the desired shape. They should also make us realize that primitive man was not the inventive genius that has so often been claimed, since there is no doubt that the pear-shaped hand axe lasted without change for many thousands of years. Speaking for myself, I am willing to admit that my Stone Age ancestors were not very bright when it came to inventing a new kind of stone tool. They appear to have collected axes as their descendants now collect bottle caps and match-folders, but with thousands of axes available for experiment, it took thousands of years before anyone tried to improve the shape of a tool which was in daily use and used for every purpose.

In both the Old and the New Worlds the progression of stone industries seems to have been the same, with one possible exception to be mentioned. In Norfolk in the Old, and Texas in the New World, the earliest stone tools were so-called eoliths which show no uniformity and were little more than stones roughly shaped to fit the hand. If you should find one, it is very doubtful if you would recognize it as an eolith, and if you did, it is even more doubtful if you could persuade anyone else that your eolith had been intentionally shaped by man.

In the Old World and probably also in Texas, the Eolithic, or Dawn Stone Age, was followed by the Palaeolithic, or Old Stone Age, which began with hand axes shaped by percussion and after some thousands of years, ended with a wide range of knives, blades, scrapers, and points shaped by pressure-flaking.

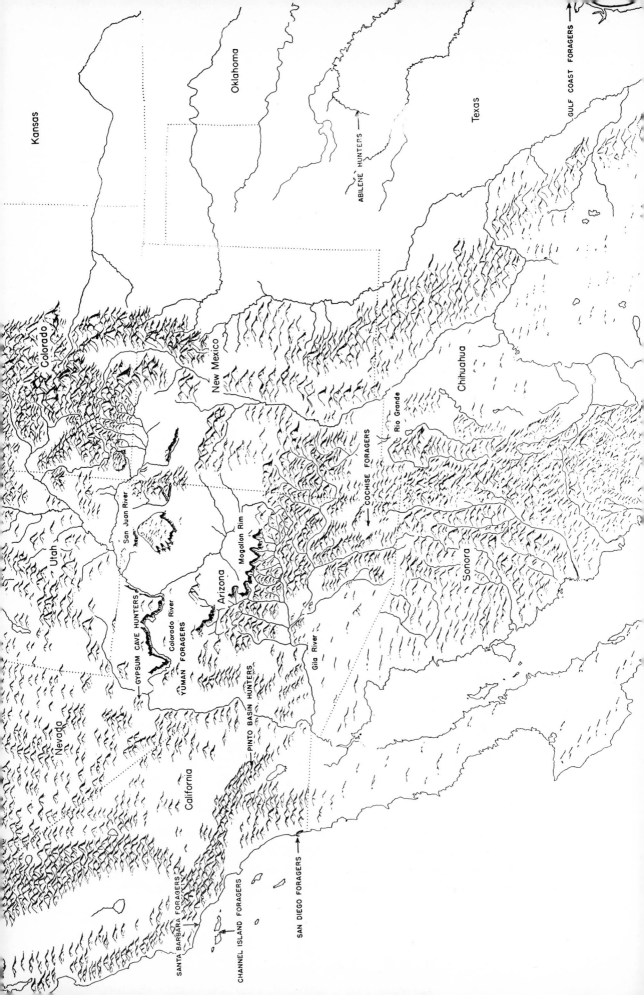

In many cases, the shapes of the tools and the techniques of making them were often so nearly the same in both hemispheres that it seems as if they must have been successive chips off the same block. But while this is probably true, it should be emphasized that there is no one Old World culture in its entirety which is the same as any one American culture as a whole. The most that can be said is that as knowledge and skills increased in Europe and Asia, there was an intermittent stream of diffusion which flowed through northeastern Asia into North America and resulted in parallel developments.

The succession from an eolithic to a percussion to a pressure-flaking method of shaping stone tools was a natural and understandable progression, since it would not be logical to suppose that primitive men could have achieved the perfection of shaping blades by pressure-flaking before they had managed to bang a hand axe into shape. It is hardly necessary to add that it would have required less skill to make a shapeless eolith than either a standardized hand axe or a symmetrical blade. So the sequence of development during the Eolithic and Palaeolithic Stone Ages is self-evident.

We come now to a method of shaping and using stone tools which cannot safely be assigned to its place in the series by any rule of thumb, and it may be that the succession was not the same in the Old and New Worlds. These are the ground stone tools, sometimes polished, which used to be regarded as one of the distinguishing characteristics of the Neolithic or New Stone Age. It is true that they have not been found in any of the Palaeolithic cultures of western Europe, but in the Americas ground stone tools are common, widespread, and in some areas—notably in southern California, southeastern Arizona, and coastal Texas—they have been found in some of the earliest sites. A few years ago, when opposition to early man in America was rampant, the discovery of ground stone tools in a site was all that was needed to discredit any claim to antiquity, since by European standards the site would automatically be classified as Neolithic, or later. There is, however, nothing inherently modern or technically advanced in rubbing one stone against another, and it would seem more reasonable to regard the presence of ground stone tools in a site as an indication of a way of life rather than to insist that such tools are, *ipso facto*, proof that their makers were more recent or more skillful than the knappers of a pressure-flaked blade.

This is a simple approach to the problem, but the acceptance of what appears to be a reasonable explanation carries some weighty implications. The vast majority of ground stone tools, particularly those in early sites, were milling stones which were used for grinding seeds and nuts. This suggests, first, that some ancient Americans depended more upon food gathering and less upon hunting than their Old World counterparts, and this, in turn, implies that the variety of edible plants, roots, tubers, seeds, nuts, and fruits may have been considerably greater in America than in Europe and Asia—an idea which is also strongly supported by the many new vegetables which were introduced into Europe from America after A.D. 1500.

◄ **Hunters and Foragers of the Stone Age in the Southwest**

Although it is undoubtedly true that hunters used vegetable foods when they were available and that foragers ate game when they could catch it, nevertheless the character and specialization of their tools usually makes it possible to draw a distinction between those people who were principally hunters and those who were primarily foragers. In central Texas, for example, sites near Abilene yield projectile points and specialized scrapers, but no milling stones, and I think the people have been properly described as hunters. Along the coast of southern California, on the other hand, ancient sites contain milling stones, but projectile points are rare or completely absent, and in such cases it seems that the people had depended chiefly upon vegetable products, such as acorns, nuts, and seeds, which were ground into meal.

When these standards are applied to some of the sites lying between the coast of southern California and central Texas, it looks as if the people on the Channel Islands and along the coast from Santa Barbara down to San Diego were foragers with main dependence on sea food and the annual crops of wild seeds and acorns. To the east, the Pinto Basin site, in the middle of what is now the desert of southern California, has been said by the Campbells to represent an ancient hunting culture at a time when this section of the country was a more favored land than it is today. So also with Gypsum Cave, in southern Nevada, where Harrington found a hunting culture in association with remains of ground sloths. In southeastern Arizona the people were foragers with minor dependence on hunting. In western Texas they began as hunters and wound up as foragers. In central Texas they were hunters, and on the Gulf Coast they were foragers.

In addition to these distinctions, which have been drawn on the strength of differences in the kinds of tools that were used, there is also the fact that sites of the hunting cultures, such as the Pinto Basin and Abilene, do not show enough depth of debris to indicate even semi-permanent habitation. In foragers' sites, on the other hand, one often finds several feet of rubbish consisting of shells, charcoal, broken and discarded implements and ornaments, and dark earth stained by organic matter, so indicating a more sedentary kind of existence. But although these remarks hold true in most instances, it is well to repeat that the two means of livelihood were not mutually exclusive, as it has been shown in some of the later sites that food gathering and hunting were often combined. The examples I have mentioned are merely intended to show that some of the cultural characteristics of some of the early people sometimes serve to indicate how they lived and that their living was largely governed by their environment.

THESE VARIOUS and scattered instances should make it clear that there is a considerable amount of early evidence to be sifted and weighed. This evidence provides us with an outline of the adaptations of culture made by the early pioneers to meet the changes in climate, fauna, and flora, which occurred in the Southwest, California, and Texas, following the Wisconsin Glaciation. These adjustments resulted in some of these groups becoming hunters, others foragers, and since these developments took place during the Stone Age when changes of culture were slow and gradual, it is to be supposed that they were spread over a long period of time. How long, in hundreds or thousands of years, is a question for which we shall have to wait for an answer until the study of Earth Sciences can provide us with a more exact chronology than is now available. In the meanwhile, all that an archaeologist can do is to guess, and it is unfortunate that our record up to date has been very poor, since we have invariably overestimated the age of the things we find.

When and if you decide to make your own guesses there are a few things to bear in mind. One of these is that even by the shortest count there is now a date of about 10,000 B.C. for the presence of man in North America, and there is no way of telling how far future discoveries or changes in present beliefs may push this date back into the past. New knowledge or ideas about the antiquity of man in America can only lead in one direction—backward in time.

Another point to remember is that if men had not reached North America before 10,000 B.C., the same men were circulating around somewhere in eastern Asia, and it would not have made them a day older to have crossed Bering Strait.

Finally, the old bare bones of animals long since dead may someday help in bringing the past to life again. One often reads, for example, that an archaeologist somewhere in the Southwest, California, or Texas has found human remains associated with the bones of strange creatures, such as mammoth, ground sloth, camel, horse, direwolf, and other extinct animals. In Europe, the discovery of man or his works mixed up with such extinct fauna has usually been regarded as satisfactory evidence that the combination was really ancient and probably harked back to the Pleistocene. In America, however, the age of man cannot thus simply be settled. On a number of occasions it has seemed that God has proposed a respectable antiquity for some of our early settlers, but in each case our scientists have disposed of the evidence as unsatisfactory. Here, when man's remains have been found in association with the bones of extinct animals, we are told that the mere presence of man proves the animals to have been recent, even though now extinct. This may be quite right, but it would be easier to understand if the lists of animals in such early sites included more of the bones of existing species. As things stand at present, it is seldom that one hears of extinct and existing creatures being found together in the same site, and this leaves us with the puzzling question of how one entire faunal assemblage could so suddenly have disappeared and have been replaced by what we have today.

As a part of general human backgrounds, speculations as to the age of ancient men and the debris they left behind them are interesting, but they have only an indirect bearing on the problems which lie ahead. As far as the Southwest is concerned, consecutive history does not begin until the time of Christ, and for the last two thousand years we have a continuous tree-ring chronology to help us in keeping the record straight. There was undoubtedly some carry-over of knowledge and techniques from earlier times as the centuries rolled along, and it would be reasonable to suppose that some of the physical features of the ancients might show up as latent but persisting factors in some of the later groups by whom they were replaced. This might account for the short stature and other peculiarities of some of the tribes in marginal and out-of-the-way places in North and South America. The problems of the early periods in American history are admittedly obscure, but this does not alter the fact that something is flitting about among the shadows, and I doubt if we shall ever realize the full significance of the American story if we slight the evidence, slim though it may be, of the high antiquity of the earliest people to reach our shores.

I V

As It Was at the Time of Christ

WITH THE ENDING of the Stone Age in the Americas at about the time of Christ, we come to the end of an era. It was a period of primitive men on the move, of ice-sheets, pluvials, and weird animals, and it belongs chiefly to the geologists and the specialists in fossils of various kinds. It is only reasonable to suppose, however, that there must have been some sort of continuity between the hunters and foragers of the Stone Age and the people who were responsible for the later cultures, and the time has come for us to identify the men and women who were concerned with the events which are about to take place.

THE DATE is within a century or two of the birth of Christ. In favorable locations, from the coast of Southern California to the Gulf Coast of Texas, men and their families had settled down to make the most of what the country had to offer. They were all interrelated to the extent that they were all descended from the earlier pioneers of the Stone Age who originally had settled in these same regions, and the fact that they had selected or had been forced into an area well below the southernmost limits of the ice-sheet is at least suggestive that they may have reached North America before the maximum of the Wisconsin Glaciation. Some, such as the foragers in southeastern Arizona, had chosen the hot open valleys of Cochise County where they could depend on the annual harvest of mesquite beans, cactus fruit, and wild seeds, with several kinds of yucca as a stand-by, and an occasional trip to the Chiricahua Mountains to collect acorns and pinyon nuts. Some had selected the broken forested country of the Upper Gila drainage where they took advantage of the caves for shelter and hunted the game which abounds in these mountains. A large number had settled in the valley and canyons of the Colorado River, from the Grand Canyon westward to Nevada and south along the river to the Gulf of California. These were the ancestors of the modern Yuman tribes who have occupied this region since time immemorial, and it is with an eastward extension of these ancient Yuman foragers that we now have to deal.

This branch of the family had penetrated eastward into northern Arizona to seek their fortune, and through no fault of their own, have come to be known as Basket Makers. That they made baskets is true, but so did their ancestors and their descendants, besides most of the other Indian tribes that are known. Nevertheless it is by this name that this particular tribe has become established in the lore of the Southwest, although no satisfactory explanation has yet been advanced to show who they were or where they came from.

In 1927 a number of archaeologists gathered together at Dr. Kidder's camp at Pecos, New Mexico, and held a conference as a result of which the legitimacy of the Basket Makers was recognized, even though no one was willing to venture a guess as to who their parents might have been. To cover their cultural progress the conferees coined three periods—termed Basket Maker I, II, and III—but of these Basket Maker I was nothing more than a notion that he must have been a hunter, since he was supposed to have lived at a time before agriculture, pottery, or houses were known in the Southwest. Basket Maker II was granted knowledge of agriculture, particularly corn and squash which had been found in the earliest Basket Maker sites; and Basket Maker III was defined by the presence of true fired pottery. Since 1927 a great deal of work has been done in the Southwest, but no one has yet succeeded in producing an acceptable Basket Maker hunter, and I think the time has come when we should be willing to compromise on a forager to fill the Basket Maker I vacancy, particularly as none of the later members of the family showed any signs of having inherited noticeable skill as hunters. It should be stipulated, of course, that such a forager knew nothing about corn or pottery, and also that he possessed something in the way of physical features or habits to link him to the later and better known Basket Makers, as otherwise we should be swamped with claims from all sorts and conditions of vagabonds that they were the ancestors of our Basket Makers.

If this proposal is acceptable, there are a number of candidates from whom to choose. There is, for example, the Forager in the Cochise district of southeastern Arizona who left his skull and some long bones in a site on the Whitewater Wash, nine miles north of Douglas. The artifacts found with the burial were nothing to brag about and, as Antevs said, "their age is somewhat indefinite." Nevertheless, the skull and bones were sent to Dr. Earnest A. Hooton who reported to us that "the incomplete picture recalls that of small Southwestern dolichocephals of the Basket Maker type." This is fine as far as it goes, but this long-headed Basket Maker type was not restricted to northern and southern Arizona, or even to the Southwest. In his *Indians of Pecos*, Hooton found this type in somewhat stunted form in the Basket Makers of northern Arizona, and it appeared as a mixture with a longer-faced, higher-vaulted, and broader-headed strain in the Pecos Basket Makers, but these and also the skulls from the Coahuila Caves in northeastern Mexico were included in "the same fundamental stock, dolichocephalic and non-Mongoloid, which was also present in the Santa Catalina Islands," off the coast of southern California.

It always pleases me when we can get in a word about non-Mongoloid people in America, as it helps to dispel the illusion of a homogeneous race of American Indians, but the most important point of these remarks by Hooton is that the people on Santa Catalina, the Arizona and Pecos Basket Makers, and the Coahuila Cave Dwellers were all members of a fundamental physical stock which once reached from southern California to northeastern Mexico.

Much the same conclusions were reached by Dr. Roland B. Dixon in his *Racial History of Man*, although in this case he referred to the type as Proto-Australoid, so suggesting an ancestral background which was certainly not Mongoloid. Dixon also included the Indians on Santa Catalina in this basic stock and added those on San Clemente, another of the Channel Islands, for good measure. He recognized a strong family likeness in the now extinct Pericue at the southern tip of Lower California; identified it as present in the Arizona Basket Makers and in the Coahuila Caves; and found that "it still survives among the Ute and Pi-ute and also among the Tarahumare and Pima of the Mexican border country."

To further round out the picture which is beginning to form, I turn to three series of skulls from Texas. One of these was from Abilene and was described by Dr. E. A. Hooton. The second was from Val Verde County and was studied by Dr. Bruno Oetteking. And the third was from the Texas Gulf Coast and was examined by Drs. Edna and George Woodbury. In their report to us, the Woodburys expressed the opinion that "if the Texas Coastal, the Abilene, and the Val Verde peoples are not closely related, they must certainly be considered as variants of the same general type as far as the crania are concerned." They then drew detailed comparisons between the Texas Coastal and the Pericue types and found that "the one difference between these series is, in fact, the strange musculature of the Pericue which may well be only a local variation. The resemblance between the two is nearly complete in every particular."

Casting farther afield, the Woodburys identified the Pericue as belonging to the Lagoa Santa physical stock, an ancient and well-recognized type which ranged from Brazil to Mexico, adding that "it would appear, from the similarity to the Pericue, that the Texas Coastal specimens may also belong to it and represent, perhaps, the northernmost extension of this southern physical type." And, as a final touch, "There is further, a distinct resemblance between crania of the Lagoa Santa type and Melanesian crania."

The gist of all these statements and opinions is that there was once a well-recognized long-headed physical stock of low to medium stature which occupied the area lying between the Channel Islands, off the coast of southern California and central Texas. This stock appears to have been very widespread in ancient times, with a southward extension to Mexico and Brazil, and there is a suggestion of relationship to Melanesian people in the southwestern Pacific—all of which points to an early, distinct, and separate migration from eastern Asia to North America.

In the Southwest, the northern boundary of the tribes included in this stock runs through southern Utah and southern Colorado, from the Nevada line to the Rockies. The southern boundary stretches from the coast of southern California through northern Mexico to the gulf coast of Texas. Within these limits were the Basket Makers, the Cave Dwellers, and the Foragers who together made up the fundamental physical stock of the Southwest.

THESE PHYSICAL RESEMBLANCES, however, are only one of several links which connect the Basket Makers to other groups in the Southwest. Starting up in the Four Corners district—where Utah, Colorado, New Mexico, and Arizona meet—sites described as Basket Maker II are spread from the DuPont Cave, in southeastern Utah; east to Grand Gulch, and over to Mesa Verde in southwestern Colorado; south to Marsh Pass; east again to Red Rock Valley; and south to Canyon del Muerto. From this rather dense concentration in northeastern Arizona, one can then drop south about two hundred miles to the mountainous country of the Upper Gila where the people whom we call Cave Dwellers made and used most of the tools and weapons that were made and used by the Basket Makers, even though the abundance of bird and animal bones in Cave Dweller sites shows a greater interest in hunting. From the Upper Gila the trail leads eastward across the Rio Grande, and the same things have been found in Cave Dweller sites in the Huecos, the Guadalupes, and the Big Bend of western Texas and even down into the Coahuila Caves of northeastern Mexico.

The resemblances between the culture of the Basket Makers and that of the Cave Dwellers consist mainly of such perishable things as string, knots, netting, matting, baskets, and tools or weapons made of wood. In many instances the similarities have been so close that the men who have written the reports have actually applied the name of Basket Makers to the people who used to live in the caves of the Upper Gila, western Texas, and Coahuila. But while it is clear that a remarkably uniform blanket of culture covered the Southwest and western Texas at about A.D. 200, there were a few rather important differences between the extremes. I prefer, therefore, to restrict the term "Basket Maker" to the people in the Four Corners area for whom the name was coined and to refer to the people in the caves of the Upper Gila and western Texas as "Cave Dwellers." As I think that both the agreements and the differences in culture are important to an understanding of the situation, I have made three lists show-

◀ **The distribution of the fundamental long-headed stock in the Southwest**

COMPARISON OF BASKET MAKER AND CAVE DWELLER CULTURES
BEFORE THE APPEARANCE OF FIRED POTTERY

Traits Possessed Only by the Basket Makers

Multiple-warp sandals	Trough-shaped milling stone
Unfired mud vessels	18-row corn*

Traits Shared by Basket Makers and Cave Dwellers

Spear-thrower	Percussion flaking
Dart with foreshaft	Pressure flaking
Bunt-point foreshaft	Flint knives
Curved fending or throwing club	Scrapers
Snares	Projectile points
Nets	Grooved maul
Matting	Winged drill
Twined-woven bag	Draw-knife
Coiled basketry	Stone pipe
Cradle	Grooved sharpening stone
String of twisted human hair	Bone awls
Rabbit-fur robe	Bone beads
Shaft wrench	Seed beads
Skin bag	Stone beads
Head-dress	Stone pendants
Bow	Shell beads
Arrow	Shell pendants
Digging or planting stick	Shell bracelet
Wooden clamp	Squash
Jar-shaped storage cists	Slab-lined storage cists

Dolichocephalic or long-headed skull-form

Traits Possessed Only by the Cave Dwellers

Fish-tail sandal	Oval-basin milling stone
Painted pebbles	Cotton
Twined basketry	8-row corn*
Cremation	Mask

* It should be noted that *all* Basket Maker corn was not 18-row, nor was *all* Cave Dweller corn 8-row. However, 12 to 18-row was rare or absent in Cave Dweller sites and 8 to 10-row was rare or absent in Basket Maker sites.

ing, first, those things which were peculiar to the Basket Makers of the Four Corners district; second, those which they shared with the Cave Dwellers of the Upper Gila and western Texas; and, third, those which were possessed only by

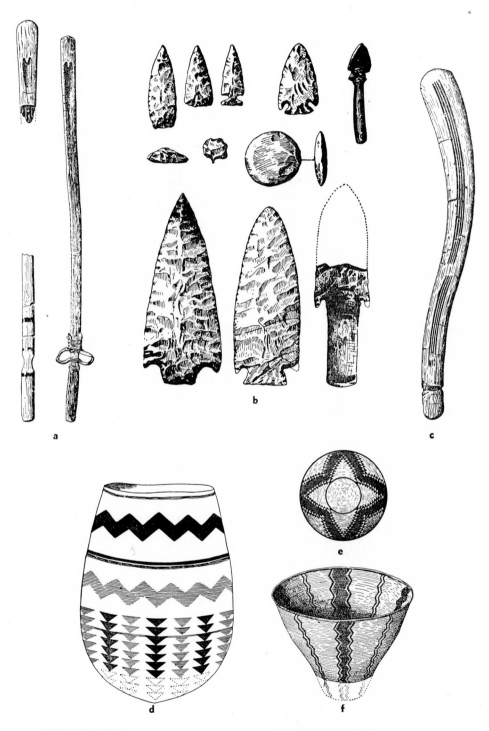

White Dog Cave
   a. Spear-thrower
   b. Projectile points
   c. Curved throwing-stick
   d. Twined-woven bag
   e & f. Baskets
   (From Kidder and Guernsey, 1921)

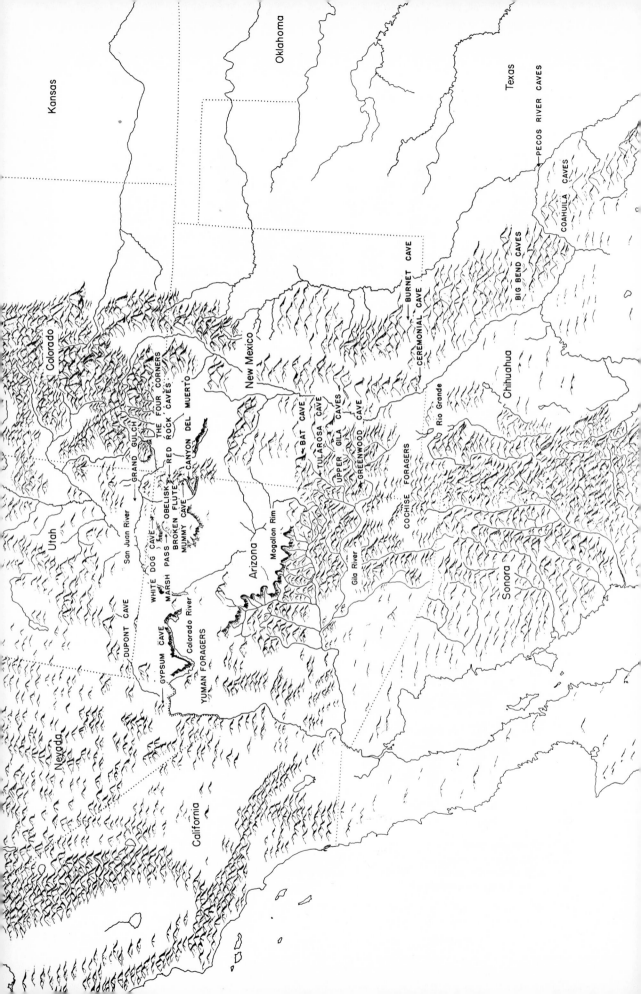

the Cave Dwellers. Without exception, all of these things have been listed from sites in which no fired pottery has been found, but this does not mean that all of these sites were occupied at A.D. 200, nor that they were all contemporaneous. Actual chronology is necessarily vague, as there are no tree-ring dates for any sites in the Southwest before A.D. 200, and the new method of radiocarbon dating is still in the experimental stage. It is quite possible that some of these sites were occupied before A.D. 200, but most of them were undoubtedly later and the comparisons are merely intended to show what Basket Makers and Cave Dwellers were doing before true pottery made its first appearance in their respective areas.

Judging by these lists, I think it is clear that the Basket Makers and Cave Dwellers were birds of a feather, but it is also equally clear that the groups at the northern and southern extremities of the Southwest were being affected by exterior contacts which, at about A.D. 200, were too recent to have leavened the entire mass of Basket Maker-Cave Dweller cultures. The problem of southern contacts will come up in due course. At present I am concerned only with the Basket Makers on the northern frontier of the Southwest and the possibility that they may have been in touch with a foreign people who hitherto have not been recognized—although Hooton gave us a lead when he identified a broad-headed strain in an otherwise long-headed people.

White Dog Cave: Marsh Pass

V

Basket Makers and Farmers: A.D. 200 to 400

THIS CHAPTER IS going to deal with one of the "Just So Stories" which Kipling overlooked or did not venture to explain, and it might well be headed "How the Basket Maker Got His Pot." It is an interesting and rather important problem, as it raises the question of whether the Basket Makers actually pulled off an independent invention of pottery, or, if the art was acquired by diffusion, who and where were the foreigners who provided the knowledge. For those who like detective stories, this one has the advantage of providing an authentic mystery without any of the usual gory details.

Fortunately there is a good deal of evidence to consider, and I begin with the four items which were listed as being peculiar to the Basket Makers in the Four Corners—multiple-warp sandals, unfired mud pottery, trough-shaped milling stones, and 18-row corn. Three of these—the sandals, milling stones, and corn—were also known to the Cave Dwellers of the Upper Gila, western Texas, and Coahuila in a somewhat different or more primitive form, so that the sudden and rather surprising advance in the Four Corners could possibly be explained by saying that the Basket Makers were somewhat harder to satisfy than their cave-dwelling brethren to the south. This, however, could not be said of the unfired mud vessels which were one of the most prominent features of true Basket Maker culture but were entirely unknown to the Cave Dwellers of the Upper Gila and western Texas.

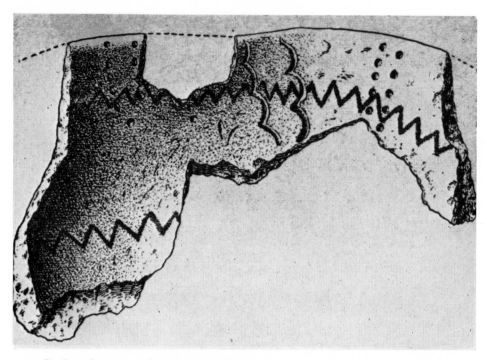

Du Pont Cave: an unfired decorated clay bowl

(From Nusbaum, J. L. 1922)

These vessels actually are rather shallow bowls or trays, made of mud which is often reinforced with fibers, or bast, or sometimes shredded juniper bark. In most cases the exteriors show the clear impressions of coiled basketry, so indicating that they had been molded in shallow baskets, possibly as a means of protecting the basket fibers when parching corn or seeds with hot embers. This has given birth to the idea that a basket which had been thus lined with mud might have caught fire or been dropped into a fire by chance, with the result that the basket was destroyed and the mud was hardened, and found to be superior to the basket for cooking purposes. In other words, this theoretical process would provide a valuable link in the chain of evidence leading up to an independent invention of pottery making by the Basket Makers.

Theoretically, it sounds like a good idea, but practically, there are some serious objections to the element of chance in the process. For one thing, a basket is not quickly destroyed by dropping it in the small fires over which Indians ordinarily do their cooking. For another, if the fire was big enough to destroy the basket, the mud, to be thoroughly baked, would have to be intentionally left in the fire, in which case it would almost certainly crack or crumble to pieces. These are merely technical objections, however, and the most convincing refutation of the theory comes from DuPont Cave in southeastern Utah, where a tree-ring date of A.D. 217 established it as the earliest dated Basket

Broken Flute Cave: an unfired mud bowl

Maker II site in the Southwest. Fragments of three mud vessels were found. In each case the surfaces bore the fingerprints of their makers, and in no instance was there any sign of a basket impression. This, by itself, is enough to show that there was nothing fortuitous in these earliest examples of mud pottery, but the strongest evidence of all was found in one of the specimens which was actually decorated with zigzag lines drawn in black paint, and in addition, was incised with scalloped lines and double rows of dots—so leaving no doubt whatever that the person who made the pot was fully aware of what he or she was doing.

Turning now to the basket-impressed mud trays, it is very disconcerting to find that such things were practically unknown in the Basket Maker II caves in the Marsh Pass district one hundred years after the start had been made in DuPont Cave. Here, Kidder and Guernsey excavated fifteen caves, including White Dog Cave which gave us a tree-ring date at A.D. 312, yet, according to their report: "The only specimen that even remotely resembles pottery was found in Cave 6. It is a fragment from the rim of a shallow dish-like receptacle nearly ½ inch thick, made of unburned clay heavily tempered with shreds of cedar bark. It was molded in a shallow basket, the print of which is plainly visible on the outer surface of the sherd." The virtual absence of mud trays in the Basket Maker II caves in Marsh Pass at A.D. 312 is all the more remarkable since Guernsey later reported: "In practically every Basket Maker III site that was found in the shelter of a cave there occurred in the rubbish fragments of objects made of unbaked clay. While no whole or even nearly complete specimens were recovered, the pieces show that they once formed parts of shallow dish-like or tray-like receptacles, 18 inches to 2 feet or perhaps more in diameter, by about 5 inches deep."

This puts an entirely different complexion on the problem, since if mud-lined trays were scarcely known in Basket Maker II but were in common use in Basket Maker III, it looks as if they must have served some special purpose, as true fired pottery was also present in large quantities in the same sites during this later period. That this explanation may be the right one is also indicated by Cushing's description in 1886 of the customs of the modern Havasupai in Cataract Canyon, in northern Arizona: "They had not yet forgotten how to boil food in water-tight basketry, by means of hot stones, and continued to roast seeds, crickets, and bits of meat in wicker trays, coated inside with gritty clay."

From all of this it looks to me as if the decorated fragment from DuPont Cave and the basket-marked mud trays from Marsh Pass represent two entirely different things. In the case of the decorated fragment it was not only painted and incised but was described by Kidder and Guernsey as a bowl about 7 inches in diameter and 4 inches deep; furthermore, it was finger-molded and showed no signs of a basket impression. To my mind it seems to have been a not altogether unsuccessful attempt to copy a piece of decorated fired pottery, and the absence of any more developed forms of the same type during the remainder of the third and fourth centuries makes it clear that this was not a step in an inventive series of pottery making. The mud trays, on the other hand, were shallower and broader than the DuPont bowl. All carry the impression of a basket, indicating a well-established custom or purpose. None were decorated; and there does not appear to be any appreciable difference between those which were made by the Basket Makers in the fifth and sixth centuries and those which were used by the Havasupai in the nineteenth century. Since it is known that the clay-lined baskets of the Havasupai served as roasting or parching trays, it would seem to me logical to suppose that the mud or clay-lined baskets of the Basket Makers were used in the same way. If this belief is right, then the cherished hope that the Basket Makers might have performed the unique accomplishment of inventing their own pottery goes down the drain, and we shall have to look for a more humdrum explanation.

IF, AS I have suggested, the decorated mud bowl from DuPont Cave was the result of a Basket Maker woman trying to copy something that she had seen elsewhere, then the implications are rather momentous, as it will now become necessary to start a search for the unknown pot which she had seen and copied, the unrecognized woman who owned the unknown pot, and the hitherto unidentified tribe to which the unrecognized woman who owned the unknown pot belonged. As a real-life whodunit this would be hard to beat, and in a situation of this kind one could not do better than follow the instructions of the Bellman in "The Hunting of the Snark":

> To seek it with thimbles, to seek it with care;
>
> To pursue it with forks and hope;
>
> To threaten its life with a railway share;
>
> To charm it with smiles and soap!

As the Basket Maker woman who made the decorated mud pot lived in southeastern Utah, the obvious place to start this search is in the Four Corners district. Here one can begin by saying that, in all the centuries before Christ, there are no signs of any strangers in this part of the country and it is reasonably certain that those people north of the San Juan were the same as those south of the river. In fact, I would go even further and say that both groups were of the same stock as the Cave Dwellers in the Upper Gila and western Texas—all being members of Hooton's "primitive dolichocephalic group, represented perhaps best by the Coahuila Cave skulls, and found in a somewhat stunted form, but otherwise identical, in the caves of Arizona associated with the Basket Maker and Post-Basket Maker Cultures."

Soon after the time of Christ, however, the Basket Makers in the Four Corners suddenly began to make and do a number of things which no one in the Southwest had made or done before, and since these innovations did not reach the Cave Dwellers to the south, there is some justification for suspecting that the Basket Makers were being exposed to some new and foreign ideas along their northern frontier. Unfortunately, the significance of this infusion of new people with a more advanced culture during the centuries after Christ has been obscured by the custom of referring to all of the groups north and south of the San Juan as *Basket Makers;* and also by the even more befuddling habit of explaining all developments of culture as having been due to local innate ingenuity. The suspicion, if not certainty, that some foreign people had reached the Four Corners gathers strength when it is realized that one of the new acquisitions was corn, of a 10 to 18-row variety, which was certainly not a local discovery, and was rare or absent in Cave Dweller sites in the Upper Gila, western Texas, and Coahuila. On the other hand, the 8-row corn which was grown by the Cave Dwellers was rare or absent in the Four Corners—a fact which was noted by Dr. G. N. Collins, of the Bureau of Plant Industry, who, when describing the corn from DuPont Cave, said: "The number of rows of seed vary from 10 to 18. The absence of 8-row ears is worthy of note."

The 10 to 18-row corn which suddenly turned up in DuPont Cave in southeastern Utah at A.D. 217 does not look, therefore, as if it had been derived from the Cave Dwellers but rather as if it had been introduced to the Basket Makers from somewhere outside the boundaries of the Southwest. As corn is one of those peculiar vegetables which requires human companionship for its survival, it seems safe to say that when it reached the Four Corners it was brought by a people who were neither Basket Makers nor Cave Dwellers—which is just another way of saying that our hitherto unidentified tribe has arrived, and it now remains to identify them. Because of the corn they brought with them and to distinguish them from the Basket Makers, I am now merely going to call them the "Farmers," which will serve as a label until they can establish their own identity.

Types of Corn from the Southwest
   Top: 8-row, Guadalupe Cave Dweller, eastern New Mexico
   Middle: 8-row, Hueco Cave Dweller, western Texas
   Bottom: 16-row, Du Pont Cave, southern Utah

(Nusbaum, J. L. 1922)

Having hauled these Farmers up out of oblivion, one can begin to look around and wonder what else they may have known beside their corn, but here one runs into a very peculiar situation. As far back as 1922, when Kidder and Guernsey described the decorated mud bowl from DuPont Cave, they mentioned a strange type of true fired pottery which had been found in the caves in Grand Gulch, in southeastern Utah, which have always been supposed to have been occupied by Basket Makers of the II variety, who, according to the Pecos conferees, should have known nothing about such pottery. According to Kidder and Guernsey:

> These pieces are now in the Museum of the American Indian, Heye Foundation, where we have had an opportunity to examine them. They are a peculiar heavy, slate-gray ware, with well-smoothed but rather uneven surfaces; in form they are unlike any other Southwestern pottery with which we are familiar; they are small, bowl-like, dipper-like, and crucible-like vessels, the latter provided with lugs and spouts. Several of them are crudely decorated with broad lines and large dots of dull-red paint. While it is not feasible to describe this pottery adequately in the present publication, we may say that to anyone who has worked much with Southwestern ceramics it is quite distinctive, and once seen could be identified at a glance, even in small sherds. We do not believe it to be of Basket Maker origin, because no similar ware was ever discovered by the Wetherill brothers in the large number of Basket Maker caves dug by them, nor have we ever found any of it in our own explorations in northeastern Arizona and southeastern Utah. On the other hand, it is certainly not characteristic of any known later phase of Southwestern culture.

I am quite sure that archaeologists would agree with Kidder and Guernsey that this pottery does not resemble any other known type in the Southwest, but coming from caves in Grand Gulch which have always been regarded as Basket Maker II, it is hard to understand why there has been no curiosity as to who could have made this pottery if it was not a Basket Maker product. Since the description and illustrations were published in the *Indian Notes* of the Museum of the American Indian in July, 1924, I do not know of a single reference in any archaeological publication, but for present purposes one could ask nothing more. Here is an unknown non-Basket Maker type of pottery, found in admittedly early sites in the heart of the Farmers' range, stored away in the attic, waiting for the day when it could be dusted off and put to use. There may be some other explanation as to how this pottery found its way into the Grand Gulch caves, but until someone else can come along and establish a better claim, I am going to say that it was made by the wife of one of my Farmers.

The unidentified tribe is taking form as the Farmers. The unknown pot has found an owner. It remains to find out what the heretofore unrecognized owner of the hitherto unknown pot looks like.

In 1944, Dr. Carl C. Seltzer announced his discovery that the Zuni Indians of Hawikuh—a pueblo in western New Mexico dating in the sixteenth century—

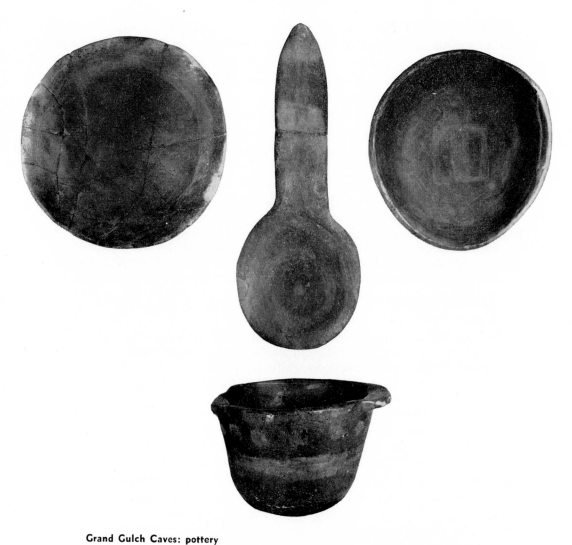

Grand Gulch Caves: pottery

(Courtesy of the Museum of the American Indian)

showed a closer physical resemblance to the ancient people in Grand Gulch, in southeastern Utah, than these old-timers showed to the Basket Makers of northeastern Arizona. To a generation of archaeologists who had grown up in the belief that the Southwest had originally been populated by a long-headed stock which was later altered by the advent of broad-headed peoples, this announcement by Seltzer was rather startling, since it seemed to demand a re-shuffling of all the old beliefs. As often happens when a new idea is broached, the first tendency was to go to the opposite extreme and say that if there were no important differences between Basket Maker II in Grand Gulch and the modern Zunis, then the entire Southwest probably represented a self-contained

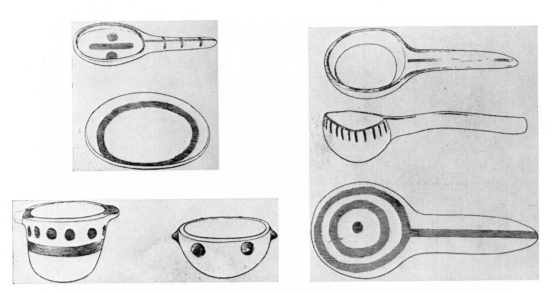

Grand Gulch Caves: pottery

(Courtesy of the Museum of the American Indian)

physical and cultural development from early to late, unaffected by any important intrusion of foreign blood or culture. In the excitement of coining new theories, however, all of the emphasis was placed on the resemblance of the modern Zunis to the ancient Grand Gulch skulls—a connection which spanned two hundred miles in space and a thousand years in time. But to me, it is much more significant to be told that the difference between the people in Grand Gulch and those in northern Arizona—their contemporaneous and supposed blood-brothers fifty miles to the south—was greater than that between the ancient Grand Gulchers and the modern Zunis. As the cowboy said when he first saw the Grand Canyon, "My God! Something's happened here!"

The reason for the present confusion is clear. During the last thirty years a great deal of work has been done in the Four Corners area. Great quantities of material and many burials have been found in the DuPont and Grand Gulch caves, in southeastern Utah; Canyon del Muerto, the Marsh Pass and Red Rock caves in northeastern Arizona; near Durango, at Ackmen, on Mesa Verde, and along the La Plata in southwestern Colorado. The time span covers six centuries, from A.D. 200 to 800, and the skulls which have come out of the burials include long, medium, and broad heads; high and low vaults; deformed and undeformed; yet *all* of these have been turned in to museums and laboratories as having been found in sites classified as Basket Maker II or III. Under such circumstances it is not surprising that a fine dividing line cannot be drawn between Basket Maker and Pueblo. Rather than a sharp break between them, as suggested in the Pecos classification, it looks to me as if the Four Corners had been a meeting ground and a melting pot from the earliest days of Basket Maker II up to about A.D. 700.

Falls Creek: dwelling or storeroom?

(From Morris, E. H. 1949)

But this does not mean that the various ingredients, physical and cultural, which went into the pot cannot be segregated and identified.

Without adding anything new, and taking the existing evidence and what has been said at its face value, it seems to me that things fall into place when we accept Hooton's and Dixon's definition of a basic long-headed stock which reached from California to Texas. Soon after the time of Christ, certain cultural changes took place in the Four Corners which I think can be explained more logically as the result of diffusion than of independent invention. On top of this, instead of the earlier uniformity of Hooton's basic stock, two distinct physical types must now be recognized according to the differences which Seltzer has drawn between the Grand Gulch people, north of the San Juan, and the Basket Makers of northern Arizona, south of the river. One wonders, therefore, if anything more is needed to herald the arrival of a foreign people with their belongings. If so, it is to be found on a side hill overlooking Falls Creek, a few miles north of Durango in southwestern Colorado.

To enjoy the full flavor of this incident, you must first realize that during all of the thousands of years which led up to A.D. 200, no one in the Southwest knew or cared anything about a house. In the old days, when caves were available, people moved in and took advantage of the shelter they afforded, but in open country the best and apparently the only protection that hunters, foragers, and Basket Makers had been able to devise had been a brush-shelter or a wind-break of which no trace remains. Then suddenly, out of the nowhere into the

A modern example of a cribbed roof to show how the Falls Creek roofs were built

here—on Falls Creek—there appeared three circular houses, 25 feet or more in diameter, complete with cribbed roofs, and four kinds of storage pits—large jug-shaped pot holes; slab-lined pits; slab-lined pits covered with mud domes; and mud domes entirely above floor level. Then—stamping the date when these people arrived—the houses burned and from the mass of charcoal Dr. Edmund Schulman obtained a number of tree-ring dates which ranged from A.D. 184 up to 324. The Falls Creek site is therefore the earliest dated ruin in the Southwest. It was contemporaneous with DuPont Cave at A.D. 217, and as, according to my reckoning, it was built and occupied by Farmers, we are provided with a valuable comparison of what Basket Makers and Farmers were doing during the third century.

There may be a few other odds and ends—such as a bow and arrow, a feather-string blanket, and some multiple-warp sandals—that I ought to claim for my Farmers, but I think they should be satisfied with the progress so far. From total obscurity they have emerged with a name (I call them Farmers, but others may call them Trouble Makers), a physique (Seltzer says they look like the Zunis), a house, pottery, 18-row corn, and a variety of storage pits. And we find that during the third and fourth centuries they have been setting the fashions for the Basket Makers with their latest imported models.

Rio Grande.

Farmers coming in from the Western Plains.

Falls Creek.

× Grand Gulch Caves

Mummy Cave.

x Bat Cave.

White Dog Cave.

Turkey Cave.

Cochise Foragers.

Colorado River.

Arizona Basket Makers

Gila River.

× Dupont Cave.

Little Colorado River.

Yuman Foragers.

THE SOUTHWEST AT A.D. 400

During the Stone Age and up to about A.D. *200, the Southwest was sparsely populated by scattered families of hunters and foragers, none of whom possessed any knowledge of housebuilding, pottery making, or the cultivation of corn.*

Beginning at about A.D. *200, the vanguard of a people whom we are calling the Farmers entered the Southwest, probably coming in from the western plains through southern Colorado, bringing:*

     10 to 18-row corn
     Pottery fired in a reducing atmosphere
     Rectangular earth-lodges with ventilators
     Slab-lined storage cists
     Multiple-warp sandals
     Twined-woven bags
     Feather-wrapped cord
     Bow and arrow

All of these things were gradually adopted by the foragers of northeastern Arizona, known as Basket Makers, but none reached the Cochise Foragers or the Upper Gila Cave Dwellers.

With the advent of the Farmers and the improvement in living conditions among the Basket Makers due to the adoption of agriculture, the population in the Four Corners district was steadily increasing at A.D. *400.*

V I

The Four Corners: A.D. 400 to 600

THE SCENE SHIFTS from the north to the south of the San Juan—to the haunts of the Basket Makers where, with some scruples and reservations, these people were testing the new ideas and gadgets which they had seen in the Farmers' villages north of the river. To learn how far the Basket Makers had progressed up to about A.D. 400, the best and most complete information comes from Marsh Pass where Kidder and Guernsey excavated fifteen caves, and as they found plenty of corn but no true pottery and only one fragment of a basket-marked mud tray, the culture can be rated as straight Basket Maker II.

The most important of these Marsh Pass sites was White Dog Cave, both because its rich haul of material helped to round out the picture of Basket Maker II as it was drawn in DuPont Cave, and because it gave us a tree-ring date which lifted the dating by one hundred years, from A.D. 217 to 312. Many of the essential features were the same as in DuPont Cave, such as slab-lined storage cists, the same type of 18-row corn, multiple-warp square-toed sandals, coiled basketry, fur robes, twined-woven bags, darts and spear-throwers, and a wide range of the same sort of ornaments and household appliances. Besides a greater number and variety, and an improvement in the quality of those things which were also found in DuPont Cave, there were several important additions, including such things as cradles, string skirts, curved grooved clubs, woven fabrics, tumplines for pannier baskets, and a rabbit-net 240 feet long by 3 feet 8 inches wide.

Each of these things is important in showing the rise in the local standard of living, but the most significant feature of Basket Maker II at A.D. 400 in northeastern Arizona is the absence of any kind of a house, two hundred years after the Farmers had built their houses on Falls Creek. It has been suggested that such houses actually were built but would be difficult to find after the timbers had rotted away, leaving neither mound nor pit to mark the spot, but I doubt if this is the true explanation. In the case of Basket Maker II, if the people had built their houses in the open and had only used their caves for storage, it is reasonably certain that such houses would have been built immediately adjacent to the caves where their corn was stored. I feel sure, therefore, that Nusbaum, Kidder, Guernsey, Morris, or some of the other men who have dug such sites would have found traces of such houses, since it would only have needed a shallow trench to have disclosed hard-packed floors and the charcoal, ash, and debris of an old occupation level, if such things were there to be found. Furthermore, it does not seem to me to be likely that a people who were fully aware of the protection afforded by a cave for storage purposes would have denied such shelter to themselves. To have done so would mean that they had deliberately chosen to expose themselves and their earth-covered huts to the weather when there was plenty of room in the caves for both houses and storage. That the Basket Makers did not build houses in the open when caves were available is clearly shown by the fact that when they finally learned how to build houses, after A.D. 400, they placed them within the shelter of their caves, alongside their storage cists, as in Obelisk, Broken Flute, and other Basket Maker III caves. In DuPont and White Dog caves, the depth of debris and the discarded miscellany of daily life are sufficient evidence to indicate that these Basket Makers actually lived in their caves, and the failure to find any trace of a house can only mean that Basket Makers had not yet started to build houses at the time these caves were occupied.

This brings us to the storage pits in DuPont and White Dog caves, and it is rather a shock to realize, with tree-ring dates showing that Falls Creek was as early or earlier than DuPont Cave, that there is no longer any justification for claiming slab-lined storage cists as an exclusive Basket Maker invention. Nothing resembling a slab-lined cist has yet been found in any site in the Southwest before the time of Christ, and we are faced with the bald fact that as the situation stands at present, each of the four kinds of storage bins found by Morris made its first appearance in the Southwest at the Farmers' Fall Creek site. Of these, the slab-lined cist appears to have been the only one which met with Basket Maker favor, and once introduced it became a standard accessory in all Basket Maker homes.

Some fifty miles to the east of Marsh Pass, in Canyon del Muerto, there are two other caves—Tse-ya-tso and Mummy Cave (see frontispiece)—both of which were occupied in Basket Maker II times and have been excavated by Earl Morris. For Mummy Cave we have an early date of A.D. 295, with a long string of dates running up into the 700's: for Tse-ya-tso the dates range from A.D. 439

Red Rock Valley from Obelisk Cave

to 739. The clustering of these dates indicates that the period of greatest building activity was late in the fifth century, but it is not possible to make any cultural comparisons, as Morris' report has not yet been published. All that can be said at present is that DuPont, White Dog and other Marsh Pass caves, Mummy Cave, and Tse-ya-tso all had their roots in a Basket Maker II culture which was slowly developing during the third and fourth centuries.

The next series of early Basket Maker sites is in Red Rock Valley, about thirty miles north of Canyon del Muerto, in the gap between the Lukachukai and Carrizo Mountains in northeastern Arizona. This is where Morris excavated several caves which had been occupied during the transition from Basket Maker II to III, and the tree-ring dates show that this took place soon after A.D. 400. All of the caves contained true pottery, so they all qualify as Basket Maker III, but Obelisk Cave stands forth as being the earliest dated site in the Southwest where pure unadulterated Basket Maker pottery has been discovered, and also, of equal or even greater importance, as the historic spot where the first Basket Maker house was found.

This house was well planned, carefully put together, and shows no evidence of the bungling efforts of an inexperienced builder. The loose surface soil was scraped away down to a hard floor, and four posts were set 10 to 12 feet apart. The tops of these were joined by four beams, forming a rectangular plate, and

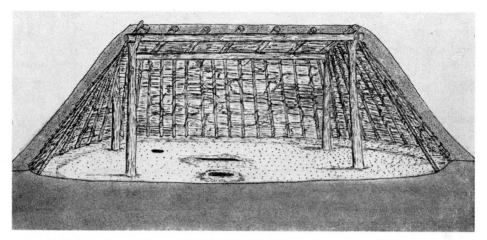

Reconstruction of the Basket Maker house in Obelisk Cave

on this rafters were laid to make a flat roof. The sides were made of inclined poles, evenly spaced, their tops resting against the plate, their butts embedded in the ground around the excavation and set back far enough to leave a low bench encircling the floor. On this framework, reeds, grass, and juniper bark were laid horizontally and lashed in place, and finally the whole structure was covered with a thick coating of mud, reinforced with plant fibers. The fireplace was near the center of the floor, so implying that an open hatchway had been left in the middle of the flat roof to serve as a smoke-vent and possibly as a means of entrance and exit, although this evidence was not preserved. Slab-lined storage cists, similar to those in earlier Basket Maker caves, were placed near the house, and as usual these were single separate units and were not joined to the house or to each other.

The details of daily life in Obelisk Cave during the fifth century are well illustrated by the things which were found. For clothes, the Basket Makers wore sandals, braided garters, a braided sash, aprons with both dyed and painted patterns, and blankets of either fur or feather-string. Tools, weapons, and other paraphernalia included such things as coiled baskets, twined-woven bags, bows and arrows, objects made of wood, bone, and mountain-sheep horn, mortars, trough-shaped milling stones, basket-marked mud trays, clay figurines, and true fired pottery. In addition, we also obtained ten good tree-ring dates at:

A.D.	424	476	484
	435	478	486
	462	481	493
	465		

Although these dates cover a spread of seventy years, it was not possible to segregate the early from the late levels in the loose dust of the cave. Nevertheless Obelisk Cave provides information of great value, as it appears to have covered the transition from Basket Maker II to III within the range from A.D. 424

to 493. No burial offerings of pottery were found in the graves, and this, plus the presence of many early traits which were inherited without noticeable change, suggests that the cave was occupied during Basket Maker II—possibly represented by the dates at A.D. 424 and 435. The addition of fired pottery, however, leaves no doubt that the people had reached the status of Basket Maker III by A.D. 493. The fired pottery in Obelisk Cave was of two kinds—plain gray, usually coarse and not well smoothed; and a pale orange or mustard colored ware, which was fine grained, rather soft, and polished over a wavy surface.

Once the art of pottery making was acquired—regardless of how, when, or where—the grayware was characteristic of Basket Maker potters throughout their range and career. It was later manipulated into coils and corrugations by Puebloan potters, but at all periods it was essentially a northern product, characteristic of the tribes on the Plateau, and was never made by the people below the Mogollon Rim, in central and southern Arizona. The orange colored ware was also a northern type but with a range restricted to the Four Corners. It did not remain in favor with the Basket Makers—if they ever actually made it, which I think is rather doubtful. It was soon to become the base of decorated pottery in the forms of red-on-orange and black-on-orange, with a center of density among the Farmers in southeastern Utah. Neither of these later decorated wares was ever made by Basket Makers south of the San Juan, and it may be that a Farmerette was responsible for the orange ware which Morris found in Obelisk Cave.

When one considers the evidence from Obelisk Cave in its general bearing on Southwestern archaeology, it seems to me that the house ranks first in importance. During these early centuries after Christ, we are primarily concerned in laying foundations and in identifying the people who are going to share in forming the societies and building the cultures with which we shall have to deal. Regarded from this angle, the Obelisk house is very significant in that it shows no evidence of having been developed from the slab-lined cists of Basket Maker II. In DuPont and White Dog caves these cists were large and carefully made, and it is clear that the Basket Makers had learned how to handle stone slabs, adobe, poles, and brush in combination, but there was nothing which even vaguely suggested that this knowledge had been extended to the building of a house. When, therefore, the Basket Makers suddenly blossomed out in Obelisk Cave with a house that was obviously based on long experience—but which bore no relationship to earlier local building methods—it could hardly be claimed that a Basket Maker had independently originated the idea. Such a claim would run still further into difficulties if it should be used to explain the fired pottery, bow and arrow, trough-shaped milling stones, mortars, and feather-string blankets —all of which made their first recorded appearance among the Basket Makers at this same time. Fortunately, however, we are not reduced to such an extremity, as the Farmers are on hand to fill the vacancy; but it is no exaggeration to say that if they had not been identified, we should have to drop everything else and go out and dig them up.

WITH ALL of these goods and chattels being received by the Basket Makers in northeastern Arizona, it is time to turn north of the San Juan and look over the Farmers who had been making the deliveries.

For the period following the early houses on Falls Creek the evidence is like the food in the picnic basket—it is very good, what there is of it, and there's plenty of it, such as it is. It consists of four large villages in the general area of Durango, with a number of smaller settlements sprinkled around between the four main concentrations. The Farmers, therefore, did their best to provide us with plenty of evidence, and it isn't their fault if no one has yet ventured to tackle the systematic excavation of any of the large Durango sites. To provide a background of these Durango villages and to give us some sort of an idea of the extent of the culture, we made a survey which included about fifteen hundred sites, all north of the San Juan and covering all periods. Finally and more specifically, we can add some pottery, some houses, and some tree-ring dates ranging from A.D. 540 up to 688.

One of the largest settlements in the area was the village on Blue Mesa, about five miles south of Durango on the west side of the Animas River. The surface indications show four long rows of contiguous rooms, stretched across the mesa, each row consisting of a double line of rectangular rooms, vaguely outlined by mounds of dirt and stones. Some of the rooms were large, some small, and some were undoubtedly used for storage, even though they were built as integral parts of the house blocks. In the open spaces between the rows of rooms there were depressions and mounds, more or less circular, which appear to have been the ruins of large single subterranean structures, and there was a scattered group of such buildings at the southern end of the mesa. All told, the total of rooms and houses must have run to several hundred units.

The other villages and smaller settlements in the vicinity of Durango all seem to have been laid out in much the same way. Although none of these ruins have been thoroughly excavated, certain points stand out from which a few deductions can be drawn. It is clear, for instance, that these villages once housed a very large population—overwhelmingly greater than the relatively few Basket Maker families that could have found shelter in the caves of northeastern Arizona. Another self-evident fact is that the uniform arrangement of these Durango villages conformed to a building code which, in the sixth century, was already well-established, apparently as a result of being based on long-founded customs. We also know—from Morris' work on the La Plata, Brew's excavations in southeastern Utah, and Martin's in southwestern Colorado—that this same style of architecture lasted without any significant change, up to the end of the eighth century. With this standardization of village planning in mind, it is therefore all the more significant, in drawing the line between Farmers and Basket Makers, that a village of this kind has not been found south of the San Juan by anybody, in any place, at any time. Judging by the distribution of the two tribes, it seems that the vanguard of the Farmer migration had arrived at about A.D. 200 and had settled on Falls Creek, which flows into the Animas a few miles above Durango.

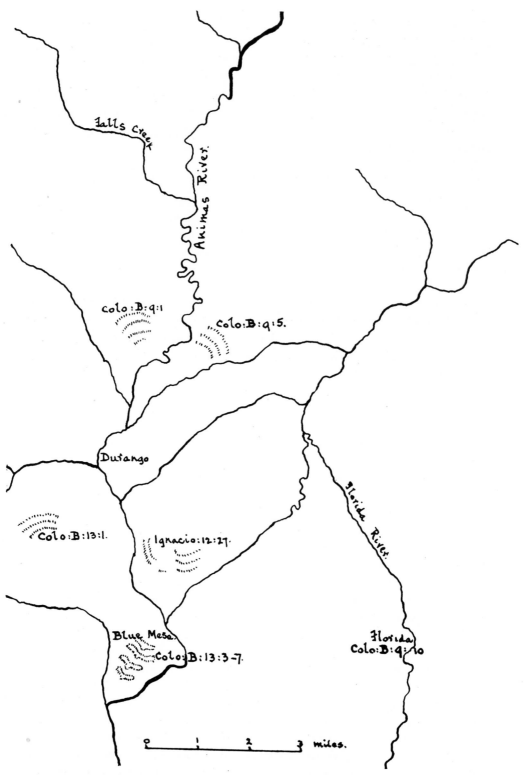

Farmer villages around Durango

An earth-lodge near Durango, Colorado

During the years which followed, the main body of the migration moved into the Durango district and by A.D. 600 the number and size of their villages are unmistakable evidence of a large population. This raises the questions of where these Farmers came from and how they entered the Southwest, and here again, the indications are fairly clear. First of all, it looks as if their earliest settlements were made along the Animas River, within a radius of about ten miles of Durango, and this suggests that these people either came down from the north—through the central valleys of Utah, west of the Rockies—or in from the east, through southern Colorado from the western plains. The same inference can be drawn from the complete lack of any signs of the Farmers in any section of the Southwest south of the San Juan, at this or any earlier time, and in their later reluctance to move south of the river. In addition to this positive and negative evidence, there is another indication which points northward and which, if it means what I think it does, carries some far-reaching implications.

In 1936, we excavated one of the large single houses which has been mentioned as lying between the parallel rows of contiguous rooms. We found that it was roughly rectangular with rounded corners, 35 feet across, and about 5 feet deep. It was surrounded by a bench or banquette about 2 feet wide, at the back of which poles had been embedded slanting inward to rest on a rectangular plate supported by four large posts. Midway of the west side, a horizontal hole, 15

West partition and ventilator

inches in diameter, had been tunnelled through the banquette to admit fresh air from a vertical shaft which had been sunk outside the west wall of the house. A low partition, about 18 inches high, separated the ventilator from the rest of the floor. No trace of a doorway or side entrance was found and it therefore seems that entry and exit must have been through a hatchway in the roof by means of a ladder, as was the custom in later houses of the same kind. This opening in the roof also served as a smoke-vent above the fireplace which was in the center of the floor.

The location and size of this house suggest that it was probably used as a ceremonial room—known in the Southwest as a kiva—but its most important feature was the ventilating system which has since been employed by all Plateau peoples to introduce fresh air into their subterranean kivas and pit-houses. Exactly the same system is being used today by the Pueblos in the upper Rio Grande Valley and the Hopi towns. The general method of construction of this Durango house was the same as that of the house in Obelisk Cave, except that the Obelisk house showed no signs of a ventilating system. This was an important omission, for it indicates that at A.D. 500 the Basket Makers had not yet gained sufficient experience in building and living in a house to appreciate the advantage of adequate ventilation. To forestall any idea that the ventilator in the Durango house was merely a later refinement of the Obelisk house, it is only necessary to point out that the same style of house and the same type of ventilating system have been found to hark back to ancient times in northeastern Asia.

In 1908, Waldemar Jochelson reported on his investigations among the Koryak in eastern Siberia and described their houses as having been derived from what he called a Palae-Asiatic-American type of dwelling—an archaic house which he regarded as ancestral to the northeastern Asiatic and some North American forms. This opinion was backed up by Roberts when, in referring to the underground houses of the Koryak, he said: "Although possessing distinct features of their own they have many characteristics in common with New World forms . . . . The similarities are too great to warrant any belief of an independent origin."

The Koryak house was rectangular, partly subterranean, and had two entrances—a covered side passage and a hatchway in the flat roof which also served as a smoke-vent. During the summer the side entrance was used exclusively and the ladder was removed from the hatchway, but according to Roberts: "Throughout the winter months when the outer doorway to the passage is blocked (by snow) the passage itself serves as a ventilator. A small round hole is left in the roof of this part of the structure and fresh air is drawn down and into the dwelling in the same fashion as through the ventilators of the Southwestern kivas." Roberts then went on to say, "It would seem that the so-called ventilator was not of Southwestern origin but goes back to certain features in the ancestral structures of northeastern Asia."

Although it is a generally accepted belief that North America was populated by a succession of migrations from northeastern Asia, it is very rare for one to be able to quote a well-known anthropologist to the effect that an important cultural trait in the Southwest can be traced back to an origin in northeastern Asia. It is a long step forward, but one wonders where the line should be drawn. Any people crossing Bering Strait with enough knowledge to build such a house would certainly know many other arts and crafts, and we may be lifting the quarantine on all sorts of Asiatic contagions if we admit the house and its ventilating system as importations from northeastern Asia.

This, I think, is a good time for me to leave well enough alone, and the only thing I have to add is that this method of air-conditioning a house was never employed in southern Arizona or in the regions to the south—in Mexico, Central or South America. For the southern type of house, I turn now to the Cochise Foragers in southeastern Arizona.

VII

Cochise and Mogollon: up to A.D. 600

To MOST OF THOSE archaeologists who have worked in the Four Corners district the red sandstone cliffs of Red Rock Valley, Tsegi Canyon, and Canyon del Muerto are as much a part of the Basket Makers as their pottery or any of the other things they made or did. In the southern sections of the Southwest the conditions are very different. The Mogollon Rim at an altitude of about 7,000 feet forms the southern border of the Plateau and is the dividing line between northern and southern Arizona. The soft footing of sand and the red cliffs of the northern country give way to lava beds and the great escarpment of the Rim. Instead of the flat sandstone slabs of the north, which were ideal for laying up walls of coursed masonry, the southern builders were reduced to round boulders or shapeless lumps of lava. And as a further handicap to artistic accomplishment, the potter's clay below the Rim was distinctly inferior to that on the Plateau.

From the Rim the land drops away sharply to the south through broken forested canyons to broad open valleys at elevations down to 1200 feet in the desert near Phoenix, and with the drop in altitude there are corresponding changes in climate and vegetation. In southern Arizona and New Mexico, the wide valleys or playas are separated by parallel mountain ranges running north and south, most of which are high enough to be forested. There is less rainfall, however, and hot dry winds from the desert are the cause of erratic tree growth. Tree-ring dating below the Rim is consequently less dependable than on the Plateau.

Both the southern terrain and its climate were primary factors in governing the lives and shaping the cultures of the ancient people, and as regards our immediate problem, they were of even greater importance in guiding archaeologists as to where to work.

During the formative period of Southwestern archaeology which ended with the Pecos Conference in 1927, the great majority of the investigations which had been made up to that time had been confined to the Four Corners, Chaco Canyon, Flagstaff, and the Upper Rio Grande Valley. The reasons for this are easily understood since most of the men who had done the work were connected with eastern institutions and could therefore only work during the summer, and southern Arizona, with daily temperatures well over 100° in the shade, had little attraction as a place to spend the summer, digging in ruins which are always exposed to the full heat of the sun.

This has brought about a situation which is badly out of balance. When, for example, a man undertakes an investigation on the Plateau, such as Earl Morris did on the La Plata, he begins with the great advantage of familiarity with the results which other men have obtained in neighboring areas. Looking over the references in Morris' *Archaeological Studies in the La Plata District*, it will illustrate my point when I say that he was able to consult over forty accounts of work done in the same general region, many of which covered actual excavations. These accounts had all been written by men whose names have been in the forefront of Southwestern archaeology—Cummings, Fewkes, Guernsey, Holmes, Judd, Kidder, Morley, Nordenskiold, Nusbaum, Pepper, Prudden, Roberts. In addition were the innumerable discussions he had been able to carry on with these and other men who were familiar with his subject and competent to express opinions.

Down under the Rim, however, when Kidder wrote his sections on the Upper and Lower Gila in 1924, his references were limited to the excavations of Cushing, Fewkes, and Hough, and half a dozen articles of general interest by Bandelier, Hodge, and Mindeleff, most of which had been written before 1900. As Cushing's only report was a paper read in Berlin in 1890, and as Fewkes published his final report on Casa Grande in 1912, it is fair to say that the archaeology of southern Arizona was not a subject about which friends were apt to argue when Kidder, in 1924, wrote his *Introduction to the Study of Southwestern Archaeology*. During the years since 1924, we and others have spent our winters rooting around in southern ruins and have now reached the point where we think some southern help is needed to explain several features of the northern cultures which otherwise are difficult to understand. If, in our eagerness to help, our life preservers should turn out to be anchors, we will gladly apologize—at least our intentions are good.

THE TALE of the Cochise Foragers in southeastern Arizona has been said by Antevs to have begun more than ten thousand years ago, but for present purposes the actual time is of no importance. It is enough now to say that from their earliest known beginnings up to about the time of Christ, the abundance of grinding tools and the scarcity of hunting gear in their sites point unmistakably to a way of life primarily dependent upon foraging. They give no indications of knowing anything about agriculture, pottery making, housebuilding, or other permanent establishments such as storage pits, and as the climate became warmer and drier in post-glacial times, they probably found it increasingly difficult to keep body and soul together. In this connection it is worth noting that the mere presence of grinding tools in a site does not mean, necessarily, that agriculture was practiced. On the one hand, milling stones are always abundant in Californian coastal sites where agriculture was unknown; and on the other, no grinding tools were found in DuPont Cave with its 18-row corn. In all of the Basket Maker caves in Marsh Pass—all with corn—the most that Guernsey and Kidder could find was one broken fragment of a milling stone—so affording one more indication that the Basket Makers preferred their corn parched or roasted in mud-lined basket trays.

At some time after the birth of Christ, things began to improve, and the tale of how the standard of living of the Cochise Foragers was raised makes an interesting comparison with the story of the Basket Makers. In each case, the benefits which came their way were basically the same and were received in the same order, but the details, the timing, and the sources were quite different and leave no doubt that the two series of events were unrelated. It all adds up to a very interesting situation which may be of some help in teaching us a lesson in the fundamental principles of diffusion.

The tale begins down in southeastern Arizona sometime around A.D. 500, but actual dates are uncertain. No beams have been found in Forager sites, for having no houses, they had no use for beams, and having no beams, there are no tree-rings to date. Dating by radiocarbon still needs to be tested and proved, and the age of recent gravel beds and silt deposits can usually be more accurately fixed by the things they contain than by guesses as to the time of the climatic fluctuations during which they were laid down. The safest approach to this angle of the problem is to work back from the known into the unknown, and for the known we have a well-established date of about A.D. 600, based on the finding of southern objects in northern sites that have been dated by tree-rings. This will be discussed in due course, but for the moment, I am concerned only with what had happened during the years which led up to A.D. 600.

Admitting the uncertainties of the dating prior to A.D. 600, I think that the culture of the Cochise Foragers during the early centuries after Christ was probably representative of the way of life in all of the open country in southern Arizona and New Mexico. The Foragers shared with the Basket Makers and the nearby Cave Dwellers those things which all had inherited from their Stone Age ancestors who had formerly lived in the same regions. When the Farmers appeared on the northern frontier at about A.D. 200, however, there is nothing to indicate that their contributions to the culture of the Basket Makers reached southward to the Foragers and Cave Dwellers below the Mogollon Rim—which is simply another way of saying that the southerners knew nothing about slab-lined storage pits, houses with ventilators, or pottery. But culture seems to abhor a vacuum, and at intervals from A.D. 500 to 600, a succession of things were absorbed by the Foragers which, judging by their character, their distribution, and their failure to reach the Basket Makers, look as if they must have come up from the south or southeast—probably along the Rio Grande Valley.

The first of these acquisitions was 8-row corn, and as Collins remarked, the absence of 8-row corn in DuPont and White Dog caves is worthy of note, but it is equally noteworthy that the 18-row variety from these caves has rarely, if ever, been found in Forager or Cave Dweller sites below the Mogollon Rim. It is quite possible that 18-row may have evolved from 8-row corn, but if it did, there is no evidence to show that the evolution occurred in the Southwest.

The next addition seems to have been kidney beans, and these again have a distinctly southern flavor. They also help to support the suggestions that have been made as to the date of the influx from the south, as beans have not been found in any Basket Maker sites before A.D. 600.

Next came storage pits in which to store the corn and beans, and one is naturally inclined to seek an analogy with the storage pits in the Basket Maker caves up north, but beyond the fact that they were both used for storage, there is nothing to compare between the northern slab-lined cists and the southern pits. The earliest southern storage pits have been found in late Forager sites along the San Pedro River in southeastern Arizona. They were very ingenious and admirably suited to the purpose for which they were designed. A hole was dug to a depth of about 6 feet; the bottom was levelled and widened to a diameter of 6 feet or more; but the opening at the surface was restricted to less than 3 feet. This kind of undercut storage pit has only been found in southeastern Arizona and southwestern New Mexico—never on the Plateau of northern Arizona —and in later times was developed to a high degree of specialization with a symmetrical arrangement of troughs and holes cut in the bottom. Some years ago, Carl Trischka took us to see some pits of this sort which he had excavated near Bisbee. I dropped down into one of them, about 6 feet deep, to examine the fancy design on the bottom, and would have been there yet if Trischka and a friend had not been there to haul me out. The undercut sides made it impossible to get a toe hold, and the overhang prevented me from crawling out by bracing against the sides. Trischka found a skeleton on the floor of one of his pits, and I wonder if it may not have been that of a man who failed to arrange for his exit.

The next acquisition was a house. It was circular or oval, about 12 feet in diameter, was excavated to a depth of about 18 inches—presumably to get rid of insects, worms, roots, and surface dampness—had a side entrance, with a step up to ground level, a fireplace, and an undercut storage pit sunk at the edge of the floor so that the owner could easily guard his belongings; and it seems to have been built along the lines of a tipi, similar to some Navajo and Apache

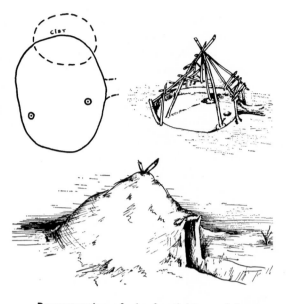

Reconstruction of circular tipi-type of house:
Pre-pottery period, circa A.D. 600

Below: Navajo and Apache houses which appear to
have been built on the same principle as the San Pedro
house.

   a. An Apache wickiup in course of construction
   b, c. Navajo hogans near Kayenta, Arizona

b

a

c

houses of recent times. It was constructed on an entirely different principle and
bore no resemblance whatever to the Farmer's type of house north of the San
Juan.

The next, the latest, and the last acquisition needed to bring the attain-
ments of the Cochise Foragers up to the level of the Basket Makers at A.D. 600 was
the very significant addition of plain brown and polished red pottery. The latter
was a good bright red, inside and out. It was coated with a layer of red paint,

known as a slip. It was hard and well fired, highly polished, well shaped, in the form of bowls and globular jars with out-curled rims. And because of its distinctive qualities and distribution, it was probably the most important single factor in, helping us to reconstruct the history of the Southwest—a statement based on six separate counts:

First, the collective peculiarities of this redware were such that the most ardent advocate of independent invention could not claim that it was the result of a local Forager's brainwave.

Second, it showed no suggestion of relationship, as to color, shape, finish, or method of firing, to the pottery which the Farmers and Basket Makers had been making up in the Four Corners district.

Third, it points unmistakably to the south or southeast as the direction from which these innovations were coming, since redware was not known to the north or west but has been found in Texas, along the east coast of Mexico, and southward all the way to Peru.

Fourth, it helps to fix the time when this migration from the south reached the Southwest, as there was no sign of polished red pottery in northeastern Arizona at A.D. 500 but it was present in Basket Maker caves which give dates in the 600's.

Fifth, the addition of plain brown and polished red pottery to the stone industry of the Cochise Foragers resulted in the creation of what is known as the Mogollon Culture in southwestern New Mexico—of which more hereafter.

Sixth, it serves as the equivalent of a dye or stain by which the people who made it can be traced throughout the arteries of the Southwest.

THIS BRINGS US UP TO A.D. 600, and a few outlines are beginning to form. Strangely enough, since they have not heretofore been recognized as an entity, the most substantial of these old shades are the Farmers north of the San Juan who have settled on the mesas along the Animas, building their houses, storerooms, and kivas, making their characteristic pottery, and keeping their noses close to their grinding stones. South of the San Juan are Basket Maker families experimenting with housebuilding, pottery making, and other new ideas which have been sifting down from the north. In the Upper Gila, the Cave Dwellers are raising snatch crops of beans and 8-row corn to supplement their diet of game, but with cave roofs to keep them dry, it will be a long time before any of them take the trouble to build a house. And in southeastern Arizona, the Cochise Foragers are in the process of losing their identity as an alien people moves in among them, bringing up new and strange ideas from the south.

For us, who are watching the slow development of a human society and trying to detect and understand the forces which are at work, the elementary lesson seems to be that when knowledge is diffused from one group to another, a new kind of food comes first—as 18-row corn to the Basket Makers, and beans and 8-row corn to the Foragers. Then come storage facilities—slab-lined

Rio Grande.

Falls Creek.

La Plata.

Durango.

Obelisk Cave.
Broken Flute Cave.
Red Rock Caves.

Mummy Cave.
Tee-ya-tso.

Bat Cave.

Cochise Foragers.

x Grand Gulch Caves.

San Juan.

Turkey Cave.

White Dog Cave.

Marsh Pass Caves.

Gila River.

Colorado River.

Little Colorado River.

x Dupont Cave.

Yuman Foragers.

THE SOUTHWEST AT A.D. 600

North of the San Juan the Farmers have been moving in to southwestern Colorado and have become firmly established around Durango and in the La Plata Valley.

In northeastern Arizona, the Basket Makers have increased and have occupied more caves in Marsh Pass and Red Rock Valley.

In southeastern Arizona, the Cochise Foragers are being affected by a migration of people who are coming up from eastern Mexico, bringing:

> *8-row corn*
> *Beans*
> *Undercut storage-pits*
> *Tipi-type circular houses*
> *Plain and polished red pottery*
> *The custom of skull deformation*

cists to the Basket Makers and large undercut pits to the Foragers. Then, with the adoption of the stay-at-home sort of life demanded by the growing, protection, and storage of crops, the idea of a house is accepted. And finally, anchored by the possession of property, the members of the family begin to experiment with the domestic arts of weaving and pottery making.

This is the stage we have reached in the Southwest at A.D. 600. From here on it will be the taste, ability, industry, and the quality of available materials that will enable us to follow the fortunes of each group through the years that lie ahead.

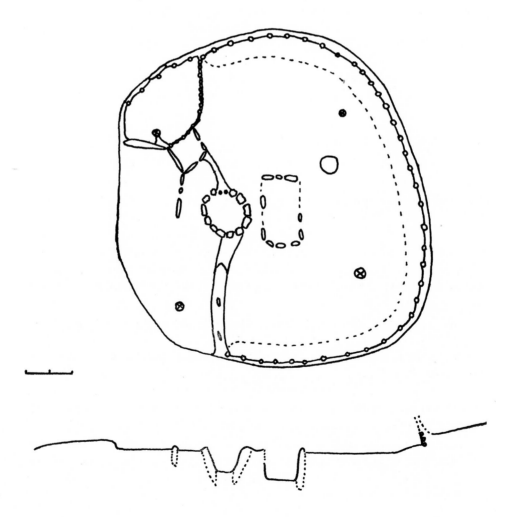

VIII

Comings and Goings: A.D. 600 to 700

DURING THE SIXTH CENTURY in Red Rock Valley the venerable culture of the Basket Makers held the even tenor of its way. At some time late in the century the family that had built their house in Obelisk Cave moved over a short distance to Broken Flute Cave, and they and their neighbors seem to have held a housebuilding bee, judging by the number of beams which have given dates in the early 600's. The style of house was much the same as in Obelisk, but in this case the hatchway in the roof has been preserved. Morris also found some traces of a side entrance, but still no sign of a ventilator. An important innovation was a low partition across the room, dividing the south section from the rest of the floor, and thereby bringing the Basket Maker's Broken Flute house one step nearer to the Farmer's Durango house. Both the houses and the storage cists continued to be built as separate units although, in some cases, there was an increase in the size of the houses, some of them running up to as much as 25 feet in diameter. The low bench was retained, beginning and ending at the points where the partition met the walls.

The general run of things that were worn, used, and made in Broken Flute Cave at A.D. 625 were about the same as the Obelisk styles of the fifth and sixth centuries, but there were two important additions to their way of life—beans and polished red pottery. Fortunately there is little doubt in either case as to the direction from which they came, as both are stamped with the hallmark of the

◄ **Broken Flute Cave: House 4**

south, if not of Mexico itself. The various kinds of beans which were grown in prehistoric times are generally believed to have been native to Central America or Mexico. Their complete absence in Basket Maker caves in Marsh Pass and Red Rock Valley with dates up to A.D. 500, and their first appearance in Broken Flute Cave at about A.D. 600 is therefore equivalent to punching a time clock to show when this drift from the south reached northern Arizona. Polished red pottery tells the same story in equally emphatic terms, and the pottery and the beans supplement one another in showing that the forces which had been affecting the Cochise Foragers in southern Arizona were powerful enough to reach as far north as the Basket Makers in Red Rock Valley. Any suggestion that the Basket Makers or the Farmers might have invented this redware would have as little to recommend it as that they might have invented their beans. From the days when pottery first appeared in the Four Corners and up to about A.D. 1300, the Farmers, the Basket Makers, and their descendants were unique in North America in consistently baking their pottery in a slow fire from which oxygen was partly excluded. This was a so-called reducing atmosphere, and the resulting pottery was gray or white. Redware, on the other hand, was the result of baking in an oxidizing atmosphere, or one in which an excess of oxygen was present due to a hot fire and forced draught. This was the practice in general use in North America—outside the Farmer-Basket Maker-Pueblo range—and was also the method employed in Mexico, Central and South America. The distinction is technical but important, for the fixed red color, as an integral part of the pottery itself, involved a technique of pottery making which was not employed by the Farmers and consequently was not used by the Basket Makers who had learned their lessons from the Farmers. As a result, the finding of polished redware in early northern sites provides the strongest kind of evidence that contact had been established with a people moving up from the south, and the time at which this event took place can be pinned down within fairly close limits. Beside Broken Flute, our survey has shown five other Basket Maker caves where polished redware has been found. These give the following ranges of dates:

In Red Rock Valley
    Broken Flute Cave   A.D. 440 to 626
    Atáhonez   625 to 670
    Twin Caves   605 to 667
South of Red Rock Valley
    Vandal Cave   607 to 683
Canyon del Muerto
    Mummy Cave   295 to 701
    Tse-ya-tso   439 to 739

From these dates it can be seen that the only time at which all of these caves were contemporaneously occupied was around A.D. 625, and the fact that neither beans nor polished redware were present in Obelisk Cave up to A.D. 493 makes it fairly sure that these things had not reached the Basket Makers at A.D. 500 and probably not before A.D. 600.

Judging by these dates, it also appears that the end of the Basket Maker occupation of Red Rock Valley came toward the close of the seventh century, the most recent date being A.D. 670 in Atáhonez. Vandal Cave, in the Lukachukai Mountains a few miles south, was occupied until 683; and still farther south, in Canyon del Muerto, Tse-ya-tso gives a final building date at 739 and Mummy Cave at 701. As suggested by the progression of these dates, the Basket Makers began a wholesale evacuation of northeastern Arizona in the late 600's, and during the eighth century we shall find that most of them had moved considerably farther south. Since their trek was from north to south, it would be logical to suppose that the cause was due to increasing pressure from the north, so it will be well to look into the situation north of the San Juan and see what the Farmers had been doing during the seventh century.

OUR TREE-RING DATES from the Durango villages range from A.D. 540 to 688, but the great majority fall between A.D. 575 and 625, and there are only a few beams with dates later than 625, which may well represent repairs rather than new construction. Although the number of beams that have been dated are only an infinitesimal fraction of those used in the houses, storerooms, and kivas, nevertheless they suggest that the peak of building activity had been reached at about A.D. 600, and the lack of dates after A.D. 700 implies that the Farmers had begun to leave the Durango area during the last half of the seventh century. Some moved due south to the La Plata Valley, where Morris has found settlements which were planned and built along the same lines as the Durango villages. Some pushed westward to Mesa Verde and Montezuma Valley, where Martin found them near Ackmen, Colorado; some as far as southeastern Utah, where Brew excavated one of their typical villages on Alkali Ridge—but in each of these cases, the dates run in the 700's and up into the 800's. Once the Durango district had been abandoned by the Farmers they did not return, and there are no indications that the area was later reoccupied by any other housebuilding or pottery making people.

One other indication that the Durango episode may have been of relatively short duration and had been terminated by about A.D. 700 is to be found in the local pottery. In 1934, Gila Pueblo acquired a collection of about five hundred bowls, pitchers, jars, ladles, and pipes which had been excavated from the rubbish mounds in the Durango villages, chiefly from the site on Blue Mesa. The collection was made up of two types of pottery, a plain rather dark grayware, and a lighter colored gray, decorated in black. None of the pottery was slipped; none was polished; there was no redware of any kind; and there were none of the later types of pottery, such as were found on the La Plata, near Ackmen, and on Alkali Ridge.

The plain gray was interesting chiefly because of its wide range of shapes, several of which were confined to the period of the Durango villages and did not again show up in the Southwest, and a few which are vaguely suggestive

An elbow-pipe from Blue
Mesa, Durango

An Algonquin elbow-type
(Willoughby, C. C. 1935)

Durango: plain gray pottery

of vessel shapes that have been found in the Mississippi Valley. This is particularly true of a baked clay elbow-pipe from Blue Mesa which appears to be identical with some of the Eastern pipes, but to the best of my knowledge, has not been found elsewhere in the Southwest at any later time.

The black-on-gray decorated pottery was valuable in illustrating the style of designs, the most popular composition being a pair of opposed panels. But again, this arrangement did not meet with lasting favor, although some of the elements of design were carried over into later types.

Taken as a whole, the Durango pottery gives one the impression of having been a rather specialized type, based on a local tradition of pottery making. Some of the plain gray pots suggest eastern influence or derivation, but neither the plain nor the decorated ware show any relationship whatever to the color, shape, finish, or method of firing of the polished redware which was being brought up

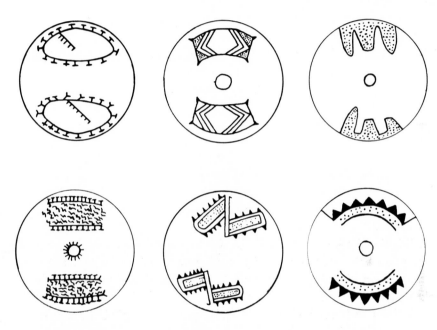

Early black-on-white: Durango District
The decoration on early Durango bowls runs chiefly to opposed panels of random elements. It is quite unlike the decoration on other early Southwestern types and appears to have been bound by an entirely different tradition of design.

(Gila Pueblo Collections)

from the south during the 600's. The lack of any later local pottery development; the absence of later pottery types from adjacent areas; our failure to obtain any tree-ring dates after A.D. 700; the marked increase in population along the La Plata, in Montezuma Valley, and in southeastern Utah after A.D. 700, all point to the same conclusion: that the Farmers left the Durango district in the late 600's and moved south to the La Plata and west to the mesas along the northern side of the San Juan. It was this southerly shift of the Farmers that was undoubtedly the reason why the Basket Makers left their caves in Red Rock Valley late in the seventh century and moved to the south—some to the west of the Chuskas, into the drainage of the Little Colorado, others southeastward into the Chaco Basin and on down to the Rio Puerco, where we will find them in the eighth century. The importance of pinning down the time and tracing the trend of these movements lies in the fact that as the Basket Makers moved southward away from the Farmers, another migration, coming up from Mexico, had moved in on the Cochise Foragers and was thrusting northward from under the Rim. It was the result of the merging, in varying degrees, of these northern and southern groups that constitutes the essence of Southwestern history. This will become increasingly clear as we drop down below the Rim and look over the situation which had been developing during the seventh century.

BY THIS TIME it will be apparent that during the seventh century there were not less than three separate and distinct peoples in the Southwest: Farmers, north of the San Juan; Basket Makers, in the middle; and some strangers from the south who were just beginning to make their presence felt. From the Farmers the Basket Makers had learned how to build a house, to make gray pottery, to weave a multiple-warp sandal, to grow 18-row corn, and to make and do a number of other things which remain to be settled. From the south, at A.D. 600, they were acquiring a taste for beans and were being told that pottery could be slipped, polished, and turned to a bright red when baked in an open fire—a lesson which the Basket Maker women promptly forgot and thereafter refused to learn.

With the Farmers and the Basket Makers accounted for, we come now to the strangers below the Mogollon Rim who had been thrusting northward, and at A.D. 600, were just beginning to make friends with the Basket Makers in Red Rock Valley.

To those archaeologists who have heretofore regarded the Southwest as a domain exclusively reserved for Basket Makers, these strangers moving up from the south will not be welcome. The prevailing attitude toward these new ideas seems to be much the same as that of the man who didn't like spinach and was glad he didn't like it, because if he did, he'd eat it, and he hated the damned stuff. But whether one likes it or not, the time has come when we are going to have to recognize these southern strangers and attend some of the courses in diffusion which they were providing for the Cochise Foragers who were starting on the long uphill climb to what we call civilization.

DURING THE SEASON when we were digging up what was left of some Cochise Foragers in a peat bog on the eastern side of the Chiricahua Mountains in south-eastern Arizona, we ran across a site at the mouth of Cave Creek where it fans out into the San Simon Valley. Sayles found the site, and how he decided that someone had once lived there I do not know, as there was not a trace of a mound or a depression to mark a house, and the few sherds lying on the surface could easily have been washed down by the creek. Nevertheless he backed his idea by cutting an exploratory trench across the area, and struck one of the most important sites we have ever found.

Excavation uncovered seven house floors, shallow and poorly defined, but well-enough preserved to show that they were circular or oval, with a side entrance and a fireplace near the doorway. The pottery was plain brown and polished red—no decorated sherds of any kind were found. A number of stone tools were turned up which could hardly be described as beautiful, unless seen through the eyes of an archaeological parent, in which case they ranked favorably with the world's masterpieces, since they appeared to be identical to those of the Cochise Foragers with whose handicraft we were already familiar. On top of all else we were singularly fortunate in finding that our Cave Creek site contained only one cultural level, so sparing us any uncertainty as to whether the houses and pottery had been properly segregated from the remains of earlier or later periods—a question which often arises in the excavation of sites which were continuously occupied for a long time.

The evidence at the Cave Creek village was clear and clean-cut. The obvious, and apparently the only, conclusion to be drawn is that the site represented a resident population at the level of the Cochise Foragers which had received an influx of a new group of people who had brought their plain brown and polished red pottery with them. Sites which show the same combination of houses, stone tools, plain and polished red pottery in their earliest levels have also been found in the San Simon, Mimbres, and San Francisco valleys, so that the Cave Creek village is not unique, even though it is the earliest and purest example of its kind so far found. In order to distinguish these sites from other groups which also were beginning to form at this time, we gave them the name of Mogollon—so called after the Mogollon Mountains in southwestern New Mexico where many of the later villages were situated.*

The recognition of the Mogollon Culture was an important step in the right direction, but it is only the first of several that must be taken to reach an understanding of one of the principal forces in the shaping of Southwestern history. In southeastern Arizona and southwestern New Mexico during the sixth and seventh centuries we are witnessing the gradual effects of a migration of people coming up from the south—their approach heralded by 8-row corn and beans, followed by storage pits and a house; the climax reached with plain brown and polished red pottery. Locally, the impact of this migration on the Cochise Foragers resulted in the formation of small communities, rarely of more than five or six houses at any one time, which are interesting in their own right, but which could not conceivably have been responsible for the far-reaching effects of this migration on the Southwest as a whole.

Looking farther afield, one can begin by saying that the same sort of house and the same kind of polished red pottery have also been found in Texas and in the southern Mississippi Valley. It is very doubtful, however, if pottery was known in Texas early enough to have been the source for polished red pottery in the Southwest at A.D. 600. It seems much more likely that both Texas and the

---

* By archaeologists, Mogollon is pronounced Muggy-own.

Cave Creek: ground stone tools and pottery

Southwest received their red pottery from the same southern source—probably the east coast of Mexico where it is known to have been made in early times.

As far as the Southwest is concerned, it looks as if the small Mogollon villages in the San Simon, Mimbres, and San Francisco valleys were merely the residue which was left as the main stream of the migration passed northward. Judging by the things which they introduced to the Foragers, these incoming people were familiar with agriculture, but the plains of southern Arizona are hot and dry and to most of the immigrants the local conditions were not sufficiently attractive to induce them to settle down in this section of the country. After crossing the Mexican Border, their trails are fairly clear. A few filtered up through the valley of the Rio Grande. Some settled in the Mimbres Valley. A considerable number pushed up the valley of the San Francisco and up onto the Plateau as far north as the Rio Puerco. A few bands drifted off to the west along the Gila. Another large body passed off to the west of the Mogollon villages and then swung north to the Rim, where some groups came to a dead end, but many were deflected westward to the Verde Valley and so up to Flagstaff and beyond, to northeastern Arizona, with some even crossing the San Juan into southeastern Utah.

This is just a bald outline of the developments which were beginning to unfold at about A.D. 600. So far it has been based chiefly on such material things as pottery and the remains of houses, but there are other extremely important clues to guide us—the physical type of the people who made up this migration from the south and the method they employed to improve their appearance.

To appreciate the full value of this evidence, it must be remembered that the First Families of the Southwest—the Basket Makers, Cave Dwellers, and Foragers—were all members of Hooton's fundamental stock, long-headed, non-Mongoloid, and that they made no attempt to improve on nature by trying to flatten the backs of their heads.

The second physical type to appear in the Southwest was that of the Farmers. Since these Farmers are an entirely new conception, no attempt has yet been made to identify them as a distinct physical group, but Seltzer's assertion that the skulls from Grand Gulch were not the same as those of the Arizona Basket Makers can only mean that some people who were not Basket Makers were circulating around the Four Corners during the early centuries after Christ. This would also explain Morris' statement that he has often found both broad and long skulls, undeformed, in early cemeteries on the La Plata. It is something for the physical anthropologists to argue about, but I suspect that when and if the Farmers' type is identified it will turn out to have been a medium-broad skull, Mongoloid, and not deformed.

The third physical type is of great value in providing us with evidence that we are dealing with an actual immigration of people who had formerly been unknown in the Southwest. This is shown by the first appearance, soon after A.D. 600, of a broad-headed, low-vaulted, Mongoloid head-form, the breadth being accentuated by an artificial flattening of the back of the skull. These were the people that we found in the San Simon village, a few miles northwest of Cave Creek, who were described by Brues as the San Simon type, with low narrow frontal region, broad-headed, and occipitally deformed.

It has sometimes been said that this flattening of the skull might have been

THE SOUTHWEST AT A.D. 700

During the sixth and seventh centuries the Farmer villages around Durango showed phenomenal growth, but by A.D. 700 the Farmers were moving southwest to the La Plata Valley and west to Montezuma Valley and southeastern Utah.

Due to this increasing pressure from north of the San Juan, the Basket Makers, at A.D. 700, were leaving their caves in Red Rock Valley and moving south along the eastern and western slopes of the Chuskas.

Below the Mogollon Rim, the people coming up from eastern Mexico who introduced 8-row corn, beans, tipi-type houses, polished red pottery, and skull deformation to the Southwest have been identified as the Reds.

In southwestern New Mexico, the meeting of Reds and Cochise Foragers has resulted in the formation of the Mogollon Culture, but other Red bands have been moving up to the Plateau, with some groups reaching northeastern Arizona where their polished red pottery and beans have been found in Basket Maker caves at dates in the 600's.

due to the use of a wooden cradle-board, so implying that the effect was the result of chance. There are, however, many skulls which show lambdoidal flattening—at that part of the top and back of our heads where many of us begin to grow bald—and if this was due to their heads being strapped to a cradle-board, the babies must have worn their cradles perched on top of their heads like a bonnet. It would also be difficult for some of us to understand why chance should not have begun to operate until after A.D. 600, since none of the earlier skulls were deformed. The practice later became so widespread that there can be no doubt it was intentional and so serves as one more clue in helping us to trace the spread of the people who introduced the custom to the Southwest. As a start along this line, it is significant that the same kind of cranial deformation was practiced in Mexico and Central America, but according to Hooton, was not known in northeastern Asia, which should help one to decide on the direction from which this migration was coming.

What to call these people is a difficult problem. When they moved in on the Cochise Foragers and the Cave Dwellers of the Upper Gila the resulting combination was given the name of Mogollon; but as this Mogollon Culture was then and thereafter confined to southeastern Arizona and southwestern New Mexico, it is obviously necessary to draw a distinction between this local mixture and the more important developments which are about to take place to the west and north. Since nothing is known of their background before they reached the Southwest one cannot be specific, so I am going to call them "Reds," after the color of their pottery, and leave it to the future to find a more appropriate name.

THIS BRINGS my tale up to A.D. 700, and it may help to keep things in order if we pause for a moment and look back over what has happened.

As I see it, the First Families in the Southwest were small scattered groups of forager-hunters sharing the same physical type and many of the same tools. Later, at about the time of Christ, the descendants of the earlier settlers—as Basket Makers and Cave Dwellers—are again shown to have possessed the same perishable things, and it would be difficult to detect any important differences within the range of their cultures.

At about A.D. 200, the vanguard of a migration of people whom I have called the Farmers arrived in southwestern Colorado and settled near Durango. During the years from A.D. 200 to 700 they increased in numbers, and it was from these Farmers that the Basket Makers acquired their knowledge of 18-row corn, pottery making, housebuilding, and a number of other things—none of which they had known before, and none of which reached the Cave Dwellers of the Upper Gila or the Foragers of southeastern Arizona.

During the sixth and seventh centuries, another migration of people whom I am calling the Reds came up from the south bringing 8-row corn, beans, a circular house, and polished red pottery to the Cochise Foragers. Some of these immigrants met and merged with the Foragers and Cave Dwellers of the Upper Gila, resulting in the Mogollon Culture. The majority, however, pushed northward to the Plateau by way of the San Francisco Valley, Tonto Basin, and the valley of the Verde.

At A.D. 700 we are entering what I believe was the most important century of Southwestern history. It was a period of comings, goings, and mergers, and it will require a great deal of care and discrimination to identify the various movements and combinations which will form the foundations of the later and better known cultures. As the eighth century opened, the Farmers who had settled around Durango were spreading out to the south and west—to the La Plata Valley, Mesa Verde, and southeastern Utah. Due to this increasing pressure from north of the San Juan, the Basket Makers of northeastern Arizona started pulling out of their caves and moving southward along the eastern and western sides of the Chuskas, and as they pushed south they met bands of Reds coming up over the Mogollon Rim from the south. Still another migration of people, with whom we will be concerned in the next chapter, was moving northward along the west coast of Mexico to reach the Gila Basin in southern Arizona during the early 700's.

Out of the stones, bones, sherds, ruined houses, and other debris which they left behind them, the various peoples who once made these things are beginning to emerge as actual creatures of flesh and blood. Lacking written records as to who they were or where they came from, it is fortunate for the purposes of history that the products of each tribe were sufficiently distinct to enable us to trace them as they circulated through the Southwest.

Snaketown: the ball-court, west half excavated

IX

Tides of Men: A.D. 700 to 800

Up to this point we have been considering the activities, variations, and combinations of three different peoples—First Families, Farmers, and Reds. We are now about to meet a fourth and extremely interesting tribe of whom, until recently, very little was known. These are the Indians who have been called the Hohokam,* and who at about A.D. 700 set out from wherever they had been living to seek new horizons, and eventually landed in southern Arizona.

Up to 1927 the identity of the Hohokam had been obscured by the belief that they represented merely an early and local stage in the cultural progress of a Puebloan tribe which overran southern Arizona in the twelfth, thirteenth, and fourteenth centuries. In 1927, however, after burrowing in the mounds at Casa Grande and sorting out the rubbish, we were able to segregate the Hohokam levels from later deposits, and when this had been done, to divide their characteristic red-on-buff pottery into three periods. The earliest of these we called the Colonial, in the belief that it represented a time of colonization. This was followed by a Sedentary Period, during which the colonists were given an opportunity to settle down. Then came a Classic Period which was approximately contemporaneous with the Puebloan influx which began in the twelfth century.

At present I am concerned only with the decorated pottery of the Colonial Period which consisted of a dark maroon paint on a buff surface which was

* Pronounced Hoho-kám, from a Pima word meaning "Those who have gone."

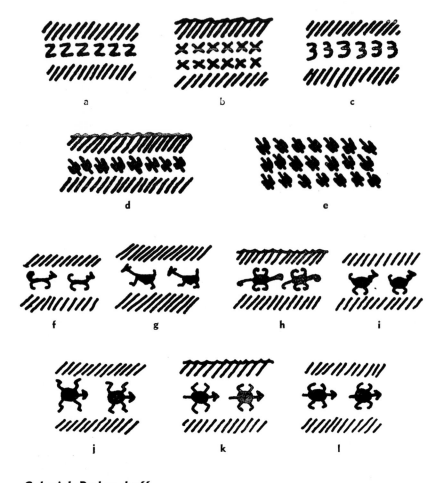

Colonial Red-on-buff
The uniformity of designs throughout the Hohokam area

a, b & c have been found at the following sites:

Arizona A	: 11 : 6	Casa Grande	: 2 : 1	Roosevelt	:	9 : 6
	11 : 9	Ft. McDowell	: 7 : 1	Sacaton	:	4 : 6
	11 : 11	Gila Butte	: 5 : 11			9 : 1
	11 : 12		5 : 14			9 : 4
	14 : 7	Mesa	: 4 : 3	Signal Peak	:	9 : 1
Arizona J	: 12 : 1	Phoenix	: 3 : 1	Tucson	:	7 : 1

d & e have been found at the following sites:

Arizona A	: 9 : 3	Gila Butte	: 5 : 4	Mesa	:	1 : 8
	11 : 10		5 : 5			2 : 3
	11 : 12		5 : 7			4 : 3
	14 : 1		5 : 9	Phoenix	:	3 : 1
	14 : 5		5 : 10			1 : 3
	14 : 9		5 : 12			2 : 1
Arizona C	: 5 : 2		5 : 16			2 : 6
	5 : 4		5 : 17	Roosevelt	:	9 : 6
Arizona J	: 5 : 1		5 : 27	Sacaton	:	2 : 1

Casa Grande	:	2 : 1	Gila Butte	:	5 : 28	Sacaton	:	2 : 4
Desert Well	:	8 : 12			5 : 29			2 : 7
Florence	:	1 : 5			5 : 30			4 : 2
		4 : 4			5 : 33			9 : 4
		5 : 2			5 : 36			9 : 12
		5 : 3			5 : 39			9 : 42
Ft. McDowell	:	7 : 1			5 : 40	Signal Peak	:	9 : 1
Gila Butte	:	5 : 1						

f	has	been	found	at	Gila Butte	:	3 :	1
g					Phoenix	:	3 :	1
h					Congress	:	2 :	2
i					Roosevelt	:	9 :	6
j					Sacaton	:	9 :	4
k					Roosevelt	:	9 :	6
l					Mesa	:	2 :	5

m    n    o

p    q    r    s

t    u    v

m	has	been	found	at	Sacaton	:	2 :	7
n					Ft. McDowell	:	7 :	1
o					Phoenix	:	3 :	1
p					Roosevelt	:	9 :	6
q					Phoenix	:	3 :	1
r					Gila Butte	:	5 :	9
s					Sacaton	:	2 :	6
t					Roosevelt	:	9 :	6
u					Sacaton	:	9 :	4
v					Phoenix	:	3 :	1

And all designs from a to v have been found at Snaketown

smoothed but not polished. Designs were composed of small figures and drawings of birds, animals, insects, and reptiles, arranged in concentric bands around the inside of a bowl, often giving the effect of a whirlpool.

With pottery which was so distinct, and was quite unlike anything that had been found anywhere else in the Southwest, we started, in 1927, on a sort of glorified paper-chase to track the Hohokam to their source. We scoured the Gila Basin and brought home the sherds and the descriptions of 167 Colonial sites, in which the decorated pottery showed extraordinary uniformity throughout its range, so implying that all of these settlements had been established within a comparatively short time. Then we went southward into the Papagueria and followed the course of the Rio Altar as far as Caborca, but when we lost the trail in northern Sonora, we folded our tents like the Arabs and as silently stole away. We searched westward to the Colorado River, northward up the Verde Valley to Flagstaff, and eastward to the Rio Grande. Failing to find what we were seeking, we decided on still wider casts and by the autumn of 1934, we had ranged east through Texas to the Mississippi; south through Chihuahua to Durango, Mexico; west to the Pacific Coast; and north into Idaho, Wyoming, and Montana. The net result of eight years of determined searching was a broadening of our horizons, but when we were through, we knew no more about the origin of the Hohokam than when we began. The only really suggestive clue we had uncovered was that our 167 Colonial sites were all clustered along the Gila and its tributaries in southwestern Arizona, so pointing to Sonora as the probable route of entry, but there was no dodging the fact that neither we nor anyone else had ever found a typical Hohokam site in Sonora.

By the autumn of 1934, having failed to run them down, we decided to dig them up. We chose the modern Pima village of Snaketown, nine miles southwest of Chandler, where our survey had shown a large site containing sixty rubbish mounds scattered over an area three-quarters of a mile north and south, and half a mile east and west. We were very fortunate in our choice, and during the two winters that we spent in excavating the site, we unearthed an immense amount of material. At this point it would be very easy to become involved in one more archaeological report, but the details have all been published, and I think that for present purposes illustrations will convey a better idea of the things the Hohokam made, used, and did than many pages of text.

When one looks over these illustrations with a discerning eye, they go a long way toward solving some of our problems. Such things, for instance, as ballcourts, mosaic plaques, copper bells, carved stone figures, earplugs, tripod trays, modelled heads of clay, designs on shell etched with acid, all point unmistakably toward Mexico, if not even farther south. These things are impressive because of the skilled workmanship which produced them, but to my mind the outstanding accomplishment of the Hohokam was their system of irrigation canals of which over one hundred miles have been traced in the Gila Basin. The engineering knowledge, the directed effort, and the cooperative labor which went into the making of these canals were unique in Southwestern history and explain

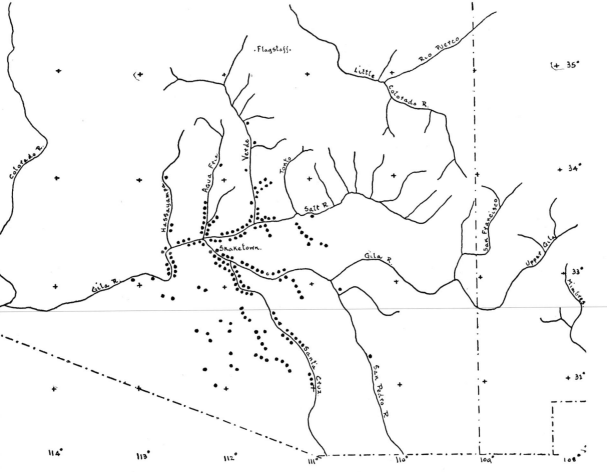

Map of southern Arizona and southwestern New Mexico, showing location of 167 Hohokam sites of the Colonial Period. (+ indicates Quadrangle Corners.)

why we have failed to find traces of the passage of these people through Sonora. Here are no hunters or foragers. We are now dealing with a people who already possessed an advanced and complex culture when they first set foot in southern Arizona. Their selection of the desert along the Gila as a place in which to settle down and go to work makes it clear that their choice was governed by certain requirements which were essential to their way of life.

The first of these was a river, but it seems that this had to be a very special sort of river: one with just the right amount of fall, so as to permit the building of brush diversion dams, low banks which would not make it too difficult to divert water from the river-bed, and flat bordering land, with not too much slope, for the irrigation canals. A second requisite would be a sandy soil, with as few boulders as possible and no rock out-crops, so as to make it possible to dig the canals with nothing more than the sticks and stones which were their

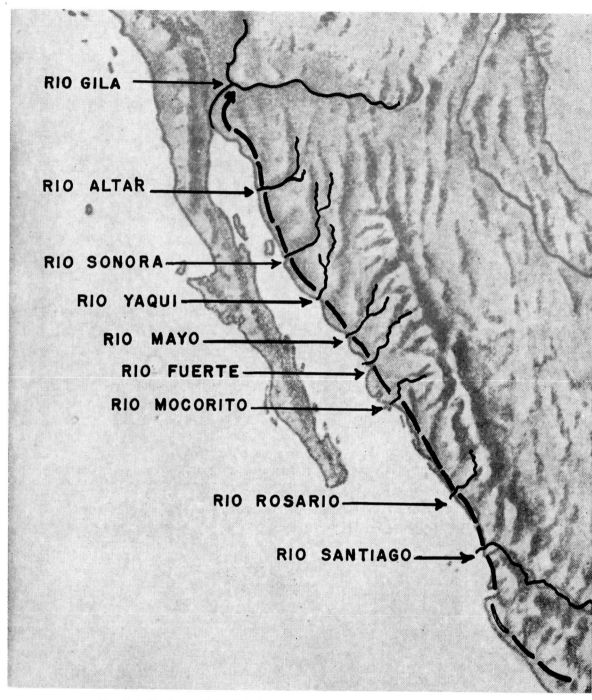

RIO GILA

RIO ALTAR

RIO SONORA

RIO YAQUI

RIO MAYO

RIO FUERTE

RIO MOCORITO

RIO ROSARIO

RIO SANTIAGO

The Probable Route of the Hohokam Migration
When the Hohokam came up from Mexico, they followed the narrow coastal plain where the rivers flowing down from the Sierra Madre are intermittent, often torrential, and not suitable for the methods of irrigation used by the Hohokam. The failure of the Hohokam to settle along any of these rivers implies that it was not until the flat flood-plain of the Gila was reached that all of the essential conditions were found to be present.

The Gila Basin, southern Arizona

only tools. Other essentials were a climate which would be favorable and a soil rich enough to enable the Hohokam to grow their crops of corn, tepary beans, lima beans, pumpkins, and cotton. And last, but by no means least, there must have been enough skilled hands to have carried out the great cooperative projects of building ball-courts and great lodges and digging the many miles of canals to irrigate the farms which were spread out along the Gila and its tributaries.

Recognizing the highly organized status of their society and the probability that the arts, crafts, and customs of the Hohokam point to a source in Mexico, it should not be difficult to understand why we have all failed to find traces of their migration. Assuming, for the moment, that they had formerly lived in southern Mexico, and that for reasons unknown, they were dislodged and started their trek northward along the west coast, they would have entered a narrowing coastal plain where all of the rivers flowing down from the Sierra Madre are either precipitous or intermittent. In Tepic they would have had to cross the Rio Santiago; the Rosario, Mocorito, and Fuerte in Sinaloa; the Mayo, Yaqui, Sonora, and Altar in Sonora. It is quite possible that the Hohokam may have halted at one or all of these rivers, but if they did, it could only have been for a short time, as there are no reports of their permanent settlements—and the size and character of the things they left behind them when they did settle down are not such as to be easily overlooked. The explanation, I think, may be that when they left their former homes their culture was already so highly specialized that certain environmental conditions were essential to its proper functioning and such conditions had not been met during the course of their journey until the Gila Basin was reached. On reaching central Sonora, some bands may have fol-

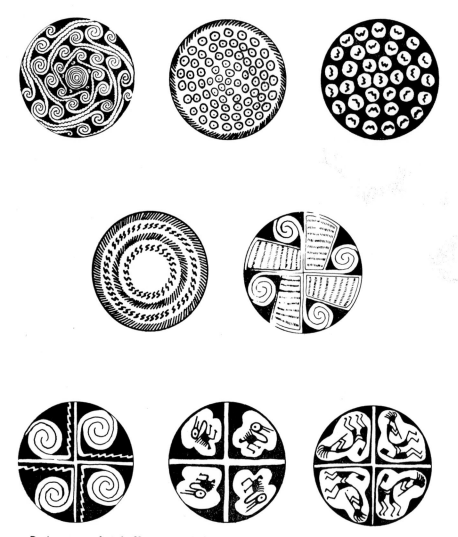

Designs on red-on-buff pottery of the Colonial Period

lowed the valley of the Yaqui, Sonora, or Altar, each of which would have led them northward to the border near Nogales or Douglas—so accounting for some of the southern Hohokam villages on the San Pedro, around Tucson, and in the Papagueria. It looks to me, however, as if the main body of the migration had followed the coast of the Gulf of California to the delta of the Colorado, then up the river for about fifty miles to the junction of the Gila, and so eastward to the Gila Basin where they settled down and went to work.

Regardless of how near the mark these ideas may be, we are now confronted with the fact that soon after A.D. 700, the Hohokam were established

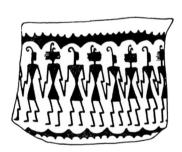

Designs on red-on-buff pottery of the Sedentary Period

in large numbers along the Gila and Salt rivers in southern Arizona with a culture which was totally unlike anything else known in the Southwest. It is extremely significant that their early culture was better in quality than that of later periods—so spoiling any theory of local origins and subsequent development. When the Hohokam reached southern Arizona they brought with them the latest ideas from the ateliers of Mexico, but after leaving these sources of inspiration behind them, their cultural initiative seems to have dried up in the heat of the Gila Basin.

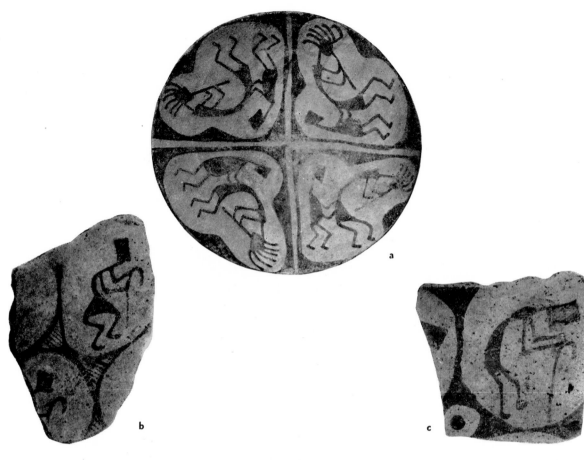

Snaketown: Red-on-buff Pottery of the Sedentary Period
   a. The hump-backed flute-player
   b & c. Old men
   d. Masked dancers

Snaketown
Horned-toad, etched with acid, and slate palettes

Snaketown: carved stone

◀ Snaketown
    a. Copper bell, cast by the lost-wax process
    b. Crescentic flints, probably inserted along the cutting edge of a wooden
       sword, as in Mexico.
    c & g. Side-notched utility arrow-points   d, e, f. Serrated points

Snaketown
   Carved stone deity (?) and pottery heads

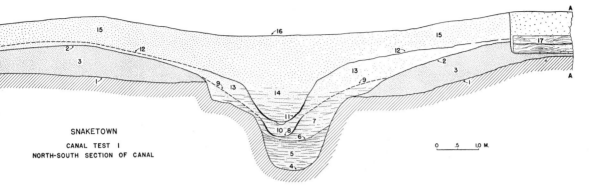

Snaketown: section through the irrigation canal showing the superposition of three canals.

LET US TURN to southwestern New Mexico, about two hundred miles to the east of the Hohokam settlements. Here, a trickle of Reds which had been filtering into the Cochise Foragers during the 600's had grown to a steady stream by A.D. 700. A number of small villages were being built in the San Simon, Mimbres, and San Francisco valleys, in each of which the same Red types of pottery and the same Cochise stoneware were being made. There were, however, some wide variations in architecture between the northern and southern extremes which raise a point that needs to be strongly emphasized—that in this early period, when groups of different peoples were moving around and various combinations of culture were beginning to form, it is very unusual to find any two villages which were exactly alike. The reasons for this are clear. In the first place, there is a vast difference between the environment of Cave Creek, the southernmost Mogollon village in the arid and exposed San Simon Valley, and that of Luna Village, over one hundred miles to the north in the pine forests of the upper San Francisco Valley. In the second, we are dealing with a time when the Red migration was entering a Southwest which was already populated by Foragers, Cave Dwellers, Basket Makers, and Farmers, with density increasing from south to north. It is therefore obvious that as they moved north from the Mexican Border, the proportion of immigrants to the resident population varied in each village. In the south, as at Cave Creek, the incoming Reds clearly outnumbered the resident Foragers, but as they worked their way up to the Plateau and began meeting more and more Basket Makers, their proportional representation declined, until by the time they finally reached the San Juan, it is rather surprising that there were enough of them left to leave any trace of their presence.

In starting on the trail of these people as they spread through the Southwest, there is one other valuable clue to guide us. This is a style of decorating pottery which made its first appearance in the southernmost Red villages at about the middle of the eighth century. Designs were drawn in broad finger-width red lines and were strictly rectilinear, in the form of chevrons, triangles, and straight parallel lines. This style of decoration was common in Mexico, but nothing of the kind was known on the pottery of the Farmers, Basket Makers, or Hohokam before Red contact, and consequently when rectilinear designs show up on their later pottery, it is a fair indication that a Red artist was somewhere in the offing. With a distinctive style of decorating pottery, the use of a slip, polished surfaces, mineral paint, and a fixed red color, we now have five good clues to detect the presence of Red potters as they moved around among the other peoples in the Southwest. If we can sometimes find that Red women had also shown other mothers how to flatten the heads of their children, so much the better. All of which goes to show that here, as usual, the female of the species was more important in the medley than the male.

SOMEDAY, someone may succeed in tracing the Reds back to their homeland in Mexico, but as things stand at present, their trail begins at the Cave Creek village, in southeastern Arizona. This is the southernmost of their sites so far found, and it also seems to have been the earliest settlement where Red men built their small circular houses, and Red women made their plain brown and polished red pottery, and where the burden of domestic chores was lightened by the help of a few Foragers who shaped the stone tools and ground the 8-row corn.

The next step takes us about twenty miles north to the San Simon village in which the earliest level showed the same polished red pottery and small circular houses. Here, an interesting innovation was started when someone set his posts and arranged the side entrance to his house in such a way that the floor, when excavated, had the shape of a bean—a peculiarity which can easily be recognized when it shows up in other sites. A little later, at about A.D. 750, brown pottery decorated with broad red rectilinear lines was added to the output of plain brown and polished red, and at about the same time the men began to flatten the entrance side of their houses. It was also here that we found the broad deformed skulls which Brues described as the San Simon type. What with the broad open valley in which they lived, their broad-line pottery designs, their broad flattened heads, and their flattened house fronts, the San Simon villagers seem to have liked things broad and flat.

A third site which can be added to this southern Red group is the Cameron Creek village in the southern Mimbres Valley about seventy-five miles east and slightly north of the San Simon village. Here Bradfield found the same polished red pottery in the lowest levels, followed by broad-line red-on-brown, and he also excavated some small circular houses and some with a flat side, similar to those at the San Simon village.

No tree-ring dates have been obtained from the Cave Creek, San Simon, or Cameron Creek villages, but in each case, the small, shallow, circular houses appear to have been earlier than those farther north. It is also true that during this early period, these three villages resemble one another more closely than any two sites to the north and west resemble each other, so implying that although Red houses were very simple, they were more or less standardized when first introduced to southern Arizona. Another feature which sets this group apart at this time is that no one of these three southern Red villages shows any sign of influence from, or contact with, either the Hohokam to the west or the Basket Makers to the north. This is an important point, as in the old days men and women took just as much interest in each other's gadgets, particularly pottery, as we today show in a new game or fashion. As a result, ideas and styles often used to spread with surprising rapidity, and it is very unusual to find a site anywhere in the Southwest which shows no evidence of intrusion from other cultures, sometimes as influence but more often in the form of sherds or other objects. The subject will frequently recur, as such trade wares and exchanges provide us with valuable time equations, but for the present it is enough to say that the absence of foreign intrusions at the Cave Creek, San Simon, and Cameron Creek villages at A.D. 700 was probably due to the fact that the Hohokam had not yet reached the Gila Basin to the west and the Basket Makers, coming down from the north, had not yet entered Mogollon territory. This, I think, will explain why these three early southern villages give us our purest examples of the meeting of Reds and Foragers. Lacking tree-ring dates, it is not possible to be accurate, but I think that the date for the founding of these three Red villages can be set fairly close to A.D. 700—possibly a few years earlier.

About fifteen miles north of Cameron Creek, up the Mimbres Valley, there is the Harris site which we excavated in the summer of 1934. Here again the lowest level contained only plain brown and polished red pottery, but the earliest houses, although circular, were deep pit-houses with long inclined side entrances. From one of these we obtained three fragments of charcoal which gave dates at A.D. 694, 704, and 712, but in each case some of the outside rings were missing and the actual date when the house was built may have been nearer to A.D. 725 than 700. A new and important addition was a great lodge, 36 feet in diameter, 5 feet deep, with an inclined entryway 15 feet long. I have called it a lodge because it was obviously too large to have served as a dwelling and it looks as if it must have been used for meetings or ceremonial purposes. The fact that large buildings of this kind were not present in the earlier and more southerly villages at Cave Creek, San Simon, and Cameron Creek indicates that these great lodges were not introduced by the Reds when they first entered the Southwest. It looks more as if the idea had been acquired from the Hohokam who are known to have built great lodges of about this same size as soon as they settled in southern Arizona. If this is the right explanation—and I think it is—it would also tend to confirm the belief that the Hohokam had not reached southern Arizona before about A.D. 700.

Some sixty airline miles west of the Mimbres Valley, the San Francisco River flows down from the Continental Divide. Here, near Glenwood in the lower part of the valley, we excavated a ruin which we called the Mogollon village. We uncovered some deep circular pit-houses and a bean-shaped great lodge, 38 feet in diameter, but if there was a pure early period of polished red

The southern country: the San Simon Valley

The northern country: the upper San Francisco Valley

a   b   c

Broad-line Red-on-brown: Quartered - Rectilinear
  a. **Harris and Mogollon villages**
  b. **San Simon Village**
  c. **Snaketown**

pottery, it could not be segregated, owing to the mixture of later deposits. A fragment of charcoal from the great lodge gave us a date of A.D. 725 which is chiefly of value in showing that the lodge could not have been built *before* 725 but may have been a few years later. No broad-line red-on-brown was found.

Up the San Francisco Valley, about thirty miles north of the Mogollon village, there are two sites which were founded in early Red times. The Starkweather Ruin, excavated by the Logan Museum, lies three and a half miles west of Reserve, and the S. U. site, excavated by the Chicago Museum of Natural History, is situated three and a half miles west of the Starkweather Ruin. At the S. U. site Martin found a number of rather shallow circular houses, all with side entrances, and two bean-shaped great lodges, each about 33 feet in diameter, with plain brown and polished red pottery, but no decorated ware of any kind. Fragments of charcoal from one of the circular houses gave us seven dates ranging from A.D. 726 to 752.

At the Starkweather Ruin, only a short distance away, Nesbit found circular houses, but they were all deep pit-houses, and some had roof entrances, which at once suggests contact with Basket Makers coming down from the north, since nothing of this kind has been found in any of the Red villages to the south or among the Hohokam. We obtained a date of A.D. 708 from one of the pit-houses with a roof entrance, but some outside rings had been lost, and the actual building date may have been A.D. 725, or later. The great lodge had a diameter of 37 feet and was over 5 feet deep; it was circular and had a side entrance, but Nesbit did not describe it as bean-shaped. There was no broad-line red-on-brown.

About twenty-five miles northwest of Reserve, the Luna village stands near the source of the San Francisco River in the heart of the White Mountains at an altitude of over 7,000 feet. The site was excavated in 1919 by Dr. Walter Hough for the U. S. National Museum, and it was shown that the village had been occupied for a long time. Unfortunately, this is another instance where it was not possible to segregate the various levels, thus one cannot be sure that the site

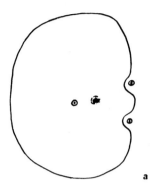 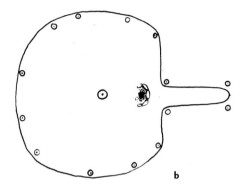

a   b

Mogollon House Plans
 a. A bean-shaped house
 b. A house with the entrance side flattened

harked back to the days when only brown and red pottery was being made. The Luna village is important, however, as all of the deep circular pit-houses were found to have roof entrances, and in this case we actually found some sherds of Basket Maker grayware when we surveyed the site in 1931, so helping to confirm the belief that Reds had run into Basket Makers when they reached the upper San Francisco. There was a great lodge at the Luna village which Hough estimated to have been over 40 feet in diameter, but it was not completely excavated and his guess may have erred on the large side.

From Cave Creek in the south to Luna in the north, the sites which mark the passage of the Reds as they moved northward through the Mimbres and San Francisco valleys have been known collectively as the Mogollon Culture—a name which applies and should be restricted to the concentrated and local culture in the San Simon, San Francisco, and Mimbres valleys. Here, for the time being, we can leave them as we follow the trail of those Red bands which continued northward to the Plateau or passed to the west of the Mogollon villages, earning new names for themselves and the various groups of people with whom they combined.

AT THE LUNA VILLAGE the Reds had reached an altitude of 7,300 feet at the headwaters of the San Francisco. The hunting was good. There was plenty of water and timber, but killing frosts come late in the spring and early in the autumn, and this usually means a growing season too short for a people chiefly dependent upon agriculture for their living. Some groups in which the Cave Dweller may have outweighed the Red strain remained and hunted the game which abounds in the forests of the Upper Gila, and these later played a part in the formation of the Cibola and Mimbres Branches. Many of the Reds, however, pushed northward over the divide which separates the Little Colorado from the Gila drainage, and dropping down the northern slope of the White Mountains, reached

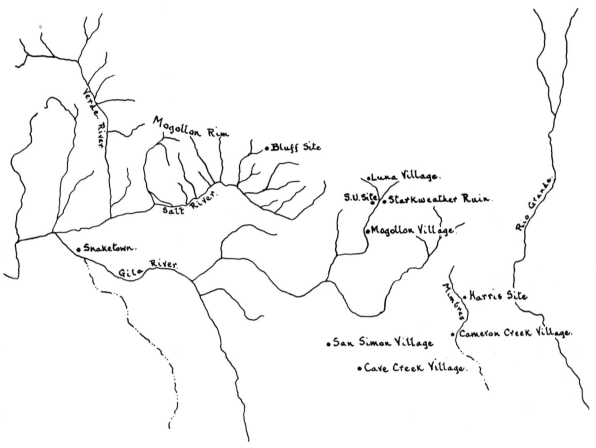

Mogollon Villages of the Eighth Century
All of these ten villages appear to have been founded within a few years of A.D.
700 when Reds coming up from eastern Mexico met and merged with Cochise
Foragers and Upper Gila Cave Dwellers to form the Mogollon Culture.

Cave Creek Village	pre (?) A.D. 700
San Simon Village	do. do.
Cameron Creek Village	do. do.
Harris Site	A.D. 694, 704, 712
Starkweather Ruin	708
Bluff Site	712
Mogollon Village	725
S. U. Site	726 to 752
Luna Village	post (?) A.D. 700
Snaketown	do. do.

the Little Colorado near Springerville. Here they spread in all directions. Some
moved eastward, up Coyote Creek, where we found some of their sites when
we were surveying this part of the country in 1927. Some drifted westward
along the crest of the Mogollon Rim and started colonies which later were
gathered up into the Salado Branch. Others followed the Little Colorado northward as it meandered through good flat farming land, past where St. Johns stands

The Mogollon Village: The village is on top of the hill.

The Mimbres Valley

today, and so up to the Petrified Forest and the Rio Puerco, which comes in from the northeast and joins the Little Colorado near Holbrook. Here, in the 700's, an important series of developments took place when these bands of Reds, moving north, met Basket Makers coming down from northeastern Arizona. In the Petrified Forest, Dr. H. P. Mera has found and described a number of sites, some of which showed only Basket Maker houses and Basket Maker pottery; some had Basket Maker houses and Red pottery mixed with Basket Maker wares; and some had Basket Maker houses and only Red pottery—which might mean either that Basket Maker architects were becoming increasingly interested in Red potters, or that Red men had come to realize the inadequacy of their tipi-like pup tents and were building Basket Maker-like houses in order to keep their women at home.

Detailed information about sites in the Petrified Forest is hard to obtain, as the country is bleak and exposed; the sites have been eroded by wind and rain, and everything on or above the surface of the ground, including sherds, has been sandblasted. The trees in the Petrified Forest are not famous for their shade or shelter.

Going up the Rio Puerco from the Petrified Forest, one soon comes to the juniper belt and the rolling hills which form the eastern boundary of the basin of the Little Colorado. Here, in the old days, the valley of the Rio Puerco was one of the main thoroughfares of the Southwest, and the sandy flats and mounds that line the stream bed are littered with the remains of those who passed through and those who stayed. An extraordinary instance of such a relic which someone left as an offering at a spring was a small ivory figurine (see page 106) now in the possession of Mr. Joseph Grubbs, owner of the White Mound Trading Post. It was found by a Navajo boy during the summer of 1936, when we were excavating the White Mound village, and it looks as if it must have been carried all the way down from Alaska or northern British Columbia, but who it was that brought it down and left it at the spring near White Mound is a question to which, strangely enough, I have no answer.

Citing Egypt and the Maya as examples, it has sometimes been said that the heavily travelled crossroads and thoroughfares of the world have been hotbeds of culture and civilization, but there is little, if anything, in the Southwest to lend support to the idea. The valleys of the Puerco, the Verde, and the San Francisco were all well-travelled thoroughfares, and Flagstaff and Gallup were prominent crossroads, but I should say that the outstanding feature in most of these cases was confusion rather than rapid advance. It is certainly true that no one of these valleys or centers was the seat of origin or the scene of later development of any of the well-known cultures in the Southwest. In the case of the Rio Puerco, it was not only the main east-west artery between the Chaco Basin and the drainage of the Little Colorado, but it was also a stream which had to be crossed by everyone travelling north or south between the Cibola country and the San Juan. Nevertheless, although the valley was occupied continuously

The Harris Site: House 29 above House 14
**The floor of an early circular house which was superimposed above the floor
of a still earlier great lodge.**

from A.D. 700 up to 1300, there is no such thing as a typical Puerco culture. At all periods the local products were affected by more powerful neighbors—Chaco to the northeast, Kayenta to the northwest, and Cibola to the south—but always in some sort of combination, so that there was never a pure Chaco, or pure Kayenta, or pure Cibola culture in the valley.

We first became interested in the Puerco in 1926, when we were sorting, cleaning, and mending the pottery of the Scorse collection which was really the beginning of Gila Pueblo. Most of this pottery came from the eastern drainage of the Little Colorado, and in 1928, in order to provide ourselves with a background for the collection, we began the intensive survey of the region lying between Holbrook and the Continental Divide which resulted during the next seven years in our finding and collecting sherds at about one thousand sites. In 1936 we picked the earliest site we had been able to find to see what more could be learned by excavation.

The Mogollon Rim: Pueblo Canyon, east of the Sierra Ancha

White Mound: an ivory figurine

THE SITE we selected is known as the White Mound village and lies about thirty-five miles west of Gallup, on the north side of the Puerco Valley. Without discussing the technical details, the essence of the results can be summed up by saying that the White Mound village turned out to be about 90 per cent Basket Maker and 10 per cent Red. The architecture was straight undiluted Basket Maker, consisting of deep pit-houses, roof entrances, ventilators, floor partitions, benches, and the customary arrangement of fireplace and deflector in front of the ventilator shaft. The great majority of the plain pottery was the typical unpolished grayware of the Basket Makers, but mixed with it, in a ratio of about 1 to 10, was the polished redware of the Reds. The decorated pottery was particularly significant in that it was black-on-white, not slipped, and not polished, according to true Basket Maker practice, but the designs were strictly rectilinear, made up of triangles, chevrons, and straight parallel lines, and drawn with mineral paint in typical Red style.

White Mound storerooms

At White Mound we were fortunate in obtaining a large number of burned beams, on twenty-nine of which the outside rings were still intact, registering the actual years when the trees were felled and presumably used for construction. The range of dates was from A.D. 760 to 801, with heavy emphasis on 786, which therefore seals off the time record of Red progress from Cave Creek, up through the San Francisco Valley, and out on the Plateau as far north as the Rio Puerco.

The White Mound village is an excellent illustration of the point I have been trying to make, and once its implications are understood the rest of the course should be easy to negotiate. Here was a site which in most of its features was typically Basket Maker. The pit-houses were of the same shape and size and contained all of the same accessories as Basket Maker houses of the eighth century in other areas. The great majority of the plain pottery was gray; the decorated ware was black-on-white; it was not slipped or polished, and had been baked in a reducing atmosphere. But in the burials, in the houses,

Black-on-white: White Mound
Late Basket Maker III (A.D. 800) in the Puerco and southern Chaco districts. Although a Basket Maker product in terms of color and texture, it has lost its Basket Maker style of decoration and shows the same treatment of Red designs as in Western Pueblo I—bands, panels, triangles, stepped figures, parallel lines, dotted lines and borders.

Compare with Shabik'eshchee (page 000) for departure from the Basket Maker tradition and with Western Pueblo I (page 000) for similarity of Red designs.

(Gladwin, H. S. 1945. Plates XI & XII)

and throughout the deposits in all sections of the site, there was polished redware which unquestionably was a Red product. It seems, therefore, that there can be no reasonable doubt that Reds and Basket Makers had come together at White Mound as two distinctly separate groups, and it is consequently of the utmost significance to find that as a result of this meeting, the local Basket Makers had adopted a style of decorating their pottery with rectilinear designs which was unknown in other Basket Maker villages of the eighth century where Reds were not present.

ABOUT THREE MILES south of the White Mound village, on the Whitewater Wash which comes up from the south to join the Rio Puerco near Allantown, there is a site which provides rather surprising confirmation for what has just been said about White Mound.

The Whitewater village was excavated by Dr. F. H. H. Roberts for the Smithsonian Institution, and detailed and well-illustrated reports have been pub-

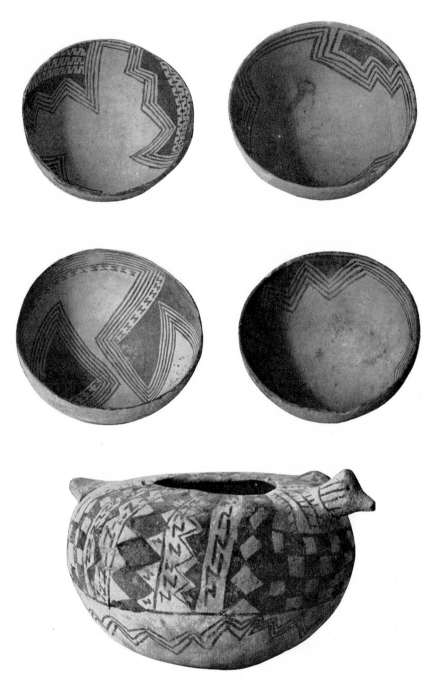

White Mound black-on-white pottery

White Mound
   Top row: Polished red pottery
   Other pieces: Plain gray pottery

lished covering the results of the work. Roberts made it clear that the village was founded by Basket Makers. Yet Roberts found no polished red pottery or other signs of Red contact in the Basket Maker levels of the site, and the many illustrations of decorated pottery from Whitewater do not show a single instance of the kind of rectilinear designs which we found on the decorated pottery at White Mound. There may be other and better explanations, but the only one I can offer is that some Red women were present at White Mound but not at Whitewater during the Basket Maker period.

To QUELL ANY SUSPICION that the White Mound village might have been unique, confirmation of its evidence can be found at Forestdale, about eighty-five miles to the southwest, on top of the Mogollon Rim. Here there are two sites, the Bluff and the Bear ruins, which were excavated by Haury for the University of Arizona, and which provide excellent examples of what happened to a Red band which by-passed the Mogollon villages, swung north to the Rim, and ran into Basket Makers.

At the Bluff Ruin, the earlier of the two sites, Haury found circular houses with side entrances; circular houses which presumably had roof entrances, since there were no signs of side doors; one house, of which Haury said: "Its resemblance to the orthodox Basket Maker house is clear"; a circular great lodge, 33 feet in diameter; and plainware, polished brown, and polished red pottery which was also said to have been slipped. On top of this batch of evidence, which is about all that an archaeological detective could ask, the Bluff Ruin also gave up sherds of Basket Maker grayware and some plain and decorated Hohokam sherds, thus putting all the eggs in one basket, so to speak, and establishing a general time level for Reds, Hohokam, and Basket Makers soon after A.D. 700.

The Bear Ruin lies upstream and about one and a half miles northeast of the Bluff Ruin, and the two sites may have run consecutively, with possibly a short gap filled by other sites near by in the Forestdale Valley. Tree-ring dates for the Bear Ruin, obtained at Gila Pueblo, range from A.D. 787 up to 889, as against an approximate top date of 712 for the Bluff Ruin, but tree-ring dates at best are merely guides and these do not mean necessarily that the occupation of the Bluff Ruin came to an end at 712, nor that the Bear Ruin was not begun before 787.

The tree-ring dates, the architecture, and the pottery show the Bear Ruin to have been contemporaneous with the White Mound village, but in this case, the proportions of Reds and Basket Makers were reversed. Most of the houses were circular, with side entrances; a few were straight Basket Maker, with benches, ventilators, and the customary accessories. So also with the pottery, most of which was some form of polished brown or red, with a minor representation of Basket Maker grayware. The small amount of decorated pottery was the same as that at White Mound in that it was black-on-white, was not polished, and had no slip; it was typical of the Reds to the extent that the designs were strictly rectilinear—triangles, rectangles, chevrons, and straight lines, drawn with mineral paint. If anything more is needed to show that the Bear Ruin was occupied by a mixture of Reds and Basket Makers, it is to be found in the skulls. These were examined and measured by Norman Gabel who reported: "It seems clear that one is dealing with a mixed population. The two best preserved crania illustrate a scaphoid ultradolichocephalic leptorrhine Basket Maker on the one hand and a hyperbrachycephalic artificially deformed Pueblo type on the other" —which is not as slanderous as it sounds, but simply means that at the Bear Ruin some Basket Makers with very long heads and rather narrow noses had met but had not, as yet, blended with some Reds whose heads were unusually broad and flattened. It seems that at this time the Basket Makers were still trying to demonstrate the facts of life in plain black and white, while the Reds were explaining how and where the straight and narrow line should be drawn.

FROM FORESTDALE WEST to the Verde no sites have been excavated, and all that is known has come from our survey. There are some sites in Pleasant Valley, north of the Sierra Ancha, that look like circular pit-houses, and the pottery on the surface is limited to plain and polished redware, but this could only be definitely settled by excavation. Most of the sites, early and late, which we have found around Payson, under the Rim, also run chiefly to polished redware— most of it of very good quality—but again, these will have to be carefully investigated before they can add details to the outline which is being drawn.

About seventy-five miles due north of Payson, however, there is one of the earliest, and also one of the best examples of a Red band which reached the Plateau and settled down. This site, known as N. A. 3996, is situated in the Cinder Basin, about twenty-five miles east of Flagstaff. It was excavated by the Museum of Northern Arizona, and it looks as if it might reach back into the seventh century and so have been contemporaneous with the early Red sites at Cave Creek, San Simon, and Cameron Creek. The architecture was described by Colton as follows:

"The dwellings which have been excavated were pit-houses with floors about 30 inches below the original ground level and with central fire pits. Two were more or less circular, 13 and 17 feet in diameter respectively, and the third was rectangular with rounded corners. Each had a long sloping entrance on the east side. The roof was of poles sloping toward the center of the room, and covered with earth. Dr. de Laguna visualized a sort of tipi construction as there was no indication of a regular system of support posts as found in later houses"— all of which leaves nothing to be desired if one is searching for my version of a Red Indian. But even if there had been no house remains, the pottery would set a Red seal with a Basket Maker imprint on the site. The total count of sherds was given as:

Basket Maker decorated black-on-gray	213
Basket Maker plain grayware	850
Polished brown or redware	5,392

These tell their own story and the only thing I have to add is to draw attention to the absence of a great lodge—a lack which was also shared by the earliest Red villages at Cave Creek, San Simon, and Cameron Creek.

ABOUT TWENTY-FIVE MILES northwest of the Cinder Basin, the Baker Ranch lies on the north side of the San Francisco Peaks. Here there is another group of five houses, also excavated by the Museum of Northern Arizona, which carries the record up into the eighth century, and in one instance up to A.D. 828. It seems that enough time had elapsed since the Cinder Basin episode for the Reds and Basket Makers to have developed some rather wide differences of opinion as to how a house should be built, with the result that when they came together at the Baker Ranch no two were alike. Some were shallow, with walls built of mud rolls and rubble. Some were deep, the sides lined with split planks and posts— a method of construction which was peculiar to the pit-houses of the Flagstaff district. Some had side entrances; others look as if they had had hatchways in the roof. In some cases, small surface rectangular rooms had been attached to the house, presumably for storage, as they had no fireplaces and it is therefore doubtful if anyone could have lived in them during the winters, when the temperature often drops below zero.

The pottery at the Baker Ranch was more interesting and helpful than the architecture. Instead of a ratio of about 5 Red sherds to 1 Basket Maker, as at the Cinder Basin, the Baker Ranch showed only 1 Red to 12 Basket Maker, and so came fairly close to the figures at White Mound which gave 1 Red to about 10 Basket Maker. Nevertheless, what the Red potters lacked in numbers of plain sherds, they made up in their influence on the decorated wares. As at White Mound, they completely monopolized the designs on the black-on-white pottery with their solid triangles and rectangles, chevrons, and parallel straight lines. Neither at White Mound nor at the Baker Ranch is there a single instance of a Basket Maker woman having managed to squeeze in an angular centipede, a boxed cross, a panel of dots, or any of the other quirks of design which their mothers used to draw, back in the old days in Marsh Pass and Red Rock Valley. The Red women at the Baker Ranch also succeeded in applying a slip and polishing the surface of the black-on-white ware, and they even managed to originate a slipped and polished black-on-red ware—so introducing techniques and processes which were never popular and were usually not tolerated in proper Basket Maker society.

As against these preponderant Red ideas and innovations, the Basket Maker women at the Baker Ranch firmly insisted that some of the decorated pottery should be baked in a reducing atmosphere, so giving them the black-on-white ware to which they were accustomed. They were probably also responsible for the paint which was used to decorate the black-on-white pottery. This was made from some sort of plant, whereas the paint on White Mound black-on-white was mineral. In most instances the difference can easily be detected, as the

Karbab
Plateau

Cedar
Butte

Tuba

Moenk

El Tovar

Tusayan
Ruin.

Cameron.

Airport.

Coconino
Plateau.

Red
Butte.

Little Colorado River

Baker
Ranch.

Wupatki.

San
Francisco
Peaks.

Medicine Valley.

Sunset Crater.

Cinder Basin

Williams

Maine

Elden Pueblo

Flagstaff.

N.

0   5   10   20
Miles.

Fine-line Black-on-white: Western Pueblo I
   Bands, panels, triangles, triangles with one side extended, F's, parallel lines,
   dotted lines, and borders.
   a. Kidder, A. V. 1924 Pl 34 f   b. Gila Pueblo collections
   c. Kidder, A. V. 1924 Pl 34 e   d, e & f. Gila Pueblo collections

vegetable paint is usually more blue than black, is faint, and sinks into the slip, whereas mineral paint gives a dense black decoration which stands out clearly and is apt to turn red when overfired. Both the Reds and the Hohokam invariably used mineral paint in an open oxidizing fire, hence the red decoration on their pots. The Basket Makers, however, preferred vegetable paint, probably as a hang-over from the vegetable stains with which they decorated their baskets, sandals, and textiles. There is no hard and fast rule, and laboratory tests have a way of upsetting snap judgments, but it is fairly safe to say that in the area from the Verde to Marsh Pass, designs on black-on-white pottery were usually drawn with vegetable paint, while those to the east and south were predominantly mineral.

Summing up the situation in the Flagstaff district, it looks as if the Cinder Basin site provides a good example of a meeting between Reds and Basket Makers at a time before either culture had been appreciably affected by the contact. Some fifty years later, the Baker Ranch illustrates the blends which resulted from the continued association of Reds and Basket Makers—shown in houses and pottery incorporating features of both Reds and Basket Makers which neither group had known in combination before their meeting. At the Pecos Conference of 1927 this mixture was given the name of "Pueblo I," the

◀ **The Flagstaff District**

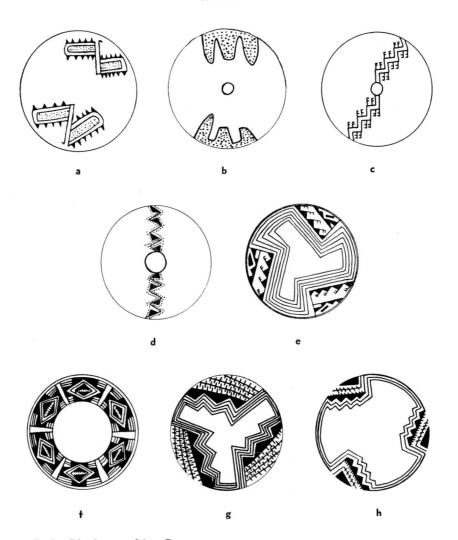

Early Black-on-white Pottery

a & b.   **From Durango, Colorado:**
Not slipped; not polished; heretofore regarded as Basket Maker III, but designs show no resemblance to those of Shabik'eshchee.

c & d.   **From Shabik'eshchee, northwestern New Mexico:**
Not slipped; not polished; Basket Maker III of the eighth century.

e & f.   **From Flagstaff district, northern Arizona:**
Slipped; polished; classified as Pueblo I and heretofore regarded as having developed out of Basket Maker III, but designs, slip, and polish show no relationship to early black-on-white from Durango or Shabik'.

g & h.   **From White Mound on the Rio Puerco:**
Not slipped; not polished; Basket Maker III, but designs resemble Flagstaff Pueblo I more than Shabik' or Durango.
Flagstaff and White Mound Black-on-white associated with polished redware: Durango and Shabik' with dull grayware.

Red-on-orange: Alkali Ridge
Many of the designs on red-on-orange pottery from north of the San Juan are
very suggestive of those in southwestern New Mexico—quarters, folds, stars,
triangles, pennons, chevrons, and parallel straight and wavy lines.
(Brew, J. O. 1946. Figs. 55, 61, 66)

classification being based chiefly on the black-on-white pottery. Very few sites
of the period had then or have since been excavated, and as no two of these
have turned out to be alike, I think it better to deal with each site individually
rather than to be governed by theoretical criteria that have not materialized.

FROM FLAGSTAFF the trail we are following leads northeastward across the Little
Colorado River, thence northward along the western side of Black Mesa to
Marsh Pass.

Four miles west of Marsh Pass, in Tsegi Canyon, there is a site, known as
RB 1002, which was dug by the Rainbow Bridge-Monument Valley Expedition.
Here, at the base of the site, Beals found a house with a side entrance and a
bench, but no ventilator, which conformed to the Basket Maker house in Broken
Flute Cave, about forty miles to the east. Superimposed or near by, at Site RB
1006, were deep pit-houses, 13 to 17 feet in diameter, which had no side entrances and no benches, but in one instance had *two* ventilator tunnels. No tree-
ring dates have been obtained, so the actual date is uncertain, but the black-on-
white pottery in the pit-houses appears to have been the same as that at the
Baker Ranch, and it therefore seems probable that they were occupied sometime
late in the eighth century.

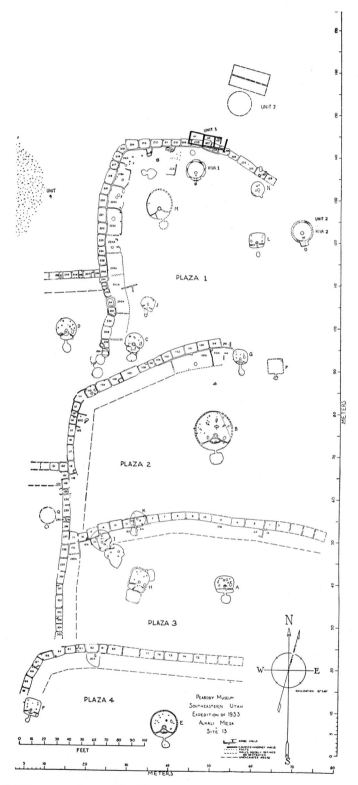

Alkali Ridge: ground plan, Site 13

(From Brew, J. O. 1946)

AGAINST THIS BACKGROUND in northeastern Arizona, it is all the more significant that as the Reds moved northward up the Chinlee and crossed the San Juan into the territory of the Farmers, the effects of their arrival were entirely different from their mixture with the Basket Makers at the Baker Ranch and in Marsh Pass. The kind of black-on-white pottery we have been tracing from Flagstaff up into northeastern Arizona disappears abruptly, and I do not know of a single site north of the San Juan where it was made. One of the most striking effects of the Red entry into southeastern Utah was the acceptance by the Farmers on Alkali Ridge of a style of decorating their pottery which more closely resembled the designs on Mogollon pottery in southwestern New Mexico than that of any intervening culture, and which was unknown north of the San Juan before Red contact. Another sensational development which took place at this same time was that after making nothing but black-on-white decorated pottery in a reducing fire for several centuries, the Farmers' wives in southeastern Utah suddenly blossomed out with red-on-orange, black-on-orange, and black-on-red types— all fired in an oxidizing atmosphere in accordance with standard Red practice. And to cap the climax, Brew reported that black-on-white pottery had been reduced to the vanishing point on Alkali Ridge during the eighth century.

The explanation that these changes and innovations in southeastern Utah during the eighth century were due to the advent and influence of Reds coming up from northeastern Arizona gathers a good deal of momentum when one moves east for some seventy miles to the La Plata in southwestern Colorado. Here Morris found that black-on-red ware (in which he also included red-on-orange and black-on-orange), amounted to only 20 per cent of the decorated pottery, whereas black-on-white ware ran up to 80 per cent on the La Plata, as against practical absence on Alkali Ridge. In other words, it looks as if Red influence had declined as the movement spread eastward along the San Juan, and had finally died out completely when the mineral (Red) paint which had penetrated into the southern La Plata towns gave way to vegetable (Farmer-Basket Maker) paint in the upper La Plata Valley. To give a further push to the ideas which are being launched, one might add that the architecture from southeastern Utah to the La Plata was remarkably uniform—long double rows of contiguous rectangular surface rooms, served by separate semi-subterranean kivas—but I do not know of a site of this kind south of the river.

These developments provide an interesting study of contrasts. From Cave Creek in the south to Alkali Ridge in the north, Red women can be traced wherever they went by their pottery styles and techniques which were among the most prominent features of Southwestern archaeology. Red men, however, appear to have had little or nothing to offer to their hosts, and if it had not been for the sherds and deformed skulls their wives left behind them, there would have been little to show that a Red Indian had ever set foot in the Southwest.

To COMPLETE THIS CIRCUIT of the Southwest during the eighth century, and also to afford another contrast, we now drop south about seventy-five miles to Chaco

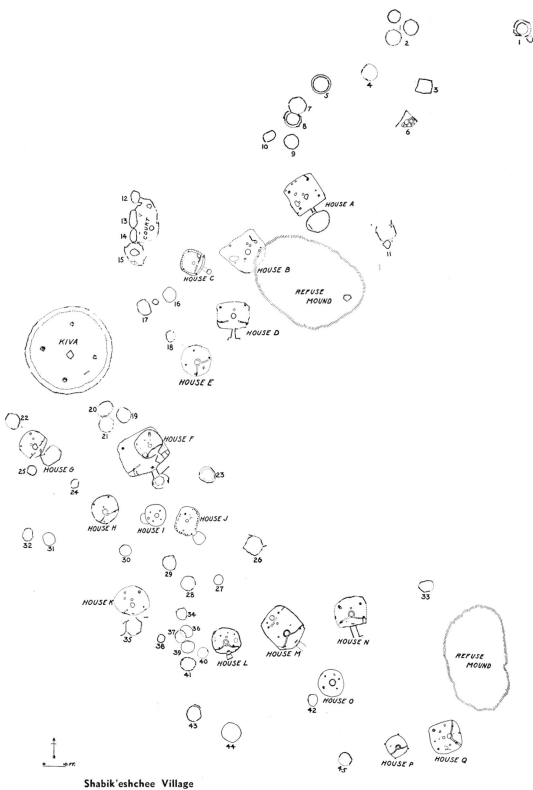

Shabik'eshchee Village

(From Roberts, F. H. H., Jr. 1929)

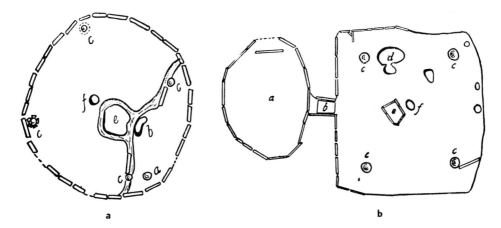

Shabik'eshchee
    a. House H had no side entrance, antechamber, bench, or ventilator.
    b. House A had a side entrance and antechamber which served as a ventilator.
                             (From Roberts, F. H. H., Jr. 1929)

Canyon, where a site known as Shabik'eshchee was excavated by Dr. F. H. H. Roberts, Jr., as a part of the investigations conducted by the National Geographic Society.

Shabik' was a Basket Maker village with a range of tree-ring dates running from A.D. 736 to 757. It was therefore contemporaneous with the Harris, Mogollon, and S. U. villages in southwestern New Mexico, White Mound on the Rio Puerco, something at Forestdale, the Baker Ranch, something in Marsh Pass, Alkali Ridge in southeastern Utah, Ackmen, and some of the La Plata villages in southwestern Colorado. *But* whereas the Reds were present in one or more forms in every one of these sites, at Shabik' itself there was not a sign of a Red— so effectually disposing of any idea that Red symptoms were pandemic.

Architecturally, instead of living and storage rooms in long rows of contiguous rectangular rooms, as on Alkali Ridge, at Ackmen, on the La Plata, and near Durango—all north of the San Juan—the plan of Shabik' shows that the people lived in pit-houses, each a separate individual unit, and that they solved their storage problems by using slab-lined cists, exactly the same as those in the Basket Maker caves in northeastern Arizona.

In addition to differences in the plans of the villages, the types of the houses, and the storage arrangements, the population at Shabik' was very much smaller than in the Farmer towns north of the San Juan. On Alkali Ridge, for example, Brew spoke of pueblos up to three hundred rooms, consisting of surface living rooms, storerooms, and semi-subterranean kivas. At Shabik', however, Roberts found only sixty-seven units in all, of which eighteen were pit-houses, and of these he expressed the opinion that not more than nine had been occupied at any one time, so implying a total population of only about thirty people.

The decorated pottery at Shabik' tells the same story. Whereas Brew found

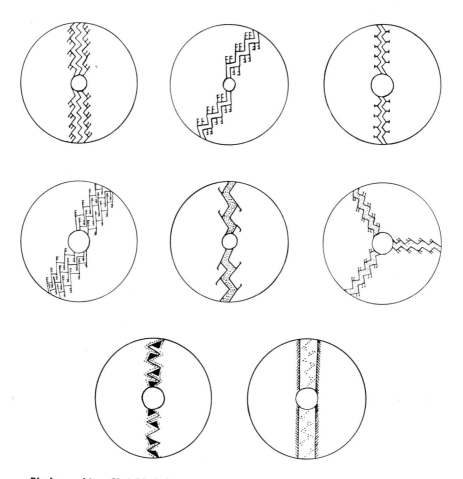

Black-on-white: Shabik'eshchee

Typical Basket Maker pottery from south of the San Juan. Note the bisecting and trisecting of the field but the absence of quartering. The zigzag is a favorite element of design, but did not persist into later types although the small extensions from each angle—often in the form of F's—are frequently found as late as the fourteenth century.

Compare with decorated pottery from Durango for the differences in early black-on-white, and with White Mound pottery for the shift to Red designs.

(Roberts, F. H. H., Jr. 1929)

that Alkali Ridge ran overwhelmingly to red-on-orange and black-on-orange, with less than 1 per cent of black-on-white, the decorated pottery at Shabik' was exclusively black-on-white, with red-on-orange, black-on-orange, and black-on-red completely absent.

Last, but by no means least, is Roberts' statement that "every skeleton had an undeformed dolichocephalic skull," so affording one more contrast with Alkali Ridge, where, I believe, all of the skulls were brachycephalic and deformed.

THE REASON for the striking differences between what was happening in north-eastern Arizona, southeastern Utah, and northwestern New Mexico during the eighth century is not far to seek. As long ago as 1939, Anna O. Shepard pointed the way in her "Technology of La Plata Pottery," when she said:

> "In the beginning we find considerable variability in technique, es-pecially as illustrated by the contemporaneous use of several very dif-ferent pigments. Is this fact explained entirely by the theory that Basket Maker III was an experimental period when a variety of materials was being tested and before the most practicable ones had been sorted out by experience, or do mineral and organic paints represent the work of two distinct groups of people having different ceramic traditions? Geo-graphic distribution as indicated by a limited number of sites and relatively few sherds seems to favor the latter theory."

In this summary, Shepard was emphasizing the difference between organic and mineral paints, but in her analyses she also drew attention to a number of other peculiar features in the early pottery north of the San Juan. Among these was the fact that there was a geographical division in the La Plata district which showed 80 per cent organic paint in the northern section, against 85 per cent mineral in the southern part of the valley. In early times pottery was never slipped, but later, during Pueblo I, decorated pottery was always slipped. Early pottery was fired in a reducing atmosphere, whereas Pueblo I potters produced both oxidized and reduced wares.

If to these clues one now adds Mogollon-like designs, polished surfaces, and skull deformation, it would seem not only that Shepard was right in suggesting that two distinct groups of people having different ceramic traditions had come together, but also that these two peoples were, first, the resident popula-tion north of the San Juan—her Basket Makers, my Farmers—and second, my Reds, who left their traces behind them all the way from the Mexican Border to the Four Corners.

With Reds pushing up into southeastern Utah from northeastern Arizona and fading out as they moved east along the San Juan, their absence at Shabik' was undoubtedly due to the fact that Chaco Canyon lies well to the east of the Chuskas and was consequently shielded by these mountains from the northward passage of the Reds. On the other hand, Shabik' was directly in the line of those Basket Makers who at about A.D. 700 had left the caves of Red Rock Valley and were moving southward along the eastern foothills of the Chuskas.

THIS BRINGS MY TALE up to A.D. 800, and the archaeological outline of the Southwest is beginning to take shape. By looking hard enough in the right places. it should now be possible to discern a few features which are sufficiently sug-gestive of things to come for one to realize that it is the same old Southwest with which most of us are familiar, even though some of the details are still obscure. The country, the people, and the things they left behind them have not changed. All that has happened is that some of the conventional barriers have been removed, with the result that Reds, Farmers, and Basket Makers have been freed to move around, visit one another, and exchange ideas. There are still a few problems which cannot be explained in terms of orthodox beliefs, but at A.D. 800 we have several pedigreed families and some country cousins around the fringes who are all waiting to set up housekeeping in various sections of the Southwest.

North of the San Juan—on Mesa Verde, in the La Plata Valley to the east, and the Montezuma Valley to the west—the Farmers were off to a flying start toward the architectural pre-eminence which they and their Mesa Verde descendants always retained. At A.D. 800, the Farmers can be identified as the authors of the Mesa Verde Branch and were rolling along their own lines to the individuality by which they can be distinguished at this and all later times from other Southwestern groups.

To the south, in the Chaco Basin—from the San Juan down to the Red Mesa Valley, and from the Chuskas across to Mt. Taylor—scattered families of Basket Makers who had left their caves in Red Rock Valley were drawing together in loosely knit villages and beginning to develop those characteristics of architecture and pottery which later were to make the Chaco Branch one of the best known in the Southwest.

To the west, in northeastern Arizona, those Basket Makers who had stuck to their Marsh Pass caves when their Red Rock compatriots moved south were bracing themselves against the influx of Reds, some of whom were pushing up from the Puerco past Ganado, some coming across from the Flagstaff region, and some gathering in the west preparatory to moving in to create what has come to be known as the Kayenta Branch.

Along the Puerco, Basket Makers and Reds were trying out various combinations, some of which were suggestive of what was to become the Chaco, others more like early Cibola developments to the south, but none achieving sufficient individuality to justify recognition as a separate and distinct culture.

Around Flagstaff, other Reds, with a sprinkling of western Basket Makers, had concocted something which some day archaeologists would call "Pueblo I," but which, perversely, would never conform to the ideal conception of what the archaeologists thought it ought to be. At A.D. 800, many of the people who had taken the advanced pottery courses in the Flagstaff school were moving across the Little Colorado to the western Chuskas, Canyon del Muerto, and Marsh Pass—spurred, possibly, by the premonitory rumblings of the local volcano which when it finally erupted left the mountain of cinders known as Sunset Crater. Whatever the reasons may have been, it seems that no one group of people ever remained long enough in the neighborhood of Flagstaff to develop a local culture which was sufficiently distinct for it to be recognized away from home. The most that can be said is that during its volcanic-free periods, the decorated pottery of the Flagstaff region suggests that it was a sort of southwestern subdivision of the Kayenta Branch, but always more heavily impregnated by Reds from the south and some Yuman infiltration from the west.

South of Flagstaff, in the valley of the Verde and off to the west of the San Francisco Peaks, bands of Reds coming up from the south and southeast during the eighth century had met and merged with some of the eastern Yuman Foragers, and with the help of a few Basket Makers had formed the Prescott Branch. From the little that is known, it begins to look as if this combination may have possessed greater significance than has heretofore been suspected and may provide a link with some developments to the west and northwest which otherwise are difficult to explain.

East of the Verde, in favorable locations under the Rim, scattered groups of Reds were producing pottery in shades of red and brown, providing the base for what Colton has recognized as the Sinagua Branch. Farther to the east, along the southern border of the Colorado Plateau, other groups of Reds were turning out the same red and brown wares, but a little decorated black-on-white ware here and there is enough to indicate that they had picked up some Basket Makers and later would play a part in helping to form the Salado Branch, destined to become one of our leading southern families.

Still farther east, around the headwaters of the Little Colorado and the upper drainage of the San Francisco, another important coalition was in the making, made up principally of Reds but increasingly diluted by Basket Makers as the Red movement spread northward toward Zuni. At A.D. 800, the Reds were strongly dominant over the few Basket Makers who had penetrated as far south as the upper San Francisco, Apache Creek, and Tularosa Valley. At the same date, Basket Makers clearly outnumbered the Reds in the Puerco-Zuni region, but as time went on, the northern and southern groups coalesced into the Cibola Branch, one of the most important in the Southwest.

South of Cibola—in the middle reaches of the San Francisco, the drainage of the Upper Gila, and the Mimbres Valley—the Mogollon people soon after A.D. 800 began to develop local quirks of architecture and pottery. To a combination which had been overwhelmingly Red with only a minor fraction of Upper Gila Cave Dweller or Cochise Forager, there was now added a slow trickle of Basket Maker groups from the north which, while gradual, instilled enough into the mixture for it later to effervesce into the Mimbres Branch.

To the southwest of these incipient Mimbres settlements—from the Chiricahuas west to the San Pedro—there were the San Simon village and a few other settlements which represented the only pure survival of what we have been calling the Mogollon Culture—meaning the original cross of Reds on Cochise Foragers, without taint of Basket Makers. During the early ninth century, the Mogollon people in these villages became increasingly interested in the Hohokam to the west, and thereafter a blending took place which was analogous to the Red-Basket Maker relationship, but in this case the farther west, the more Hohokam, the less Mogollon; the farther east, the more Mogollon, the less Hohokam.

West of the Mogollon settlements and south of the Verde, in the Gila Basin

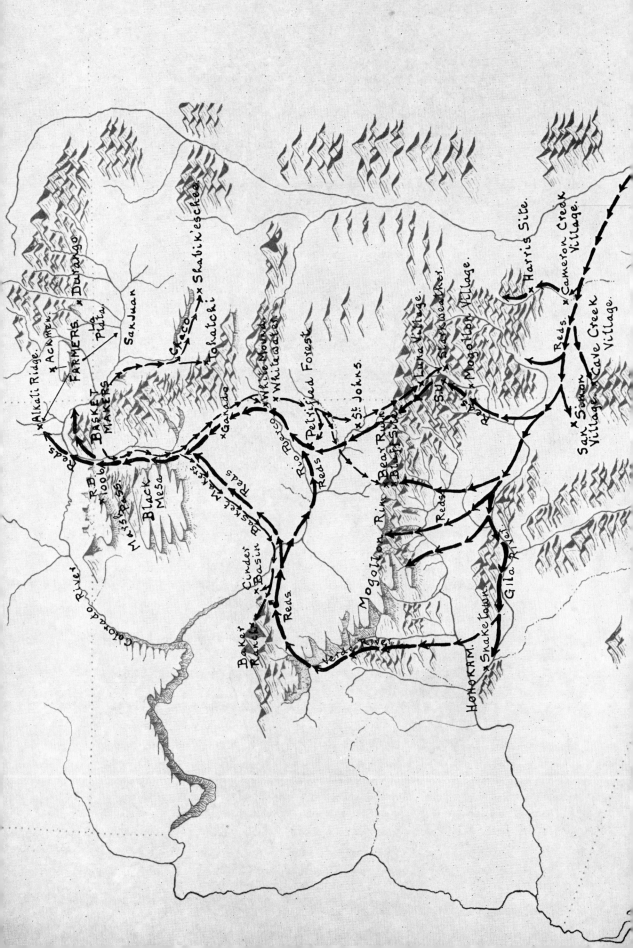

THE SOUTHWEST AT A.D. 800

During the eighth century the foundations for all later developments between the San Juan and the Gila were laid when Basket Makers moving south from northeastern Arizona met Reds coming up over the Mogollon Rim from the south. In the early days of their meeting no two sites were alike, but soon after A.D. *800 the various well-known cultures of the Southwest began to take shape.*

North of the San Juan, the Farmers were firmly established in the La Plata and Montezuma valleys, on Mesa Verde and Alkali Ridge. As the Reds moved north through Marsh Pass, however, and crossed the San Juan into southeastern Utah, their influence brought about some marked differences between Alkali Ridge in the west and the Farmer villages to the east. A few Red bands also seem to have penetrated eastward along the San Juan as far as the southern La Plata Valley, where they were responsible for the differences in the black-on-white pottery between the northern and southern La Plata towns.

In the Upper Gila district, regional variations began to develop between the Mogollon villages in the San Francisco, the Mimbres, and the San Simon valleys as Basket Maker families began to filter down from the north and new ideas were acquired from the Hohokam to the west.

In the Gila Basin, the Hohokam migration had arrived in the early 700's and the people were developing their irrigation systems, digging their ball-courts, building their great lodges, and practicing the arts and crafts of their Colonial Period.

of southern Arizona, were the Hohokam, busily engaged in digging irrigation ditches, building ball-courts and great lodges, turning out great quantities of their red-on-buff pottery, and otherwise going about their lawful occasions.

THIS BRIEF SUMMARY is merely intended to give the names and home grounds of the various cultures which were beginning to take shape at A.D. 800. There were a few other nebulous groups which withered on the vine before attaining cultural identity—possibly because they were marginal, such as those on the Fremont in central Utah, or possibly because of unfavorable surroundings, such as some of the sites in the barren wastes of the Little Colorado Basin.

To the south, in upper Sonora and Chihuahua, there were people who were related to those in southern Arizona and southwestern New Mexico through a common strain of Red blood and culture. To the east, in the upper Rio Grande Valley, the early black-on-white pottery indicates that some Farmer families had penetrated eastward to lay the foundations for what later would become the Rio Grande Branch, but at A.D. 800 they had not yet attained cultural distinction. From what is known at present, one gains the impression that the people on these eastern and southern peripheries exerted little, if any influence on the course of Southwestern history. In later times, some groups moved eastward into the Rio Grande Valley and others southward into Chihuahua, but I doubt if there was any appreciable infusion of blood, culture, or ideas *from* these areas until after A.D. 1300.

And now, with all of this as an outline, we can go ahead to fill in some of the details.

Here and There, in the South and West: A.D. 800 to 900

THE BEST place to start the ninth century is down in the Mogollon country where, sometime around A.D. 800, the broad-line red-on-brown, mentioned in the last chapter, developed into a type which was decorated with fine straight lines, often in the form of chevrons bordering solid triangles. Designs were invariably rectilinear and were drawn with red mineral paint on tan or brown slipped and polished surfaces. Changes in architecture were also taking place at about this same time. During the middle-to-late 700's, when broad-line red-on-brown was the fashion, a trend in architecture began in which the front, or entrance side, of the earlier circular houses was flattened. At about A.D. 800, with the change from broad-line to fine-line red-on-brown, a further development took place when all four sides were flattened and the central roof-support was replaced by four corner posts, calling for a flat instead of a conical roof. Floors were sunk lower in the ground and as the depth increased, step-entries such as those in the bean-shaped houses could no longer be used, and the side entrance became a long narrow incline. Firepits were placed near the entrance, and since this must have been very inconvenient for anyone entering or leaving the house, it can best be explained by supposing that the entrance was also intended to serve as a smoke-vent.

It was also during this period that the peak of population was reached in the Mogollon villages, judging by the number of houses that were built at this

Broad-line into Fine-line Red-on-brown: Quartered, Triangular Solids, Rectilinear
a & d.   Harris and Mogollon villages
b & e.   San Simon Village
c & f.   Snaketown

time. At the San Simon village five houses can safely be assigned to the period. At Cameron Creek there were not less than twelve. At the Harris site there were at least eight, from four of which we obtained tree-ring dates at A.D. 843, 845, 853, and 857. And at the Mogollon village six houses gave a series of dates running from A.D. 812 to 829, dating the period as having lasted approximately from about A.D. 800 to 850.

By A.D. 850, the minor differences in both architecture and pottery which had gradually been developing between the northern and southern sites had become so pronounced that it is no longer possible to cover all of the villages in the San Francisco, Mimbres, and San Simon valleys under one Mogollon blanket. In southern pottery, the change was marked by the application of a white slip or coating to all decorated surfaces, providing a more brilliant contrast between the red designs, and a white instead of a brown background. Fine-line rectilinear designs were carried over without much change, but it is interesting to find that scroll designs were often added, since these were a clear indication of contact with the Hohokam settlements to the west where the women were adept at this style of decoration.

The local housebuilders were also experimenting with new ideas. There was a shift from square to rectangular plans following the lead of Hohokam architects, and in the San Francisco and Mimbres districts there was an increasing use of

The Mogollon Village
House 10, early circular, with House 4, later rectangular, above

masonry to bolster weak places in the walls. In some houses there were stone-lined firepits with an occasional up-ended slab suggesting a deflector. Benches were sometimes built across the opposite ends of a house. Side entries were changed, and in the upper San Francisco there was a greater emphasis on roof entrances— all of which hark back to Basket Maker practices.

During the latter half of the ninth century there were some rather surprising shifts in population. At the San Simon village we could find only two houses that could be assigned to this period, and our survey does not encourage the belief that there were many other contemporaneous Mogollon settlements. In all of the upper San Francisco Valley there are, at present, only five houses which were associated with red-on-white pottery—two at the Luna village, and one each at the Mogollon, S. U., and Starkweather villages.

When one turns east to the Mimbres Valley, however, one finds eleven houses and a great lodge at the Cameron Creek village, all of which look as if they belonged to this period, and at the Harris site were thirteen houses and two great lodges which had been built during the days when red-on-white pottery was being made.

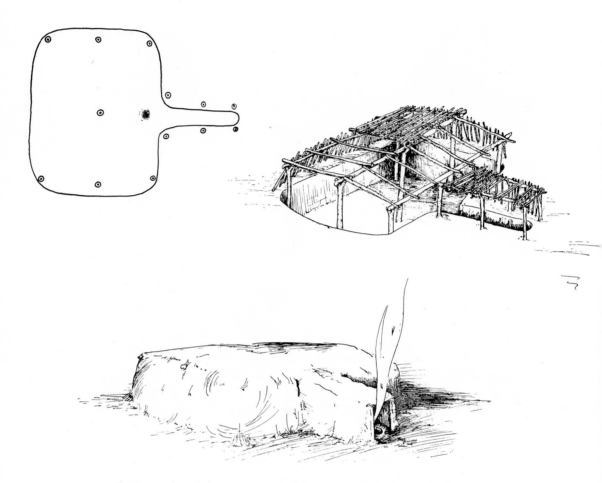

Reconstruction of deep rectangular pit-house: San Simon, Cameron Creek, Harris, Mogollon, and Starkweather villages. Period of fine-line red-on-brown. A.D. 825.

No tree-ring dates have been obtained for houses of this time at the San Simon, Cameron Creek, S. U., Starkweather, and Luna villages. At the Mogollon village, however, we got twenty dates running from A.D. 888 to 899, and at the Harris site forty-one beams from four houses of this period gave dates from A.D. 840 to 911, so establishing the stage of red-on-white pottery as about A.D. 850 to 900, and preserving the continuity of the series.

In general, there was a noticeable increase in the southward drift of people from the Plateau during the ninth century. The villages in the upper San Francisco Valley were naturally the first of the Mogollon groups to be affected, and this may have been one reason for some of them moving over to the Mimbres Valley. Of those who remained, the people who had settled around Luna and in the Tularosa Valley were well along the road, at A.D. 900, which led to Cibola. To the southeast, the colonies which were farther removed from the Plateau were developing those traits which stamp them as Mimbres. And still farther south, the Mogollon remnants in the San Simon and Sulphur Springs valleys show

Broad-line into Fine-line into Red-on-white or Buff
a, d & g.   Harris and Mogollon villages
b, e & h.   San Simon Village
c, f & i.   Snaketown

no signs of having been affected by anything coming down from the north, but were establishing closer relationships with the Hohokam to the west, in the Gila Basin.

From all that is known at present, it looks as if the Mogollon population at all stages had been relatively small. I doubt if they ever numbered more than three hundred, and they seemed to have chosen the kind of country where their remains have been found because they relied more upon hunting and foraging than on agriculture for their living. Their undercut storage pits are typical, but there are rarely enough of them to indicate that the people were mainly dependent upon stored grain for food. Bones of birds and game animals are

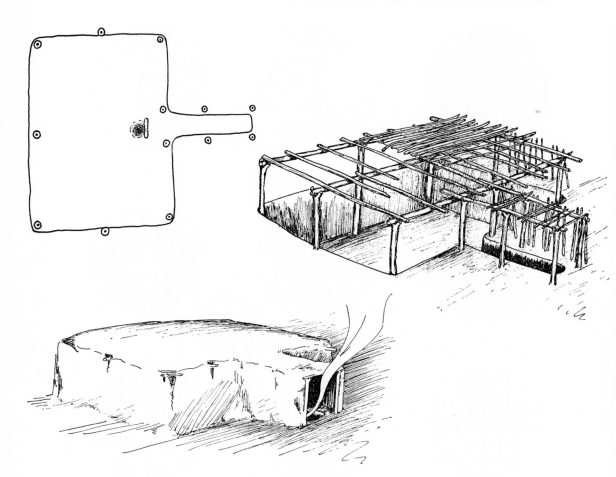

Reconstruction of deep rectangular pit-house, Cameron Creek and Harris villages: Period of red-on-white pottery. A.D. 875

usually abundant in their sites—more so than in Basket Maker caves—and while one occasionally finds a corncob or a few burned beans, these suggest small snatch crops rather than established agricultural practice.

As MENTIONED in an earlier chapter, there were some people to the south, in Chihuahua, who were related to the Foragers in southeastern Arizona and southwestern New Mexico, and later were affected by Red contact in much the same way as in the case of the Cochise Foragers. Since it seems to be clear that the Red migration came up from Mexico, there is a temptation to wonder if the route may not have led up through Chihuahua. Possibly it did, but there is little or nothing to support the idea, and there is a good deal against it.

The earliest evidence of man's activities which we have been able to find in Chihuahua consisted of twelve sites containing handstones, flint knives, blades, points, and chips, but no pottery of any kind and no signs of a house. These

Snaketown, looking east toward Gila Butte

sites were usually situated in sand dunes near a lake or river and indicate that once upon a time, there were hunting or foraging groups in Chihuahua who were probably southern extensions of those in western Texas, southern New Mexico, and Arizona.

The next later stage consisted of twelve sites scattered through the middle of Chihuahua from north to south, represented by camp-sites, hearths, and low house-mounds, strung along watercourses for as much as a mile or more. The feature which characterized this stage was a fine-line red-on-white pottery decorated with red rectilinear designs of zigzags, triangles, and parallel lines on a chalky white or gray slip.

Associated with this decorated pottery was a polished redware which was present in all pottery periods throughout the length and breadth of Chihuahua and later reached a degree of excellence that was not matched at any time in any other culture of the Southwest. Although this redware was one of the most important local products, it was so universal that it cannot be used as a criterion for any one period or locality. It was always abundant, but more so in early times, and it may eventually turn out that the earliest pottery making culture in

Chihuahua was confined to polished red and plain wares as in southwestern New Mexico. On the strength of what is known at present, however, the earliest pottery was fine-line red-on-white accompanied by polished red, and as this was often found in association with decorated pottery from the Mimbres, it would be stretching the evidence to claim that fine-line red-on-white was being made locally much before A.D. 1000, and it might have been considerably later. The probability that this type of decorated pottery in Chihuahua was relatively late—as compared to similar developments in New Mexico—is also indicated by the fact that the twelve pieces of fine-line red-on-white in the Gila Pueblo collections were all found near Colonia Dublan in sites which were occupied during the thirteenth and fourteenth centuries.

Besides the positive evidence afforded by these associations which imply that the local form of red-on-white should be dated later than A.D. 1000, there is also the negative evidence that at present there is no indication in Chihuahua of any of the three stages represented by polished red, broad-line, and fine-line red-on-brown which preceded the period of red-on-white in the Mimbres district.

Rather than a Red migration coming up from Mexico through Chihuahua to reach the Southwest in the 600's, it looks more as if the Red traces in central Chihuahua had filtered down from southern New Mexico at A.D. 1000 or later.

WHEN ONE LEAVES these Red manifestations and turns west to the Hohokam, one must resort to a rather roundabout method of dating their cultural periods. The only trees in the Gila Basin which could be used for construction were cottonwood, mesquite, palo verde, or an occasional juniper, and these were either too short-lived or too erratic in their habits of growth to be of any value for tree-ring dating. But although there were no tree-ring dates, we were very lucky at Snaketown in finding large numbers of sherds of foreign pottery types which had been traded or carried in from neighboring cultures. Many of these had come down from the Flagstaff area, some hundred and fifty miles to the north, and there was also a considerable quantity from the Mogollon villages, about two hundred miles to the east. Nearly all of these foreign types have been dated in their home districts, and consequently they serve as a date-stamp for the local horizons with which they were associated. Some were found lying on the surface of the ground and so had no dating value other than to indicate intercultural traffic while Snaketown was occupied. Some were mixed with local pottery and burned bones in the remains of cremation burials, and it seems fair to suppose that such foreign and local types were contemporaneous. Some were in the fill or on the floors of old houses, but by far the greatest number were found in the rubbish mounds. To grasp the full significance of what this means a short explanation is needed.

One of the most prominent features of the culture of the Hohokam are the mounds, large and small, which occur at all their sites. On two separate occasions —in Compound B at Casa Grande and in Mound 29 at Snaketown—we have found what seemed to be the original core of the mound, and the character, the thickness, and the tilt of the strata made it seem reasonably certain that the mounds were nothing more nor less than the waste products of the daily life of a large community. The deposits were made up largely of fine silt, of about the consistency of flour, which fills the air with dust as soon as it is disturbed. Mixed with the silt were sand, gravel, ashes, sherds, and broken or discarded artifacts. It is only rarely that one finds anything of value, such as an unbroken piece of pottery, and strangely enough, no burials were ever made in these mounds, although the soil is loose and digging is easy. The only explanation appears to be that the mounds represent the gradual accumulation of rubbish swept up by Hohokam housewives, and as such they provide us with a stratified sequence of the day-to-day collections of trash which were thrown on the mounds.

At Snaketown there were sixty of these mounds, some as small as 20 feet in diameter and only a couple of feet deep, others larger, ranging up to Mound 29 which had a diameter of 170 feet and a maximum depth of 18 feet from the crest to the bottom of the underlying pits. As the dissection of Mound 29 served us as a guide in our reconstruction of the cultural progress at Snaketown, it may add a touch of realism to this tale if I describe how one goes about an operation of this kind.

When we began work at Snaketown in September, 1934, we were familiar with two kinds of red-on-buff pottery—an early, representing the Colonial Period, and a later type which was characteristic of the Sedentary Period. Both of these types were abundant all over the site, and if these had been all we had to consider, our task would have amounted to little more than digging up cremations, clearing house floors, ball-courts, and irrigation canals, and so amplifying and confirming what already was known of the culture of the Hohokam. While all of these things would have been of value, our principal object was to try to discover the origin of the Hohokam, and we had hardly started to work when we turned up some sherds of a red-on-gray ware which none of us had ever seen before.

The surface of these strange sherds was sometimes brown but more often discolored to a smoky gray. Designs were rectilinear and drawn with mineral paint, sometimes broad finger-width straight lines, but more often narrow parallel lines which were used to fill triangles, or free-flowing scrolls and pennons. Knowing next to nothing in 1934 about Mogollon pottery, we thought at first that these red-on-gray types were local products of the Hohokam and that they might represent the pre-Colonial Pioneer Period for which we had been searching for so many years. We found that there was a concentration of this kind of pottery just south of Mound 29, so we decided to make what is known as a stratigraphic test by cutting a trench right through the middle of the mound from end to end and from top to bottom.

Our first rough trench was cut down to desert level with a team of mules and a scraper, but thereafter the rest of the work was done by hand. The next step was to cut a sheer vertical face along the south side of the trench. This face

Snaketown, red-on-buff pottery of the Colonial Period

was then divided into measured rectangles, one-half meter deep and two meters long, each identified by a letter for its column and a number for its layer. When this had been done, it was only necessary to trowel into the face of the mound to a depth of half a meter, and each section, except those on the surface, gave us exactly half a cubic meter of rubbish (0.5 x 0.5 x 2.0 meters).

Snaketown, red-on-buff pottery of the Sedentary Period

Broad to fine-line red-on-gray at Snaketown

(From Haury, E. W. 1937)

Broad-line red-on-gray at Snaketown

(From Haury, E. W. 1937)

Broad-line red-on-brown at San Simon Village

(From Sayles, E. B. 1945)

a

b

Snaketown
  a. Mound 29
  b. The preliminary cut was made with a team and scraper.

a

b

Mound 29
  a. The side of the trench marked off in sections
  b. Removing sections and screening sherds

The contents of each section were then screened through a half-inch-mesh sieve, and all sherds were saved, sacked, and the bags marked with the letter and number of the section. The sherds were then washed, sorted, and divided into their various types, and the number of each type entered on a large sheet of graph paper. Every precaution was taken to avoid any mixing of the sherds from different sections, even to the extent of covering exposed surfaces with paper at the end of each day's work to guard against possible caving of the face of the trench.

Sections contained from eight hundred up to as many as four thousand sherds. We screened one hundred forty sections from this main trench, and when the operation was finished 108,305 sherds had been identified and listed according to type. The actual counts were as follows:—

Sedentary red-on-buff	19,829
Colonial red-on-buff	13,439
Narrow-line red-on-gray	208
Broad-line red-on-gray	80
Polished redware	453
Intrusive pottery	47
Plainware	74,249
	108,305

As plainware was of no value in helping us to define the succession of culture, the significance of the proportions of the local red and decorated wares can be more easily understood when these are reduced to percentages of the total of these types:—

Sedentary red-on-buff	58.4%
Colonial red-on-buff	39.5
Narrow-line red-on-gray	.6
Broad-line red-on-gray	.2
Polished redware	1.3
	100.0

The point which at once stands out from these figures is that during the period represented by the formation of Mound 29, the polished red and red-on-gray sherds amounted to only 2 per cent of the total decorated pottery content of the mound. Based on mere numbers, it might be argued that this poor showing was due to the fact that the postulated Pioneer Period had lasted for only a short time, or possibly that the population was small, so accounting for the relative scarcity of Pioneer rubbish. But herein lies the value of stratigraphy, since if these red and red-on-gray types had actually been pre-Colonial, they should obviously have been concentrated in the lowest levels of Mound 29, with only a few persistences into the supposedly later Colonial layers. Their true status is shown when one draws diagrams of cross sections of Mound 29 and marks the presence of these sherds as they were found in the various sections. This at once makes it clear that fine-line red-on-gray was manufactured throughout the life of the mound and was actually more abundant in the upper Sedentary layers than in the lower Colonial sections. More important than anything else, however, is the evidence that Colonial red-on-buff was present in the lowest sections of the mound, in *direct association* with both polished red and broad-line red-on-brown. This association during the earliest days of Snaketown is even more strongly emphasized when it is found that Colonial red-on-buff and polished red were both present in Section 0.11 at the bottom of Pit 1—the lowest section of Mound 29—under 18 feet of undisturbed rubbish. When it is realized that these associations occurred in sections containing only one-half cubic meter of rubbish—roughly the equivalent of a good-sized wheelbarrow load of dirt—it provides convincing evidence that at one and the same time Colonial red-on-buff

A   B   C   D   E   F   G   H   I   J   K   L   M   N   O   P   Q   R   S   T   U   V   W   X   Y

Snaketown: cross-sections, Mound 29
 Top: Distribution of red-on-buff sherds of the Colonial Period
 Middle: Distribution of red-on-buff sherds of the Sedentary Period
 Bottom: Distribution of fine-line red-on-gray sherds

and polished red were being made, used, smashed, swept up, and thrown with other rubbish into the bottom of Pit 1.

This effectively disposed of most of the theories we had been cherishing, but it also opened up some new leads that had to be followed. Once convinced that polished redware and the red-on-grays did not represent a pre-Colonial period, it did not take long to pin down the people who had caused all the trouble.

Although all of the polished redware at Snaketown appeared superficially to be exactly the same, the paste itself was of two different kinds—one in which relatively fresh volcanic material was the main constituent, the other low in volcanic particles, but high in granites and mica schist. These distinctions were clearly brought out by Nora Gladwin through the examination of thin sections under a petrographic miscroscope, but this was only the first step in the solution of this problem. The second was to demonstrate, by the same means, that all other native Snaketown pottery showed a high percentage of local granites and schists, with a small showing of volcanic material, in rounded, well-weathered particles, difficult to identify. And the third was to show that in pottery which was actually made in the Mogollon villages in southwestern New Mexico, volcanic rocks, or minerals derived from them, were the major, if not the only, constituents.

It was a beautiful example of the successful application of highly technical laboratory methods to an archaeological problem, and the results were extremely important. Nora Gladwin had provided us with convincing evidence that Mogollon women had not only been present when Snaketown was founded—as shown by their volcanic-tempered redware—but also that they had settled down and continued to make their polished red pottery out of local materials when their Mogollon clays were no longer available to them—as shown by the redware composed of the local granites and mica schist.

With this as a guide, it was later discovered that the broad-line red-on-gray at Snaketown was so similar to broad-line red-on-brown at the San Simon village as to be often indistinguishable—but we had to excavate the San Simon village to find this out.

Fine-line red-on-gray at Snaketown also closely resembled the fine-line red-on-brown that we had found in the Harris and Mogollon villages, and the greater tendency toward scroll designs at Snaketown could be attributed to the contemporary influence of Hohokam potters, who always preferred the longest way around a design rather than to draw a straight line.

The identification of the cultural parentage of this Mogollon-like pottery at Snaketown was of great help in establishing a dependable chronology for the site. When one applies the Mogollon time-scale to the local series at Snaketown, one finds it possible that the earliest deposits of polished redware were laid down as far back as A.D. 700, when some of the Mogollon villages to the east were being founded. Broad-line red-on-gray would then have made its first appearance at Snaketown at about A.D. 750—the date at which it also showed up for the first time in the Mogollon villages. Fine-line red-on-gray would therefore have come in at about A.D. 800 and have lasted until about A.D. 850, by which time the Mogollon influence seems to have faded out, since at Snaketown there was no equivalent to the red-on-white pottery in the Mogollon district.

This scale of time also agrees very well with the chronology of the Flagstaff area, represented by black-on-white and black-on-red pottery types which were found in Mound 29 and which in their home district have been dated as ranging from A.D. 750 to 900.

Besides the positive evidence provided by these cultural and chronological equations, there are also two negative features which set rather definite time limits. The first of these is the total absence of any kind of Basket Maker pottery in Mound 29, implying that these types of pottery had already ceased to be made by the time the mound had begun to form. The second is the complete absence of any type of pottery from the Classic (Pueblo III) Period of any Southwestern culture in Mound 29, indicating that the formation of the mound had come to an end by the time these Classic types had begun. Entirely aside from all other evidence, the absence of intrusive sherds from these two periods establishes the lower limit of the mound as not earlier than A.D. 750, and the upper limit as not later than A.D. 1000. It is consequently reassuring to find that the tree-ring dates of all of the intrusive pottery types fall well within these limits, and furthermore it even inspires confidence in the accuracy of the dating of the intrusive types themselves to find that their dates agree with their mutual associations in various sections of Mound 29.

The stratigraphic testing of Mound 29 showed that during the ninth century the Colonial culture of the Hohokam changed slowly to that which we have called the Sedentary, unaffected by any foreign influence. The transition was gradual, spread over a number of years, and at the time was imperceptible. As regards pottery, the same bowls of inverted bell shape were made, but the trailing red lines on exteriors were dropped. Designs of small repeated elements were sometimes included in more complicated patterns which often suggest that they were derived from textiles—none of which have survived.

Architecturally, there was a gradual change from the square house of the early Colonial Period, through a long rectangular shape in which the length was often more than twice the breadth, to an elliptical plan in which the ends of the houses were rounded. Grooves or gutters were dug around the edges of the floor to receive the ends of reeds, set vertically to form a wainscoting. The entrance passage was provided with a step, and instead of four roof supports, posts were placed close together around the periphery of the floor with two main posts on the center line of the long axis, presumably calling for a gable rather than a flat roof.

By A.D. 800, several large communities had been founded and had become well established, as shown by rubbish mounds and houses strung out more or less continuously along the rivers, streams, and washes within the Gila Basin. In some of these watercourses, such as the Santa Cruz Wash which now is dry for most of the year, water is said to have flowed the year around, but many undoubtedly dried up during the summer and the colonists were compelled to withdraw to settlements more favorably situated. By the beginning of the Sedentary Period, during the ninth century, most of the outlying camp-sites and small isolated villages had been abandoned and the Hohokam had congregated in the large communities where the great irrigation projects were already well advanced, such as Snaketown, which had been forming in the Gila Basin. Another very large community once flourished on and near what is now the Casa Grande National Monument, one and a half miles south of the Gila River. This settlement obtained its water from a canal, the remains of which can still be seen near Adamsville, which had its intake about eighteen miles east of Casa Grande. One of the largest Hohokam settlements was near Cashion, where the Gila, the Salt, and the Agua Fria came together about eighteen miles west of Phoenix, and there were many others stretching off to the east, often so close together that it is hard to tell where one ends and another begins. It is in these large farming communities that one finds the culture of the Hohokam at its best. There are some single isolated villages such as Roosevelt: 9:6, which we excavated in 1932, and a number of other outlying sites as far west as Bouse, near the Colorado River, which our survey has listed. But while these were certainly early Hohokam sites on the evidence of their pottery, none of them showed any indications of ball-courts, great lodges, or irrigation systems, and when excavated, none contained copper bells or any of the beautifully carved stone, bone, and shell objects which have been found at Snaketown, the Grewe site, and the other large settlements at Casa Grande, Cashion, and Phoenix.

WITH THE HOHOKAM at Snaketown busily engaged at A.D. 800 in building up the rubbish in Mound 29 for us to take apart in A.D. 1934, we can now leave them for a time while we follow the Reds as they swarmed up to the Plateau. From the Gila Basin at an elevation of about 1,000 feet, the easiest way up to the Plateau in the old days was up the Verde Valley which provided a natural thoroughfare up to Flagstaff at 7,000 feet.

We first became interested in this section of the country in 1926 when we made a survey of the Verde and its tributaries and ran across a type of pottery which was new to us and which has not since been found, even as sherds, anywhere outside of the Verde drainage. It was thick, rather crude, not slipped or polished, with a surface which was dull gray and heavily flecked with mica. Bowls were large and decorated on the inside with broad finger-width black lines arranged in rectilinear designs. Pottery of this kind was most abundant west of the Verde, running north up Chino Creek, down through Skull Valley, and dying out in the pine forests of the Bradshaws, south of Prescott. Still farther west, the black-on-gray ware of the Verde faded out into the red-on-brown decorated pottery that was made by the western Yuman tribes, which also carried geometric designs of broad finger-width lines drawn with mineral paint.

The houses of the Prescott Culture were square to rectangular, four-posters, with a side entrance, resembling the houses of the Hohokam. Contact with the Hohokam was also shown by sherds of Colonial red-on-buff which were found in most of the local sites, but there the connection ended. The dead were buried at full length in shallow graves, so breaking abruptly with the Hohokam custom of cremation, and there were no signs whatever of great lodges, ball-courts, irrigation systems, or any of the arts and crafts which were distinctive of the Hohokam. The Prescott Culture provides a shining example of country cousins trying to act like city folks. On a base consisting of local Yuman yokels, one can see the impressions made by three other peoples—the Hohokam, as noted above, Reds, and Basket Makers. The Red influence in the local pottery was represented by broad-line rectilinear designs, drawn with mineral paint, and by plain red-brown ware, baked in an oxidizing fire. The presence of Basket Makers is clearly indicated by the use of a reducing fire for the black-on-gray ware, and also by the incorporation of elements of design on the local decorated pottery which were typically Basket Maker. It is an unusually interesting situation for those who like their problems well scrambled.

GOING NORTH from Prescott, the pine forest is left behind, and one comes to the broad open plain of the Chino Valley. Straight ahead lies the high country between Ashfork and Flagstaff, with the San Francisco Peaks rising up to 13,000 feet. To the east, the Chino Valley contracts to become the Verde and leads up to Flagstaff by way of Sycamore and Oak creeks. To the west, Chino Creek comes down past Seligman from the western section of the Coconino Plateau, and it is with this western region that we are now concerned.

For the greater part, the Coconino Plateau is rather flat and exposed, with a thin stand of grass and clumps of junipers, and little to offer to a people looking for a place in which to settle down. Along Chino Creek there are a few sites— enough to mark the trail—but about twenty-five miles south of the Grand Canyon the character of the country changes to forests of pinyon and juniper, and ruins increase rapidly in numbers. In 1930, we ran a survey along the south rim of the Canyon and found over 250 sites, all situated in the forest where the hunting was good and open glades made it possible to raise crops on a small scale. Some of these sites were what we call sherd areas, where fragments of pottery were the only indications of former occupation and where houses, if any, must have been subterranean, as no surface traces are now to be seen. The great majority of sites showed the remains of one-room square or rectangular houses, outlined by rows of rocks which may have served as foundations for adobe or wattle-and-daub walls, as there were never enough stones in the debris to have carried the walls up to their full height in masonry.

The decorated pottery in these small one-room sites was a broad-line black-on-white which has generally been recognized as characteristic of Pueblo II, but it is hard to see how this simple broad-line black-on-white could have developed

The Prescott Culture: sites in the forest south of Prescott

from the solid triangles bordered by fine parallel lines which are the hallmark of Pueblo I. The same is true of architecture, since it would be difficult to derive the local rectangular surface houses, outlined by rocks, from the semi-subterranean pit-houses on the Baker Ranch which have been called Pueblo I— particularly as pit-houses lasted into Pueblo II in Medicine Valley. It is not safe

Broad-line Black-on-gray: Verde Valley
   Showing the use of stars, nets, triangles, the boxed cross, dotted lines, and borders, and the characteristic zigzag of the Basket Makers.

to put too much reliance on the results of a survey without excavation to fill in the details, but from the evidence now available, it looks as if there once had been a movement of people, marked by broad-line black-on-white pottery, which had passed to the west of the San Francisco Peaks and had mushroomed east and west upon reaching the Grand Canyon of the Colorado. It further seems that this movement was contemporaneous with the culture known as Pueblo I, rather than that it had developed out of Pueblo I.

These doubts as to the validity of Pueblo I as a widespread cultural stage are again raised by the fact that in southern Nevada and southwestern Utah there was a local culture where broad-line black-on-white was associated with a plain grayware which appears to have been identical to Basket Maker plainware, but there was no trace of an intervening Pueblo I stage.

RETURNING NOW to the upper Verde, we can pick up the trail of those Red bands which followed Sycamore and Oak creeks up to the Plateau and moved northward, east of the San Francisco Peaks. Here, from Flagstaff northeast to Medicine Valley, there was a combination made up of Reds and Basket Makers, and it would be hard to decide which was the dominant strain. The pottery consisted of a black-on-white ware, heavily slipped, polished, decorated with broad-line rectilinear designs drawn with vegetable paint; a black-on-red ware, slipped, polished, and decorated with a mineral paint; and polished red or brown ware with black smudged interior surfaces.

A Chino site on the Coconino Plateau

The houses were deep square pit-houses, the walls lined with horizontal split planks, held in place by vertical posts. Entrance was through a hatchway in the roof which also served as a smoke-vent above a central fireplace. Outside the wall a vertical ventilator shaft was sunk to connect with a tunnel at floor level to supply fresh air. And scattered around among the pit-houses were shallow surface circular or oval, one-room houses, outlined by stones, which give the same tree-ring dating as the pit-houses, and which were probably used as store-rooms, since they had no fireplaces.

The tree-ring dates which have been published by the Museum of Northern Arizona sustain the doubts which have been expressed above as to the succession of Pueblo I and II. The first series includes the most recent dates for sites classified as Pueblo I at which no broad-line black-on-white was found:

N.A. 1531	The Elden Pit-house	A.D. 708 to 885
N.A. 1925 b	Pit-house, Bonito Terrace	833 to 859
N.A. 2798	Pit-house, Baker Ranch	710 to 828

The second series includes some of the earliest dates for sites containing broad-line black-on-white and classified as Pueblo II, at which no Pueblo I black-on-white was found:

South Rim of the Grand Canyon: a small house site

N.A.	408 a	Surface house, stone outlines	A.D. 824 to 976
N.A.	1244 b	Plank-lined pit-house	817 to 948
N.A.	2001 a	Plank-lined pit-house	825 to 965

From these dates it can be seen that broad-line black-on-white—classified as Pueblo II—overlapped on sites which were classified as Pueblo I for a period of not less than sixty-eight years, from A.D. 817 to 885, so helping to confirm the belief that the differences between Pueblo I and II were regional rather than developmental.

HAVING REACHED THE PLATEAU at Flagstaff, and using this as a vantage point, it will be well to pause for a few moments while we look over the country lying off to the east, since this played an important part in the problem to be considered.

When one leaves Flagstaff at 7,000 feet and heads east, the country changes rapidly. The pine forest dies out at 6,000 feet, about fifteen miles east of Flagstaff, and one enters the zone of junipers which encircles the basin of the Little Colorado. Travelling east on Highway 66 or by train on the Santa Fe, one leaves the junipers behind after crossing Canyon Padre, and one hundred miles of open barren windswept land lies ahead until the juniper belt again is reached around Navajo Springs on the Rio Puerco.

Broad-line Black-on-white: Flagstaff District
Some form of the maze or meander is very common in broad-line black-on-white; note also seamed, folded, and banded designs, keys, pennons, interlocking scrolls, dotted lines, and borders.

The desert bounded by the juniper belt covers an expanse of about ten thousand square miles—one hundred miles east and west from Canyon Padre to Navajo Springs, and a little more than one hundred miles from the junipers along the Mogollon Rim up to the Hopi towns on the southern edge of Black Mesa. I speak of this great area as desert, and it should be emphasized that in many ways this stretch of the Plateau is actually more desertlike than most of southern Arizona. There is less vegetation; game is not as abundant; annual rainfall is about the same, sometimes dropping down to 3 inches or less at Winslow in the center of the basin; and while it may not be quite as hot in summer, it is much colder in winter.

From the east, south, and west, everything slopes down gradually to the Little Colorado River. Rising in the White Mountains, near Greer, as a small trout stream, it drops sharply down to Springerville, and then meanders through flat meadows past St. Johns, picking up a few creeks and washes coming in from the east. At Holbrook, the Rio Puerco joins the Little Colorado, after draining one hundred miles of country east to the Continental Divide, and the river flattens out to a broad shallow bed where sandstorms alternate with floods according to the season of the year. At Winslow, the Highway and the Santa Fe cross the Little Colorado, and the river bends northwestward to Grand Falls where it has cut a deep gorge through which it flows to join the Colorado River a few miles east of Desert View, on the south rim of the Grand Canyon.

This is the desert of the Little Colorado Basin which, with a few rare exceptions, was a cultural vacuum which proved to be an effective barrier to east-west or north-south intercourse. Some contacts undoubtedly were made, as shown by a few Flagstaff sherds in the White Mound village, but by intercourse I mean the sort of cultural exchange which once was carried on between the people in Chaco Canyon and those on Mesa Verde, or between the Hohokam and the Flagstaff villages by way of the Verde Valley. It is reasonably certain that relations on any such scale were not maintained across the wastes of the Little Colorado Basin, and the difficulty of communication between the various groups around the periphery of the basin was an important factor in the development of local cultures.

SOUTHEAST OF FLAGSTAFF, in the general region drained by Canyon Diablo, we have run across a number of small isolated sites in the open desert, east of the juniper belt which surrounds the basin of the Little Colorado. These ruins are rarely more than one or two rooms in size, outlined by rows of rocks which may have served as foundations for walls of masonry. Polished redware is abundant and the decorated pottery consists of black-on-white carrying broad-line geometric designs, applied with a vegetable paint on a white, slipped, polished surface.

None of these sites have been excavated. No tree-ring dates are available, but the approximate period is suggested by the fact that the Canyon Diablo colony seems to have been an offshoot of the people who were spreading broad-line decoration through the western reaches of the Southwest during the ninth century.

SOUTH AND SOUTHEAST of Canyon Diablo, along the Mogollon Rim from the Verde east to Showlow, there once were some other people about whom little is known. They later played an important part in the history of the Salado Branch, below the Rim. Scattered through the forest of junipers along the southern border of the Plateau, there are a considerable number of sites outlined by rows of stones, consisting of not more than one or two rooms, with an L-shaped extension or windbreak usually open to the east, suggesting a sort of patio.

The pottery is of three different kinds—polished redware, mostly bowls with black smudged interiors; a redware, not slipped or polished, but decorated with broad-line rectilinear designs; and a black-on-white ware, heavily slipped, well polished, carrying broad-line ribbon designs, applied with a dense black mineral paint. A few scroll designs on the black-on-white ware suggest friendly relations with the Hohokam, but otherwise decoration was strictly rectilinear.

None of these patio houses have yet been excavated. There are no tree-ring dates, and some of them may have been later than the ninth century. They seem, however, to belong in the general class of small one- and two-room houses con-

The Little Colorado Basin: sites near Canyon Diablo

Mogollon Rim: a patio house

taining broad-line black-on-white, and it would probably not be far wrong to say that these various groups were beginning to form during the 800's. In the present survey of the situation, the people who built their patio houses along the Rim are important, as they formed the southern arc of the crescent of broad-line

Broad-line Black-on-white: Mogollon Rim
   Showing folded and band designs, keys, pennons, interlocking scrolls, and
   dotted borders.

groups which enclosed the basin of the Little Colorado around its northern, western, and southern borders.

WE TURN NOW to the northern arc of this crescent, and this brings us to the Kaibito Plateau, about fifty miles east of the Grand Canyon. This is where Noel Morss found and described conditions which in many ways resembled those which we had found along the south rim of the Canyon. In this case, the culture was described as part of the Kayenta Branch and was classified as Pueblo II, but Morss found that Pueblo I "peters out rather suddenly west of Kayenta," and that "in Nevada and Utah the Pueblo II stage is found following close upon Basket Maker III without any apparent Pueblo I horizon." Morss therefore ran into the same difficulties that we had met in trying to derive Pueblo II out of Pueblo I; in fact, he actually said, "The two cultures were to a large extent geographically complementary and probably overlapped in point of time." After what has already been said above, I think it only fair to chalk this up as a bona fide instance of a "duplicate independent discovery."

The houses which Morss found were usually larger than those along the rim of the Canyon, and the decorated pottery may have been of somewhat better quality as to the clarity of the white slipped surfaces and the broad-line ribbon designs. The plain pottery was gray, as at Flagstaff and the Canyon, but no mention was made of polished redware—which is all as it should be, since Red influence could be expected to decline as the Reds penetrated deeper into the home grounds of the Basket Makers and their descendants.

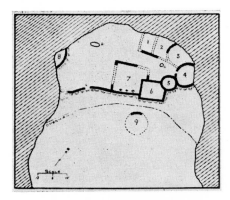

Ruin I: Monument Valley

Ruin II: Sayod Neechee Canyon, Monument Valley

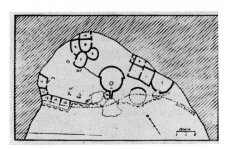

Ruin VII: Laguna Creek

Ruin VIII: Marsh Pass

Four ruins excavated by Kidder and Guernsey in which no two kivas were alike.
(From Kidder and Guernsey, 1919)

FROM THE KAIBITO the scene shifts to Marsh Pass and the haunts of the Kayenta Branch. This used to be one of the favorite playgrounds for Southwestern archaeologists, and we have the benefit of the investigations made by Kidder and Guernsey during the years from 1914 to 1923 which provided the skeleton of the Pecos Classification. More recently, there is the report by Beals, Brainerd, and Smith on the Rainbow Bridge Expedition which found that the skeleton was just a bag of bones which could not be articulated. After excavating five sites and making a detailed analysis of the pottery, Beals and his associates concluded:

> It is evident that much remains to be done in the Tsegi region and that the work of the expedition thus far has been primarily of value in defining problems. It is clear that Basketmaker problems have not been conclusively solved and the transition from Basketmaker to Pueblo I remains obscure. More work on Pueblo I with special emphasis on the transition to Pueblo II is needed. Pueblo II also presents many variations which need to be understood more thoroughly, while redefinition of the demarcation between Pueblo II and Pueblo III is required.

Broad-line Black-on-white: Marsh Pass District
   Seamed patterns, triangles, maze, pennons, interlocking scrolls, and negative
   design.

(From Beals, Brainerd and Smith, 1945)

Beals finally wound up by saying, "Pueblo I and Pueblo II black-on-whites were made by the same people simultaneously"—which comes very close to hanging up a new record as a "triplicate independent discovery."

Beals agrees with Morss and ourselves that the two cultures overlapped in time. His statement also agrees with the conditions which we found on the Coconino Plateau, and also with those at Snaketown where we found sherds of Pueblo I and II associated in the same deposits. These associations, however, do not demand, necessarily, that both types were made by the same people. They simply mean that these two kinds of pottery were contemporaneous rather than successive, as formerly supposed.

For the architecture in Marsh Pass at this time, it is enough to glance at the plans of Ruins I, II, VII and VIII which Kidder and Guernsey excavated, to make it clear that Kayenta architects were not governed by any fixed rules. Speaking of kivas, Kidder and Guernsey said, "The kivas are characterized, to permit ourselves a paradox, by their lack of character . . . they vary greatly in size and interior arrangement, some having small recesses, some very large ones, many none at all."

Under the circumstances, I do not think it possible to explain the conditions in Marsh Pass by the conventional idea that Basket Maker III developed locally through Pueblo I into Pueblo II under its own power without any outside contacts or intrusions. It looks to me as if we are dealing with three regional

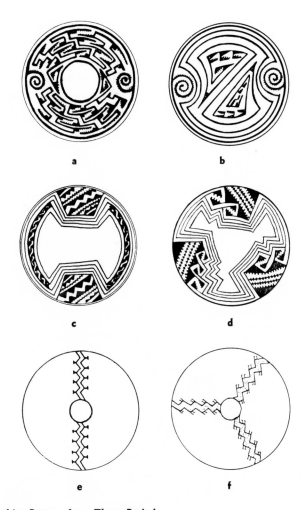

Black-on-white Pottery from Three Periods
  a & b.   Classified as Pueblo II
  c & d.   Classified as Pueblo I
  e & f.   Classified as Basket Maker III
  Heretofore regarded as a consecutive series of development, but there does
  not appear to be any continuity or relationship between the designs of any two
  groups.
  a, b, c, d.   Slipped and polished
  e & f.   Not slipped; not polished

groups—Basket Makers in Marsh Pass, Pueblo I at Flagstaff, and Pueblo II in northwestern Arizona—all of them at least partly contemporaneous, but owing to the order in which they came together in Marsh Pass—Pueblo I on Basket Maker III; Pueblo II on Pueblo I—they have given the appearance of a local cultural progression. This impression has been further strengthened by the application of a terminology which in itself conveys the idea of a self-contained development.

SOUTHEAST OF MARSH PASS, information for the Canyon de Chelly-Ganado district is limited to surface surveys. These show sites containing broad-line black-on-white as far east as the Chuskas. Nothing is known of the architecture, and there are no tree-ring dates. I mention them merely because they mark the easternmost limit of the northern arc of the broad-line crescent enclosing the northern, western, and southern borders of the Little Colorado Basin.

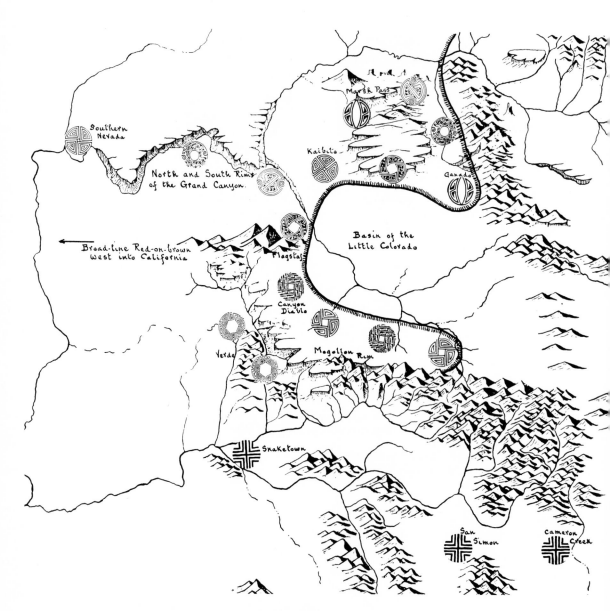

The Distribution of Broad-line Decoration

WITH THE DYING OUT of broad-line sites in the western foothills of the Chuskas, we come to the end of a trail which started in the southernmost Mogollon villages in southwestern New Mexico; ran west to Snaketown and north up the Verde; continued northward up Chino Creek to the Coconino Plateau; west to California and southern Nevada; east from the Verde along the Mogollon Rim and out to Canyon Diablo; north along the eastern side of the San Francisco Peaks past Flagstaff; east to the Kaibito Plateau and Marsh Pass; and east to the Chuskas.

In view of such a wide spread, it may seem that I have placed too much emphasis on a mere style of pottery design and that the inclination to dip one's finger in a pot of paint and draw straight lines is inherent in all people—but I doubt it. To bolster my doubt, I can point, first, to the fact that the spread was continuous, without any gaps; second, there was no alternative form of decorative treatment competing with the broad-line within its area; and third, that neither the Hohokam, the Farmers, nor the Basket Makers showed any desire to paint with their fingers or draw rectilinear designs. And finally, I think it is also significant that throughout the broad-line range one finds polished redware, plain or decorated, in association; *but* again, polished red, plain or decorated, was not favored by the Hohokam, the Farmers, or the Basket Makers.

Against this background, the distinctive value of broad-line decoration will become increasingly clear as soon as we leave the western section of the Southwest and move eastward into western New Mexico. Here we shall find an entirely different, but equally characteristic, style of pottery decoration which was just coming into fashion in the early 800's.

When and Where, in the East and North: A.D. 800 to 900

THE VARIOUS GROUPS of people who chose during the ninth century to decorate their white pottery with broad black ribbon designs were spread in a long unbroken curve around the southern, western, and northern borders of the Little Colorado Basin. This leaves a gap of about one hundred miles, from Showlow in the southeast to Ganado in the northeast, still to be accounted for and it is with this eastern quadrant, and the peoples back of it, that we are now going to deal.

The country covers the area lying between the Little Colorado and the Continental Divide—an east-west distance of about one hundred miles and a north-south spread of about 175 miles, from the San Juan to the Upper Gila. The entire region is cut into two approximately equal halves by the Rio Puerco, which heads on the Divide and flows west through the Red Mesa Valley, past Gallup, White Mound, and the Petrified Forest to join the Little Colorado at Holbrook. The northern half includes the Chaco Basin, with the Chuskas forming a barrier between the Chaco drainage and the Little Colorado to the west. The southern half covers the Province of Cibola, made famous by the Conquistadores in their search for the fabled Seven Cities of Cibola, and is separated from the Chaco Basin by the Zuni Mountains, running east and west from Mt. Taylor to Zuni.

In the northern half, the people of the Chaco Branch—fundamentally Basket Makers—undoubtedly owed a great deal of their culture to the Mesa Verde

The Red Mesa Valley

Farmers north of the San Juan, with whom they had maintained close relations for six hundred years or more. But protected as they were by the Zuni Mountains along their southern border and the Chuskas to the west, the only Red influences which reached the Chaco were those which had already been filtered through their Cibola neighbors to the south or the Kayenta people to the west.

In the southern half of this eastern area, from Zuni down to the Upper Gila, the conditions were very different. Basket Makers had come down from the north during the eighth century, as shown at White Mound, Whitewater, Zuni Creek, the Petrified Forest, and the Bear Ruin. They were the dominant factor in the Cibola district. Their influence was strong in the upper San Francisco drainage and extended in a descending scale as far south as the Mimbres. In fact, the Cibola Branch might be said to have been founded on a Basket Maker base, and was consequently closely allied to the Chaco Branch, but it was affected by Red influences from the south and west to an extent that was unknown in the Chaco area.

With recognition of the fact that Chaco and Cibola were sisters under the skin, so to speak, I come now to a style of decorating pottery which put the family brand on four cultures—Chaco, Cibola, Mimbres, and Salado—in western New Mexico and eastern central Arizona. This is the technique known as hatching, which consists usually of two so-called framing lines which outline the pattern, the space between them being filled with fine parallel lines, although

Types of Hatched Designs
  Fine Parallel Lines
a.   St. Johns, Arizona: Gila Pueblo Collection
b.   Mimbres Valley: Cosgrove, C. B. 1932.
  Opposed Hatched and Solid
c.   Mimbres Valley: Cosgrove, C. B. 1932.
d.   Tularosa Valley: Gila Pueblo Collection

  Oblique Hatching
e.   Red Mesa Valley: Gladwin, H. S. 1945.
f.   Toadlena: Gila Pueblo Collection
  Wavy Hatching
g.   Rio Puerco: Gila Pueblo Collection
h.   Red Mesa Valley: Gladwin, H. S. 1945.

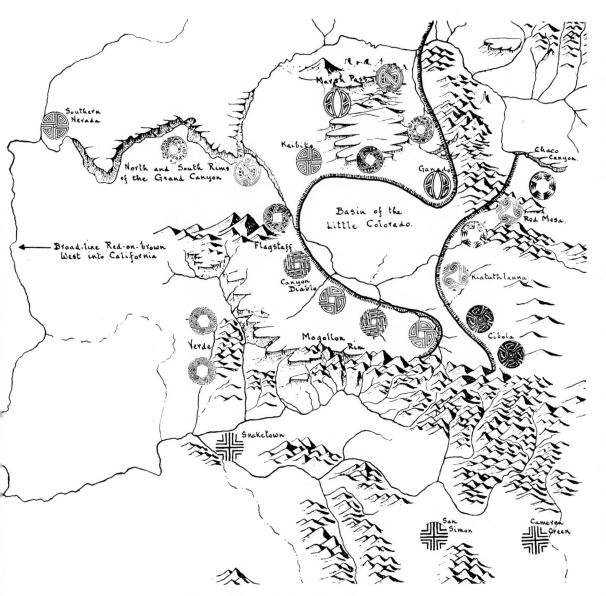

The Distribution of Broad-line and Hatched Decoration

rectangles and triangles sometimes also served as frames. There are three types of hatched designs.

First, there is the kind in which the framing lines were parallel and the space was filled with wavy lines. This was the earliest, showing up at about A.D. 800 in Chaco Canyon, the Red Mesa Valley, and the Zuni district, but dying out in the Chaco-Cibola area by A.D. 900. A few examples have been found in the Mimbres Valley at a date of A.D. 900, or slightly later, and the design hung on in some Salado pottery—of which more later—until about A.D. 1200.

The second kind had the same parallel framing lines, but in this case, the space was filled with fine straight oblique lines which were more widely spaced in early examples than in later times. This type was particularly characteristic of the Chaco potters, and it may not be too much to say that when it is found on the pottery of other people, it almost certainly indicates Chaco influence or derivation.

The third method of hatching employed two parallel framing lines, but the filling lines were drawn parallel to the framers in rectilinear patterns, and at random angles in curvilinear designs. An even more marked characteristic of this method is that the hatched elements of the design were invariably opposed or balanced by solid elements of the same shape. This type was the hallmark of the Cibola potters, but it is also found on Mimbres and Salado pottery. It is rare, but occurs occasionally in the Chaco.

A variant of hatching shows up in the custom of filling rectangles, triangles, or large uneven blank spaces with fine parallel lines. This was often done in the Mimbres, where the potters were remarkable for the accuracy of their line-drawing, but these same potters were also accustomed to drawing half a dozen fine lines parallel to the rim of a bowl, and it would be hard to know where to stop if all parallel lines should be regarded as hatching. For present purposes I am concerned only with certain styles of decorating pottery which can be used to trace the peoples who drew them, and I think it is very fortunate that the rigid adherence to form, as seen even today in the pottery and dress of their descendants, makes it possible to identify each group with a good deal of assurance even when found far from home.

THE TECHNIQUE OF HATCHING appears to have begun in western New Mexico early in the ninth, or possibly late in the eighth century. For the early type of wavy hatching there are three sites, well distributed—one in the northern half, one in the middle, and one in the southern section—and no one of them shows any sign of the later oblique hatched designs.

The first of these is in Chaco Canyon where Neil Judd found and excavated a pit-house one mile east of Pueblo Bonito.

Most of the pottery was plain grayware, similar in color and texture to that of the Basket Makers, but some of the pots had banded necks—a feature which has often been regarded as a symptom of Pueblo I, and which was also present at the Baker Ranch and in the last days at White Mound. The black-on-white pottery was a sort of combination of White Mound and Baker Ranch types in that all three sites shared the same rectilinear designs, made up of rectangular or triangular solids bordered by parallel lines. The local Chaco ware, however, was heavily slipped and well polished, as at the Baker Ranch, but was decorated with dense black mineral paint, as at White Mound. This is interesting in adding still one more variety to the heterogeneous Pueblo I brood, but the item of greatest present importance was that a large egg-shaped jar carried a spiral design

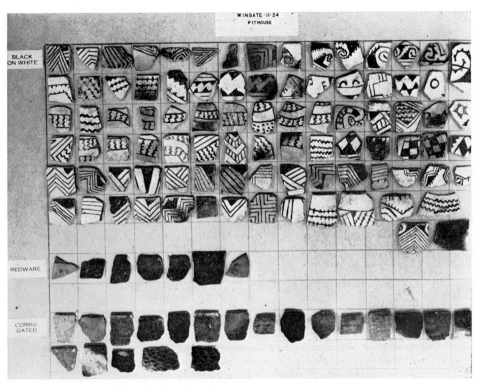

The Wingate pit-house: pottery types

of wavy hatching—showing beyond a doubt that this style of design had made its appearance on the Plateau by about A.D. 800.

THE SECOND INSTANCE of a site of this kind is a lone pit-house in the Red Mesa Valley, about three miles west of the Continental Divide. We had been excavating a small surface house and were running a trench from the ruin to the rubbish mound to define the occupation area, when we came to a soft pocket of earth in which charcoal specks were embedded. We followed these traces down for 8 feet and finally came to the floor of a circular pit-house, 13 feet in diameter, with a central firepit, four roof supports, a ventilator, but no bench. None of the charcoal fragments were large enough to be dated, but although no whole pieces of pottery were found, we saved all the sherds, and these showed gray pots with banded necks, and black-on-white ware with a thick white slip, highly polished, and decorated with wavy hatching and rectilinear designs applied with dense black mineral paint. For reference the site was named the Wingate pit-house.

THE THIRD SITE of this kind is the village of Kiatuthlanna, about forty miles south-west of Zuni, near the Salt Lakes in eastern Arizona. The village was excavated

Black-on-white: Kiatuthlanna
This pottery, which is sometimes referred to as Eastern Pueblo I, is strongly suggestive of Mogollon or Red influence. It shows the same treatment of straight lines in the forms of quarters, folds, stars, squares, triangles, pennons, chevrons, parallel straight and wavy lines.
Compare with fine-line red-on-brown (pp. 187, 188) and early Mimbres black-on-white (p. 213).   (From Roberts, F. H. H., Jr. 1931)

in 1929 by Roberts for the Smithsonian Institution, and is the only site which gives a complete picture of this type of settlement. I might add here that while there may be many other sites of the same kind, they are not easy to find unless they lasted long enough to leave some surface indications. Of the other two that are known, the pit-house in Chaco Canyon was exposed by the undercutting of the arroyo wall, and I stumbled on the Wingate pit-house when I was digging an entirely different kind of ruin.

The architecture at Kiatuthlanna was just what it should have been. All of the dwellings were pit-houses. All were deep, circular, provided with four roof supports, and had flat roofs, central firepits, ventilators, and roof entrances which also served as smoke-vents. The earlier houses had sheer vertical sides from floor to ground level, as in the Wingate pit-house. The later houses had benches with poles embedded, as in the Chaco Canyon pit-house, White Mound, Whitewater, Bear Ruin, and Shabik'.

The pottery also was all that one could ask. There were numerous examples of triangular solids bordered by parallel lines and a number of wavy hatched designs, but no oblique hatching. There was a noticeable increase in both scroll and quartered designs, and also a greater tendency to elaboration through the addition of little curls and hooks to designs which already were rather busy. One's

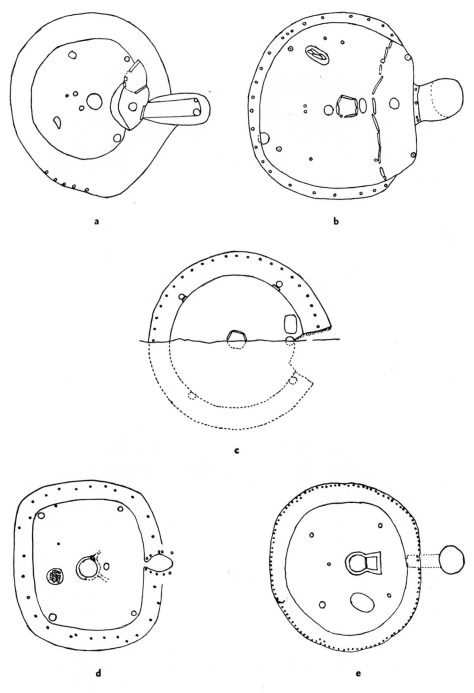

Houses with Benches and Inset Posts

a.	Whitewater Village	House 16	Roberts, F. H. H., Jr. 1940 b
b.	White Mound	House 3	Gladwin, H. S. 1945
c.	Chaco Canyon	House 2	Judd, N. M. 1924
d.	Bear Ruin	House 1	Haury, E. W. 1940 b
e.	Kiatuthlanna	House C	Roberts, F. H. H., Jr. 1931

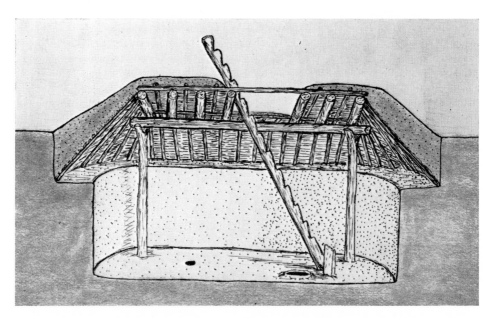

a

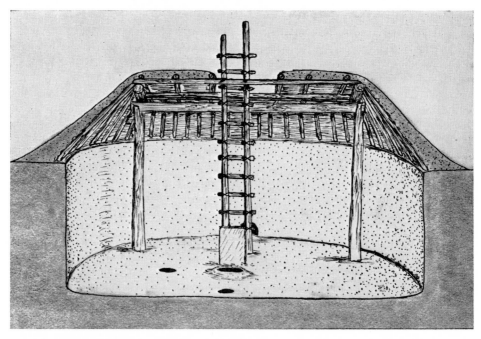

b

Pit-house Reconstruction
    a.   With bench as base for wall supports
    b.   With wall supports embedded on ground surface

(From Roberts, F. H. H., Jr. 1931)

general impression from the range of architecture and pottery is that Kiatuthlanna may have begun at about the same time as the Wingate pit-house and lasted somewhat later than the Chaco Canyon pit-house.

One other item in the report on Kiatuthlanna is of particular interest in connection with some of the suggestions which have been made. This is Roberts' comment:

"The skeletal remains show striking contrasts. The crania from the pit-houses exhibit long and broad forms, and show slightly deformed and undeformed examples in both groups. This is considered to indicate an unquestionable mixing of stock and customs."

THE SITE ON WHITEWATER WASH, just south of the Rio Puerco in eastern Arizona, which was also excavated by Roberts for the Smithsonian Institution, covered the transition from wavy to oblique hatching. As this settlement was continuously occupied for over two hundred years—from A.D. 800 to 1000—it is not possible to pin down the exact date when the change took place, but it is probably safe to say that it occurred during the ninth century.

Equations with Kiatuthlanna as the common denominator for the period include gray pots with banded necks, egg-shaped decorated jars, triangular and stepped figures bordered by parallel lines, wavy hatching, and the same kind of house-construction with a bench serving as a base for the butts of inclined poles. Resemblances to the later period at Kiatuthlanna consist of the same tendency toward scrolls, quartered designs, hooks, curls, and small key figures attached to lines and solids.

An important innovation at Whitewater was the use of parallel lines in such a way as to give the effect of longitudinal hatching, which seems to have been leading up to the balanced type of solid and hatched patterns which were the hallmark of the Cibola Branch.

FROM KIATUTHLANNA AND WHITEWATER in the western Cibola district, I now turn to the Red Mesa Valley in the southern Chaco area where hatching was being developed into one of the fine arts.

The Red Mesa Valley heads on the Continental Divide and drains westward to Gallup where it becomes the Rio Puerco. The northern side of the valley is bounded by a rampart of red sandstone cliffs of the Wingate formation, and the southern side by the Zuni Mountains. Highway 66, paralleling the tracks of the Santa Fe, bisects the valley throughout its length, the land on either side sloping gently up to the foot of the cliffs to the north and the mountains to the south. The altitude rises from 6800 feet at Gallup to 7500 feet on the Divide. Winters are cold, temperatures dropping sometimes to zero, with occasional heavy snowfall. Summers are pleasant with warm days and cool nights, but are not ideal for agriculture, for the growing season, from May to September, is apt to be too short.

Red Mesa Valley: the Red Mesa Ruin

The floor of the valley is pock-marked with the remains of houses and what in some cases appear to have been villages. A good example of such a cluster of houses is to be found in the ten isolated units which are spread along the rim of a low plateau just north of Crafts del Navajo, at Coolidge, New Mexico. Our first impression, in 1928, was that all of these units had been approximately contemporaneous, but excavation disclosed distinctions in pottery and architecture which made it seem more probable that no two sites had been occupied at exactly the same time, and that the ten units might represent the shifting around of one or two families over a relatively short period of time. Much the same effect is given today by Navajo families who abandon one hogan and build another near by whenever a death occurs in the house, or sometimes for other reasons that to us may seem trivial.

A good example of a single unit of this period is the Red Mesa Ruin, near the head of the valley. The six rooms of the house showed very uneven wall construction. Some were of adobe; one room had walls of adobe reinforced with poles; in others, the adobe had been stiffened with sandstone flakes; and the foundations of the outer walls were masonry, laid in adobe, and capped at a height of about 15 inches with flat sandstone slabs carefully shaped by flaking the edges. No fireplaces were found inside the rooms, although one often finds a windbreak

The Red Mesa Ruin: pottery types

extension enclosing a firepit on three sides and open to the east, suggesting an outdoor kitchen. This alfresco kind of life is also indicated by the numerous post-holes—the remains of brush shelters—and the slab-lined firepits which are scattered over the occupation areas to the south of the houses.

About 20 feet southeast of the house at the Red Mesa Ruin there was a pit-house, 12 feet in diameter, which satisfied all of the requirements of a kiva, and the only doubts as to its use for ceremonial purposes were raised by the lack of fireplaces in the rooms of the house and the question of why a family should want a kiva all to itself. To a people who had only recently emerged from sub-terranean rooms, the old pit-houses must still have had a good deal to offer in the way of coziness and warmth on cold stormy nights in winter—particularly when there were no fireplaces in the rooms of the surface house near by.

There was a perceptible decline in the quality of black-on-white pottery be-tween the period of Kiatuthlanna and that of the Red Mesa Ruin. The clear polished surfaces at Kiatuthlanna, which sometimes gave the effect of an enam-elled coating, had given way to a soft porous surface covered with a thin white wash rather than a hard white slip. Wavy hatching had entirely disappeared in favor of the oblique type; the tips of hatched triangles were often filled; and there was a marked increase in the use of solids, often with ticked borders. In laying out their patterns, the Red Mesa potters showed a preference for encir-cling band designs on bowls, instead of the quartered field of the Kiatuthlanna artists. The trend can be summed up in a sentence by saying that black-on-white pottery of this period was beginning to show those features which were char-acteristic of the Chaco Branch at all later times.

The bands on the plain gray pots at Kiatuthlanna had become true spiral coils and by the time of the Red Mesa Ruin the neck-coils were being pressed together by the potter's finger and thumb so as to leave deep indentations, some-times arranged in diagonal rows to give a waved effect. Polished redware was rare or completely absent, and there was no sign of any black-on-red ware.

We obtained twenty-two tree-ring dates from the Red Mesa Ruin, running from A.D. 875 to 916, with most of them falling between A.D. 880 and 890. In addition, we also have a few dates from other sites of the same period to help in rounding out the picture. One of the units at Coolidge, known as Wingate: 11:47, which had walls only of adobe and could therefore be expected to have been somewhat earlier than the Red Mesa Ruin, gave us five dates from A.D. 852 to 873. Another unit at Coolidge, Wingate: 11:49, which had the same kind of pottery and architecture as the Red Mesa Ruin, yielded seven dates from A.D. 862 to 927, and the kiva at the same site gave six dates from A.D. 891 to 922.

AND NOW, while Kayenta potters are learning to hatch their designs and Chaco women are messing themselves up trying to paint with their fingers, it is time to look north to see how the Mesa Verde Farmers have been handling their prob-lems during these turbulent years.

Chaco-Kayenta
Black-on-white pottery of Toadlena, northwestern New Mexico, bearing Chacoan designs but polished and decorated with vegetable paint suggestive of Kayenta potters.

For anyone in the ninth century who wished to travel from the Red Mesa Valley north to Chaco Canyon or beyond to the San Juan towns, two routes were open. One led to the east around Powell Mountain, through Satan's Pass and across thirty barren wind-swept miles to the Canyon, the other to the west over the Chaco-Puerco divide to the foothills of the Chuskas and so northward past Tohatchi and up past Bennett Peak to Shiprock. Judging by the relative numbers of ruins along these two routes, it looks as if most of the north-south traffic in the old days had flowed along the eastern slopes of the Chuskas.

There has been a great deal of pot-hunting in these foothill sites, but there are no published reports. Our survey includes over five hundred sites in the Chaco drainage, and these reveal some interesting but rather scrambled conditions. All along the foothills there are large numbers of sites of all periods. Some contain pottery that seems to be the same as that at Shabik'; some have black-on-white which looks like the decorated pottery at White Mound; while a short distance away, there are the same designs in mineral paint, but the surfaces are slipped and polished as at the Chaco Canyon pit-house. Near Toadlena and up to Mitten Rock, there are several sites with decorated pottery suggestive of the so-called Pueblo I at the Baker Ranch, but the vessels seem to have been larger than those at Flagstaff and of better quality as regards paint, slip, and finish. That some of these sites were considerably later than the Baker Ranch is also indicated by the presence of black-on-white ware which appears to be exactly the same as that in some of the Red Mesa villages, so pointing to a date in the 800's, as against the 700's at Flagstaff. Scattered around and about among these ruins— particularly in the valley west of Newcomb's on the road to Toadlena where they almost touch one another—we have found many sites with the same types of gray and decorated pottery as in the Red Mesa Valley, and the surface indications of architecture are the same as regards size and plan. It was surprising, however, to find that ruins of this kind, and also those of all earlier periods, were very scarce in Chaco Canyon itself, and I think there can be little doubt that the early stages of the Chaco Culture developed chiefly along the western and southern borders of the basin, from Shiprock down to Tohatchi and east to Mount Taylor.

Another prominent feature—particularly in the Red Mesa type of sites from Toadlena up to Shiprock—is the evidence of intercourse between the Chaco villages around Mitten Rock and Toadlena, and the Kayenta settlements west of the Chuskas. In the Chaco-Red Mesa sites at the eastern end of the pass formed by Red Rock Valley, one finds black-on-white pottery, some fine-line, some broad-line, slipped, polished, and decorated with vegetable paint, for which only a Kayenta potter could have been responsible. On the other hand, in the Kayenta sites in and to the west of Red Rock Valley, there are numerous examples of hatched and Red Mesa designs—some in vegetable, some in mineral, paint—and this combination runs up as far north as the San Juan and can often be found in sites of the ninth and tenth centuries on Mesa Verde and in Montezuma Valley.

My reasons for describing these conditions along the northern end of the Chuskas is that the best way to understand what was happening north of the San Juan during the ninth century is to approach the problem by following the Chaco bands which were moving northward. The trend has been reversed. From A.D. 200 to 700, the Basket Makers in northeastern Arizona had been acquiring knowledge as it was diffused southward from the Farmers. Then during the eighth century Basket Makers took over the Chaco Basin and pushed their colonies down to the Province of Cibola and out into the basin of the Little Colorado along the Mogollon Rim and west to Flagstaff. Meeting Reds coming up from the south, they acquired new traits which filtered back to their settlements in Chaco territory. Here, left to themselves, the people in the Red Mesa and Chuska villages flourished and increased in numbers up to about the middle of the ninth century when some of them started to trek northward. I am not now concerned with the reasons for this reversal of trend, as these can be more intelligibly discussed after more of the evidence has been reviewed. At present, the point of chief importance to establish is the fact that beginning in the middle 800's and lasting up to about A.D. 1100, there was a definite northward movement of people from the southern section of the Chaco area up to the Mesa Verde towns, north of the San Juan. A few examples will make this clear.

ON A PROMINENT MESA between Johnson and Greasewood canyons, a few miles southeast of Mesa Verde, there is a ruin excavated by Earl Morris with the impersonal title of Site 33. It is large, 280 feet long and 20 feet wide, with two parallel rows of surface, rectangular rooms, with walls of mud reinforced with poles and sometimes strengthened with a veneer of vertical stone slabs set on edge.

There were six subterranean kivas, 12 to 20 feet in diameter, about 6 feet deep, and one great kiva, 62 feet in diameter, with an oval firebox, 70 x 58 inches, which may have been one of the earliest examples of the large fire-vaults which later were characteristic of the great kivas in Chaco Canyon. One of the huge logs which supported the roof of the great kiva gave a date of A.D. 831, which will help us to keep things in their proper order.

Illustrations of the decorated pottery from Site 33 are of particular interest in that there does not appear to have been a single piece which might be said to have come from a Chaco site in the Red Mesa Valley, along the Chuskas, or in the Chaco Canyon. At A.D. 831, there was not a sign of any hatching, wavy or oblique, on the black-on-white ware at Site 33, and if there was any other indication of Chaco influence or intrusion at the site, it was not mentioned by Morris.

THE SECOND SITE in this series is known as Site 102, from our survey of Mesa Verde in 1929. This ruin is situated on Chapin Mesa in the Twin Trees area and was partly excavated by Gila Pueblo in 1947.

Site 102 was of the standard Farmer-Mesa Verde type, consisting of a row of surface, rectangular rooms in one continuous building about 100 feet long, served by three subterranean kivas, about 6 feet deep, and provided with all of the essential features. The main house was shallow, with floors about 2 feet below the present ground level, and walls of adobe or wattle-and-daub, stiffened with upright stone slabs.

The surface rooms and two of the kivas had been destroyed by fire, and from the resulting charcoal a large number of dates were obtained, all of which fell within the range from A.D. 799 to 844.

In its bearing on the problem now under discussion, the most important evidence at Site 102 was the decorated pottery. This consisted of black-on-red and red-on-orange wares which were the same as those found by Brew at Alkali Ridge, and also black-on-white types typical of the La Plata and Piedra villages in southwestern Colorado. Since Mesa Verde lies between Alkali Ridge and the La Plata, this is just about what one should expect. It is therefore the more significant that in an otherwise normal Mesa Verde community, 5 per cent of the decorated pottery consisted of White Mound black-on-white which can only be explained as having been made by people who were coming up from the south.

THE THIRD SITE in this progressive series is Site 1, on the south rim of Cahone Canyon, about seven miles west of Ackmen, Colorado, which was excavated by Paul Martin for the Chicago Museum of Natural History.

The ruin consisted of two groups of rectangular contiguous living rooms backed up by parallel rows of smaller storerooms, and the only change from the houses at Sites 33 and 102 was that instead of adobe or wattle-and-daub, the walls at Ackmen appear to have been carried up to their full height with crude coursed masonry laid up in clay. The kivas varied in size from 15 to 21 feet in diameter and conformed to Mesa Verde standards in all essential features. There were also two so-called great kivas at the site, one 43, the other 80, feet in diameter, but there is doubt as to their true status, since Martin did not find any firepits or ventilating systems and expressed the opinion that neither one had been roofed—possibly they were never finished. Getty succeeded in obtaining eighteen tree-ring dates from Site 1, all of which fell within the range from A.D. 837 to 872.

The decorated pottery was extremely important to the problem under consideration. Of all the black-on-white ware that was illustrated in the report 43 per cent showed Chaco hatched designs—20 per cent wavy and 23 per cent oblique—and since it also looks as if most of these had been drawn with mineral paint, this would indicate the presence of actual Chaco potters rather than that Mesa Verde women had adopted Chaco designs.

THESE THREE SITES provide us with a timetable of the movement of people from the southern and western sections of the Chaco area up to the Mesa Verde towns north of the San Juan. At A.D. 831, Site 33 in Johnson Canyon showed no evidence of Chaco people coming up from the south, in spite of the fact that it was the southernmost of the three sites and hence nearest to Chaco Canyon.

By A.D. 844, 5 per cent of the decorated pottery at Site 102 was White Mound black-on-white and definitely of Chaco derivation, regardless of whether the focus of this type was on the Rio Puerco or along the eastern Chuskas.

By A.D. 872, 43 per cent of the decorated pottery at Site 1 consisted of Chaco hatched designs, although Ackmen was the northernmost of the three sites of the series and consequently the farthest removed from the Chaco villages.

This evidence is also supported by our survey which shows that at about A.D. 900 Mesa Verde sites were running up to 50 per cent or more of Chaco pottery, and in view of its historical importance, I think we have been very fortunate in being able to establish the beginning of this northward movement within such close limits.

Aside from the effects which resulted from the influx of people from the Chaco, the development of pottery north of the San Juan from A.D. 800 to 900 followed along the lines of the eighth century. Plain grayware greatly outnumbered all other types, both in the quantity of vessels and in their larger size, so resulting in more sherds when the pots were broken. At some time during the early 800's, banded necks appeared on plain gray pots, and waved corrugating at Site 33 stamps this technique as having started in this area before A.D. 900.

As regards decorated pottery, it is again shown that red-on-orange and black-on-red types were more abundant in the west than in the east. At Ackmen, the combined collections from surface rooms and kivas gave the following percentages:

Black-on-white	Black-on-red	Red-on-orange
8%	2%	90%

whereas at Site 102, on Mesa Verde, the figures were:

63%	31%	6%

Morris did not publish any pottery statistics, but it is clear from his text and illustrations that black-on-white heavily outnumbered black-on-red and the various orange wares in the La Plata district. This continues and helps to confirm the distribution of these types during the eighth century, and the spread of Red influence is further indicated by the rapid increase in the use of slip, polishing, rectilinear designs, and mineral paint during the ninth century. All of these things are of importance in helping us to understand the conditions north of the San Juan at about this time, but the event which overshadows all others in importance was the northward movement of Chaco people which began at about A.D. 850. Prior to this date, Mesa Verde decorated pottery showed no connection whatever with the hatched designs of the Chaco or the broad-line decoration of the Kayenta Branch. We are dealing with three distinct and separate entities, of which Chaco and Kayenta had already begun to exchange ideas and techniques in the early 800's. Their single and combined influences were just beginning to make themselves felt north of the San Juan at about A.D. 850, but the changes which took place at Sites 1, 33, and 102 between A.D. 831 and 872 point to a sudden large-scale movement of which some explanation will have to be found.

With this account of what was going on north of the San Juan the circuit of the Southwest during the ninth century has been completed. What with one thing and another, a good deal has happened since A.D. 800 and it may make it easier to keep the over-all picture in focus if I wind up the century with a short summary.

The Southwest at A.D. 900

THE HISTORY OF the ninth century revolves largely around the activities of a people who, regardless of their other qualities, were certainly good mixers. At A.D. 800, this tribe of Red Indians was still testing what the Southwest had to offer in the way of human relationships and physical surroundings. From the deserts in the south to the forests in the north, the Reds had mixed in varying degrees with Cochise Foragers, Upper Gila Cave Dwellers, Hohokam, Yuman Foragers, Basket Makers, and Farmers, and at A.D. 800 it would have been hard to find an unadulterated Red man or woman. By A.D. 900, however, instead of the mixtures of the eighth century, when everyone was choosing partners but no two couples were dancing to the same tune, these various combinations had begun to set into forms which can be recognized as ancestral to later and better known cultures. In this summary we are concerned primarily with the identification and make-up of these incipient communities, so I begin in the south where the Reds first made their presence felt.

The Mogollon Branch. To find a remnant of the Mogollon people at A.D. 900, one would have to scour southeastern Arizona, since the earlier Mogollon groups in the San Francisco and Mimbres valleys had been showing an increasing interest in Basket Maker-Pueblo habits, styles, and customs as these northern people filtered slowly southward. But even in southern Arizona, beyond the reach of northern influence, the men and women at the San Simon village were turning from their old Mogollon ways as they were won over to the new ideas which were percolating eastward from the Hohokam villages in the Gila Basin. Great lodges, ball-courts, new styles of architecture, some pottery designs, slate palettes, carved stone bowls, and three-quarter grooved axes had all found ready acceptance in the Mogollon villages, but it is worth noting that cremation and irrigation were not included—in the latter case an added indication that Mogollon people were not deeply interested in farming.

As the old Mogollon groups in the San Francisco and Mimbres valleys were drawn more and more into the Basket Maker-Pueblo orbit, and as the San Simon people established more intimate relations with the Hohokam, the center of Mogollon population was shifted westward to Dragoon, the valley of the San Pedro, and Tucson. At Dragoon, Hohokam influence was apparent but relatively weak. At Tucson, although fundamentally Mogollon, enough Hohokam were present to form a distinct local culture.

The Hohokam. In summing up a century of Southwestern history, particularly one such as this which is so concerned with the movements of peoples and their effects on one another, there is a temptation to pass lightly over the accomplishments of the Hohokam since they did not move and exerted little or no effect on the peoples of the Plateau. It is very remarkable that such a large number of people, possessing such an advanced culture, could have moved in, settled down, and attended to their own affairs so exclusively that they aroused no interest among other Southwestern tribes. It is even more extraordinary that the Hohokam were practically unknown to a large, active, and inquisitive corps of Southwestern archaeologists until a few years ago. One would suppose that miles of irrigation canals, with the implied fields of corn, beans, cotton, and other crops, would have attracted the attention of other near-by peoples who were themselves vitally interested in all forms of agriculture. Or regarded from a modern point of view and our attendance at games of all kinds, one might expect that men would travel from the farthest corners of the Southwest to see the World's Series between the Gila Monsters and the Mogollon Rattlers, played out on the ball-court at Snaketown. Possibly they did come and laid their bets with the sherds we found in Mound 29, but if they did, they returned home with empty heads and pockets, as there is not a vestige of Hohokam currency on the Plateau.

The Kayenta Branch. Of all the tribes on the Plateau, the Kayenta people were the least Puebloan—undoubtedly due to the fact that they had more Red in their make-up than the tribes to the east and northeast. While the people of the Chaco and Mesa Verde Branches were building and living in pit-houses equipped with slab-lined walls, benches, floor partitions, and ventilating systems, some of the Kayenta groups were lining their subterranean rooms with planks, as in Medicine Valley; some were combining pit-houses with surface rooms, as at the Baker Ranch; some were living in surface rooms outlined in masonry, as on the south rim of the Grand Canyon; and when some of them reached Marsh Pass and tried their hand at building a regular pit-house, they added an extra ventilator tunnel. The same is true when the time came to build kivas. Kidder found that in three contemporaneous cliff-dwellings in Tsegi Canyon, the men in Bat Woman House built their kivas round and subterranean; those at Betatakin built them square and above ground; while those at Kiet Siel built both square and round, above and below ground. In addition to all else, the Kayenta Branch was the only one of the four major Plateau cultures in which no great kiva has been found.

Although Kayenta men were decidedly erratic in their architectural ideas, Kayenta women succeeded in turning out a series of well-known pottery types which were remarkably uniform throughout their range. In the ninth century Kayenta potters were making broad-line black-on-white, and regardless of where it started, this particular and easily recognized type of pottery covered a wide range of country: from the Verde Valley up past Flagstaff to the east of the San Francisco Peaks, up the Chino Valley to the west of the Peaks, over the Coconino Plateau to the south rim of the Canyon, on the Kaibab Plateau, north of the Canyon, west to the Virgin River, east to the Kaibito Plateau, northeast to Marsh Pass and the Canyon de Chelly, and out through Red Rock Valley to the western margin of the Chaco Basin. From the Verde to the Utah border the distance was over two hundred airline miles, and from the Virgin to Red Rock Valley over three hundred miles, or about five times the area covered by the Cibola, Chaco, or Mesa Verde Branches. In spite of this vast difference in the area covered by each culture—or rather the pottery types by which they are recognized—there is nothing in the later history of the Kayenta people to indicate that they greatly outnumbered the people of Mesa Verde, Chaco, or Cibola. The only explanation which seems to account for these conditions during the ninth century is that bands of people who were making broad-line black-on-white pottery must have been moving around and covering a great deal of ground, but it is obvious that such an explanation cannot be reconciled with the

conventional idea that the Kayenta Culture originated in Marsh Pass and thereafter developed along orthodox, Puebloan lines. So, from an entirely different
starting point, I come back to the belief that rectilinear designs, slipped, polished
surfaces, mineral paint, red and black-on-red pottery, erratic ideas of domestic
architecture and kiva construction, and skull deformation all point to a Red
source. These strains—cultural and physical—were more pronounced in the
Kayenta than in the Mesa Verde, Chaco, or Cibola Branches, and were responsible
for those features wherein the Kayenta differed from the other Plateau cultures.
From this point of view, the distribution of broad-line black-on-white, accompanied by black-on-red, was simply the northern continuation of the Red migration which entered southern Arizona at some time before A.D. 700, and which was
modified—culturally and physically—as new contacts and combinations were
formed with the earlier residents of the western Plateau.

The Salado Branch. There is little that can be said about the Salado people at
A.D. 900. The Bear Ruin at Forestdale was occupied during the ninth century,
but its architecture and pottery were clearly mixtures of Reds and Basket Makers
at the White Mound level. By the end of the ninth century the culture at the
Bear Ruin had not sufficiently crystallized for it to be recognized as ancestral
to the Salado Branch which later occupied this area. In the thirteenth and fourteenth centuries the Salado people were one of the most powerful forces in the
Southwest, but at A.D. 900, for reasons which will be discussed in due course,
it had not yet started to take definite form.

The Cibola Branch. By A.D. 900 the Cibola Branch had begun to take form when
the women in the upper San Francisco Valley agreed on and started to produce
the kind of pottery which was to distinguish them from all other Southwestern
potters. Their choice was a black-on-white ware, heavily slipped and well
polished, and decorated with geometric patterns made up of a kind of hatching
which became typical of the Cibola Branch. This consisted of two parallel framing lines with the filling lines drawn parallel to the framers and each such element
balanced by a solid figure—all drawn with a dense black mineral paint.

The great majority of decorated ware was turned out in the form of small
pitchers which were rather squat, with globular bodies and cylindrical necks.
But there was evidently something in the Red make-up which could not stand
monotony, and just as Red men refused to adhere to the rigid conventions as
to how a kiva should be built, so the pent-up Red strain in the Cibola women
found expression in the handles of their pitchers. Some were provided with
simple flat straps, others had round rods—single, double, triple, quadruple. There
were twisted ropes and braids of clay, but it was in the variety and the modelling
of their small animal head handles and lugs that the Cibola women really excelled.
And as a sidelight on conventions and customs, I hope that someday someone

will be able to explain to me why the Cibola women decorated their pitchers and used plain brown bowls, while the Mimbres women next door made plain brown pitchers and decorated their bowls.

The best example of a site of this period is the Starkweather Ruin, near Reserve, but our survey shows a number of other sites of the same kind scattered through the pine forest on the Spur Ranch and around the headwaters of the San Francisco. At Starkweather, two pit-houses which were assigned to this period gave dates at A.D. 918 and 927. These lift Starkweather out of the ninth century, but it is probably safe to set the beginning of the period at A.D. 900, or a few years earlier, as we found the same black-on-white pottery at the Harris site in a pit-house which gave us twelve dates from A.D. 876 to 879.

The Mimbres Branch. While the Mogollon villages in the upper San Francisco Valley had begun to develop characteristics typical of the Cibola Branch at A.D. 900, those in the lower San Francisco and Mimbres valleys were tending toward a recognizable Mimbres Branch. At the Mogollon village near Glenwood on the lower San Francisco, we found four black-on-white bowls, crushed on the floor of a pit-house which gave us twenty cutting dates between A.D. 888 and 899. These four bowls made it obvious that the earlier period of red-on-white pottery had ended and that black-on-white pottery typical of the early Mimbres series had begun. This change was also indicated in several houses at the Harris site, in the middle Mimbres, with dates in the late 800's. As in the early stage of the Cibola Branch, it is not safe to try to define an architectural style to accompany the beginning of typical Mimbres pottery other than to say that the people were still living in pit-houses at A.D. 900, but these show a good deal of variation between Cameron Creek, the Harris site, the Mogollon village, and the S. U. site— at each of which early Mimbres pottery has been found. Polished red and brown pottery appears to be indistinguishable from that in the early sites of the Cibola Branch in the upper San Francisco.

The Chaco Branch. During the ninth century the people of the Chaco Branch began moving up from their subterranean pit-houses to living rooms built at ground level. The lack of fireplaces in what otherwise appear to have been living rooms suggests that the shift may have been seasonal, but at any rate, it marked the beginning of a way of life which thereafter showed a progressive development up to a full-fledged pueblo. By A.D. 900, the walls of some of their surface houses look as if they might have been carried up to their full height in masonry, and it may be that by the end of the ninth century their old pit-houses had been converted into small kivas suitable for use by one or two families. One reason for thinking that this may have been the case is that there is a peculiar absence of great kivas in sites of the Chaco Branch during the 800's. In the Red Mesa Valley we found over three hundred sites, none of which was large enough to contain more than one family, all of which belonged in the ninth or early tenth century, but there was no sign of a great kiva between Gallup and Mount Taylor, and I think the same is true of the area from Gallup up to Shiprock.

Potterywise, the century began with the wavy type of hatching. This soon changed to the oblique kind with lines rather widely spaced, and this led up to the typical Chaco hatching which stamps the culture, or its influence, wherever found. Redware of any kind was rare or entirely absent, and the only trace of Red influence was in the geometric patterns of the hatching, drawn with mineral paint. By A.D. 850, contact had been established with Kayenta people through Red Rock Valley, and as a result, Chaco hatching made its appearance in vegetable paint on polished surfaces—neither of which is known in pure Chaco sites. Singly, and in combination with Kayenta, Chaco colonies were working their way northward to the San Juan in the late 800's, but in spite of these new contacts, there is surprisingly little evidence of either Kayenta or Mesa Verde influence on the culture of the Chaco Branch during the ninth century. The conditions around the southern and western borders of the Chaco Basin give one the impression of a large number of individual family units working out their problems along remarkably uniform lines without much, if any, outside interference—so affording a marked contrast to the vagaries of the Kayenta people and the heterogeneous groups in the southern section of the basin of the Little Colorado.

The Mesa Verde Branch. The archaeology north of the San Juan during the ninth century provides a good test case for the ideas which have been advanced. At A.D. 900 there were enough similarities between the Mesa Verde and Chaco cultures to compel a choice between two explanations—either the two began as one and were growing apart, or they both had separate origins and were gradually being drawn together. To my mind, the evidence denies the first of these alternatives. Falls Creek in the third and fourth centuries was markedly different from Du Pont, White Dog, or Mummy caves. The Durango settlements in the seventh century had nothing in common with Broken Flute or the other Basket Maker caves in Red Rock Valley. In the eighth century, Alkali Ridge, Ackmen Site 2, and Site 23 on the La Plata differed from Shabik'eshchee in Chaco Canyon, and the southern Chaco villages on the Puerco. Instead of diverging from an earlier common stock, it therefore looks more as if the Chaco and Mesa Verde peoples were converging as both cultures grew, the two tribes increased in numbers, and the gap between their borders was narrowed. This seems clearly to have been the case during the ninth century, since the one-family unit sites of the Chaco resembled those of Mesa Verde more closely than their respective sites at any earlier period. But besides the similarities, there are some differences which demand the choice of alternatives mentioned above. I think there can be very little doubt that the surface rectangular rooms with walls of coursed masonry on Mesa Verde were more advanced than the adobe walls reinforced with sandstone flakes in the surface houses in the Red Mesa Valley, yet the dates from the Mesa Verde sites are somewhat earlier than those from Red Mesa. It also seems to me—judging by La Plata Site 33, Ackmen Site 1, and Mesa Verde Site 102—that the plan of the Mesa Verde units was more uniform than the rather random agglomerations of the Red Mesa units. Great kivas were the rule rather than the exception throughout the region north of the San Juan, yet none were found in the Red Mesa Valley and none have been reported from anywhere south of the San Juan during the ninth century.

Other differences between Mesa Verde and Chaco at this time are to be found in the decorated pottery. These are so marked, both as to design and texture, that a Chaco sherd on a Mesa Verde site can usually be spotted without difficulty, and this has made it possible to give exact counts of the two types when found together in sites of the ninth and following centuries. There is also the fact that decorated red and orange wares were the prevailing types in the western section of the Mesa Verde range, but entirely absent in the Chaco villages.

These differences appear to have been due to the Red factors which were considerably stronger in the western Mesa Verde sites in southeastern Utah and in Montezuma Valley than on the La Plata, and which were practically absent in the Chaco Branch. This is also emphasized by the remarkable resemblance between some of the designs on the red-on-orange ware at Alkali Ridge and those on the red-on-brown pottery from the Mogollon villages in southwestern New Mexico. That this was not just a random quirk of decoration is further shown by an unbroken chain of sites beginning in the Mimbres Valley, running west to Snaketown and the Verde, then north past Flagstaff to Marsh Pass, across the San Juan to southeastern Utah, and eastward to the La Plata. From one end of this chain to the other, during the ninth century, one can find scroll, star, quartered, and fold designs in cultures where none of these designs occurred on the pottery of earlier periods. And on top of all else—particularly their heads—there is skull deformation which follows the same trail.

When all of these clues are added together, I think we are provided with an explanation of the conditions during the ninth century which otherwise are difficult to understand. On the one hand, the Mesa Verde Culture on Mesa Verde and in the La Plata Valley, the Chaco, and Hohokam Cultures—in each of which Red influence was a minor factor—were relatively homogeneous within themselves. On the other, the conditions were abnormal or erratic during the ninth century on Alkali Ridge and in the Kayenta, Flagstaff, Puerco, Cibola, Mimbres, and Mogollon districts—in each of which the Reds were strongly represented.

Although Mesa Verde and Chaco were drawing together during the latter half of the ninth century as Chaco bands moved northward, each was distinct from the other and both were entirely different from the Hohokam. Nevertheless, within each of these three cultures there was remarkable uniformity from site

NORTH

Toadlena

St. Johns

Puerco

Mogollon Rim

Mimbres Valley
(Cosgrove, C. B. 1932)

Tonto Basin

San Simon

Snaketown

SOUTH

The Scroll Design: the northward spread of southern traits

NORTH

La Plata
(Morris, E. H. 1919)

Alkali Ridge
(Brew, J. O. 1946)

Pueblo Bonito
(Morris, E. H. 1927)

White Mound

Verde Valley

Kiatuthlanna
(Roberts, F. H. H., Jr. 1931)

San Simon

San Simon

SOUTH

The Star Design: the northward spread of southern traits

NORTH

Southeastern Utah

Alkali Ridge
(Brew, J. O. 1946)

Kiatuthlanna
(Roberts, F. H. H., Jr. 1931)

Kiatuthlanna
(Roberts, F. H. H., Jr. 1931)

Verde Valley

Snaketown

Mogollon

Mogollon

SOUTH

The Quartered Design: the northward spread of southern traits

NORTH

Alkali Ridge
(Brew, J. O. 1946)

Alkali Ridge
(Brew, J. O. 1946)

Flagstaff

Mogollon Rim

Kiatuthlanna
(Roberts, F. H. H., Jr. 1931)

Snaketown

Mimbres
(Bradfield, W. 1929)

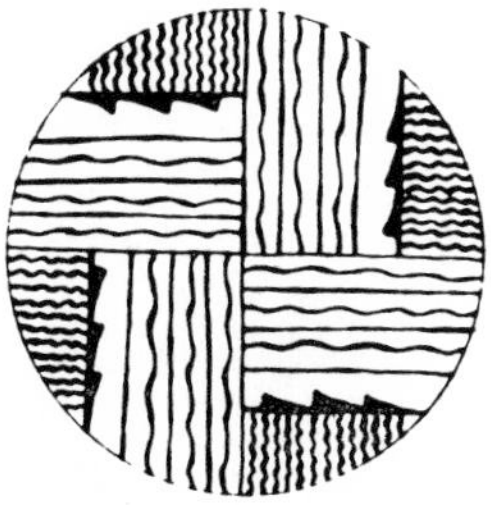

Mogollon

SOUTH

The Fold Design: the northward spread of southern traits

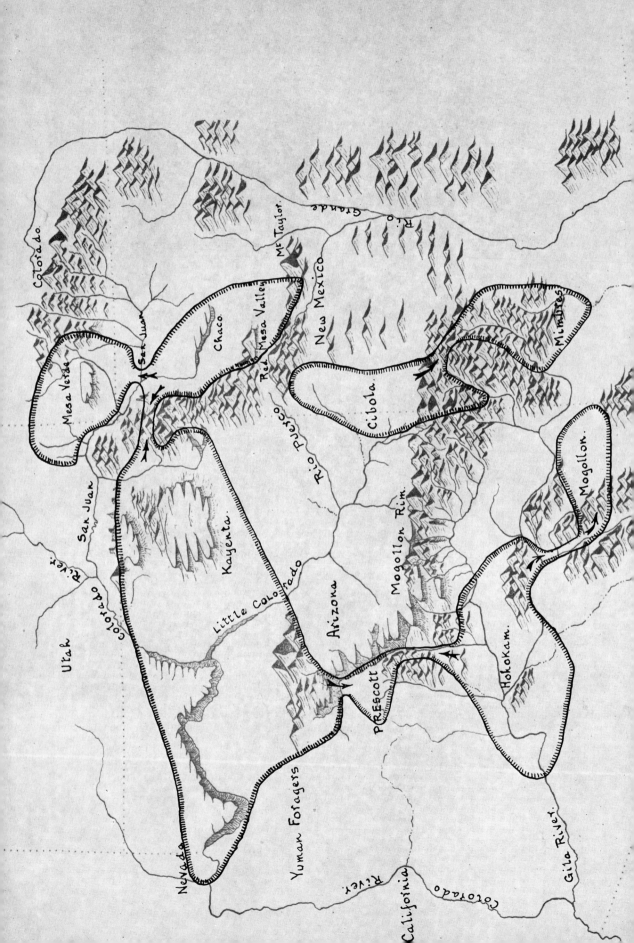

Colorado.

Rio Grande.

M⁹ Taylor.

New Mexico

Mimbres.

San Juan.

Chaco.

Red Mesa Valley.

Cibola.

Mogollon.

Mesa Verde.

San Juan

River.

Rio Puerco.

Mogollon Rim.

Kayenta.

Colorado

Little Colorado

Arizona

P⁹ Escott

Holokam.

Utah

Nevada

Yuman Foragers

California

Colorado

Gila River.

River.

THE SOUTHWEST AT A.D. 900

During the ninth century the Farmers north of the San Juan had been developing those characteristics of their culture by which they have come to be known as the Mesa Verde Branch. Their colonies in southern Colorado extended eastward as far as the Piedra and it was probably at about this time that a few Farmer families first moved down along the Chama and settled in the Upper Rio Grande Valley.

In southern Arizona the Hohokam were concentrated in the Gila Basin, but some colonies had pushed northward up the Verde Valley as far as Flagstaff and others had penetrated eastward to Tonto Basin and the Mogollon settlements in the Sulphur Spring Valley.

In the central Southwest, between the Farmers and the Hohokam, scattered and heterogeneous groups of Reds and Basket Makers had combined and had begun to crystallize into distinct cultures.

At A.D. 900 a number of shifts were taking place:
Some families from the Chaco district were moving north to Mesa Verde.
Contact between Chaco and Kayenta had been established through Red Rock Valley with consequent interchange of influence.
Cibola and Mimbres had both broken away from their Mogollon controls but still shared much in common with one another.
Mogollon people were moving westward and were becoming increasingly affected by the Hohokam.
Kayenta groups were filtering down into the Verde Valley and setting their stamp on the Prescott Culture.

to site. It is therefore all the more significant that wherever Reds were present, during the eighth and ninth centuries, the conditions were very variable from site to site as regards architecture, or pottery, or both.

THIS BRINGS US up to A.D. 900, and after a good many twists and turns, the road is beginning to straighten out into more familiar surroundings. Isolated colonies around the periphery of the Southwest—such as those in central and western Utah, southern Nevada, and south-central Colorado—have either died out or have withdrawn, to be absorbed in more powerful communities. The Mogollon Culture has split apart, some to become Cibola, some Mimbres; and the small remnant in southeastern Arizona is leaning heavily toward the Hohokam. The Salado Branch has not yet taken definite shape out of the various groups which are scattered along and below the Mogollon Rim. But the foundations of the Mesa Verde, Chaco, Kayenta, Cibola, Mimbres, and Hohokam communities have been laid.

It has taken a long time to assemble all of these clues, but I hope that they will simplify the task of following the course of development in the Southwest as it winds through the centuries which lie ahead.

X I I

Growing Up: A.D. 900 to 1000

REGARDLESS OF THE WAYS by which they reached their status at A.D. 900, seven of the eight cultural groups with which most of us are familiar—Mesa Verde, Chaco, Kayenta, Cibola, Mimbres, Mogollon, Hohokam—with Salado in suspense, had begun to take shape in their various districts. With the slow and often tedious steps of laying foundations and building backgrounds behind us, we can now go on to the relatively simple task of following the careers of these seven different tribes as they worked their way through the tenth century.

Beginning in southeastern Arizona, a few scattered villages strung out from San Simon in the east to Dragoon in the west were all that was left of Mogollon at A.D. 900, after subtracting the Cibola and Mimbres contingents. One speaks of them as Mogollon, but actually the only characteristic trait which had survived was their red-on-brown pottery. At A.D. 950, they were living in houses a little longer than broad, shallow, with a side entrance and a flat roof—similar to the rectangular houses of the Hohokam at a somewhat earlier time. The San Simon men had also borrowed the idea of a ball-court from the Hohokam; three-quarter grooved axes had been introduced from the Hohokam; and the San Simon women were showing an increasing use of Hohokam designs on their decorated pottery.

This and a number of similar incidents provide an example of how archaeological evidence can sometimes provide an understanding of a people for which one might look in vain in written records. In this case, it is interesting to find that although the Reds introduced techniques and styles of pottery making which spread like an epidemic through the Southwest, there was no such thing at A.D. 900 as a pure Red culture. When they entered the Southwest at about A.D. 600, they promptly merged with Cochise Foragers, and started the Mogollon Culture on its way. For a few years, in southeastern Arizona and southwestern New Mexico, this combination followed the Mogollon line. It was not long, however, before the western groups made friends with the Hohokam and began borrowing some of their ideas—notably a great lodge for their cere-monies and a square living room with a flat roof which had obvious advantages over the circular tipi-type of house which the Reds had been using when they arrived. During the years from A.D. 700 to 900, the more northerly groups of Mogollon people, in the San Francisco and upper Mimbres valleys, had been taking to their bosoms a steady stream of people filtering down from the Plateau. By A.D. 900, they had become so saturated with northern blood and ideas that they were losing their Mogollon identity in the beginnings of the Mimbres and Cibola Branches, both of which were more Puebloan than Red—judging by their pottery and architecture.

As the Reds spread northward to the Plateau, it is again a succession of mergers with Yuman Foragers, Basket Makers and Farmers, the results of which were the creation of cultures which varied in accordance with the proportions of their composing elements. The point which stands out in all of these meetings and mergers is that they were invariably peaceful. Wherever the Reds went, whether as a family or a crowd, they seem to have been welcomed with open arms, and as soon as the women could get their heads together they all started making the new red pottery and drawing straight lines. And speaking of heads, the rapidity with which skull deformation spread through the Southwest when once the Red pediatricians had shown Pueblo mothers how the operation should be performed reminds one of the way a Parisian model affects our modern womenkind—the uglier and more inconvenient it is, the more they seem to like it.

GOING WESTWARD from the westernmost Mogollon villages, one comes first to the San Pedro and then over a low divide to the Santa Cruz Valley. Here, centering around Tucson, there was another example of a meeting of Reds and Hohokam which helps one to understand the relationship of these two peoples. Not much is known, as no report has yet been published, and my only information is derived from some notes which were taken during the winter of 1937-1938, while Mr. and Mrs. Wetmore Hodges were excavating their site, a few miles northwest of Tucson.

Tucson lies about midway between Snaketown and the San Simon village, and one is tempted to speak of the Red factor at the Hodges site as Mogollon. Neither at Snaketown nor at the Hodges site, however, was there any evidence of what I would call a Mogollon village—meaning the sort of settlement that has been found in the San Simon and San Francisco valleys. So I think that Tucson is probably a good place to draw the line between Mogollon and Reds. As the early period at the Hodges site was more strongly Red than at any later time, I think that it may provide a good example of a settlement which was founded and left behind as the Reds passed through at about A.D. 700 on their way to the Plateau. Some time after the village was established and the main Red tide had flowed northward, the Hohokam entered southern Arizona and explored the limits of the Gila Basin. Some of them reached Tucson, their presence at the Hodges site marked by cremation, a ball-court, and square or rectangular houses with four roof supports and side entrances. The pottery was particularly interesting in showing a pronounced leaning to a rectilinear or Red treatment of Hohokam designs. During the early period bowls were decorated on the interior, but by A.D. 950 or soon after, the buff exteriors were invariably decorated with red designs and the interiors were smudged to a dark gray or black. This practice of smudging was typical of many of the cultures in which a Red strain was present but was never used by the Hohokam, so it looks as if the Red probably outweighed the Hohokam component near Tucson. This belief is further strengthened by the relative scarcity of the fine arts of the Hohokam, such as slate palettes, mosaic plaques, copper bells, finely modelled heads in clay, and carved or etched shell and bone.

The incident is important because it provides a milestone of the passage of the Reds through southern Arizona on their migration northwestward, and also because the evidence at the Hodges site points strongly to the probability that this movement took place a short time before the Hohokam arrived on the local scene.

FROM TUCSON the trail of men and their debris leads northwestward across a wide stretch of desert to the Casa Grande National Monument, a mile or so south of the Gila River, and about seventy miles northwest of Tucson. Our survey has shown a number of small Hohokam encampments on some of the washes between Tucson and Casa Grande, but I do not know of any full-fledged settlements, including such things as ball-courts and great lodges, and I doubt if there ever was water enough in the intervening area to make it possible to practice irrigation. Beginning in the east with the Casa Grande villages which received their water from a diversion dam a few miles east of Florence, there was an almost continuous series of settlements strung along the Gila, reaching as far west as Cashion, where the Agua Fria and the Salt River join the Gila. In addition, there was another more or less continuous chain of villages along the Salt, from Mesa west to Cashion; and at least one large settlement had been founded in the desert between the Salt and the Gila, at Los Muertos, near Chandler. Here the people had supplied themselves with water by means of a canal which they had dug to connect with the Salt River, some ten miles to the north.

In these villages change had been very gradual. Hohokam architects had given up the early square type of house and after trying out a rectangular shape.

Notched stone posts from House 11

House 11 at Roosevelt: 9:6 in Tonto Basin
Rows of notched stone posts were used to raise the floor above the damp earth.
Entrance at left; firepit near entrance.

by A.D. 1000, had arrived at an elliptical plan for their houses, some of which showed great care and ingenuity in their construction. In many instances, gutters were dug around the edge of the floors to receive the ends of reeds, set upright around the walls to form a wainscoting. Peripheral posts carried most of the

House 11 at Roosevelt: 9:6
  As reconstructed at Gila Pueblo. It was interesting to find that the Pima
  workmen used strips of mesquite bark to tie all joints. No nails were used in
  the reconstruction.

weight of the roof, leaving the floor clear of roof supports, and at Roosevelt 9:6, on the Salt River, we found that the floors in several of the houses had been raised on stone piers to obviate the dampness resulting from rain and floods. Each pier was carefully notched and set in line; then the joists were set in the notches and lashed in place; then fine brush and reeds were laid across the joists; and finally, a layer of mud or adobe was spread on the brush, resulting in a raised floor above an airspace about 12 inches in depth. Entrances were always placed in the middle of the long side, provided with one or two steps with stone treads, and protected by a hood covering the top and sides. The firepit was set near the door of the entrance which also served as a smoke-vent.

Pottery had been changing slowly, and the differences between the old and the new are often difficult to detect. Earlier designs persisted, being frequently included in decoration suggestive of textile patterns, but the most obvious changes were in the shapes of vessels. More were made as the population increased and as a general rule, vessels were larger in order to meet the demand for greater storage facilities—no storage cists or rooms having yet been found in any Hohokam site. One of the principal characteristics which has been used to distinguish the Sedentary from the earlier Colonial Period were the large decorated jars which show a sharp angle at their greatest diameter. This angle resulted from the custom of starting the bottom of a large jar in a shallow basket or pottery tray which could be revolved on its base in much the same way as a potter's wheel. When the bottom of the pot under construction reached the edge of the basket or tray, it could obviously be extended no farther and the potter, perforce, was compelled to build up the sides, so forming the angle which has come to be known as the Gila Shoulder. While on the subject of Hohokam pottery making, it is also interesting to note that in making their large jars they used the so-called paddle-and-anvil method. This consisted of adding lumps or short ropes of damp clay and patting these into place with a wooden paddle while a flat stone was held as an anvil against the inside of the jar to prevent the wall from collapsing. The process had a wide distribution both in the Americas and the Old World, but was not used by the potters on the Plateau, who made their pots by laying up bands or coils of clay and smoothing them with a scraper, usually made from a sherd or the rind of a gourd.

In their pottery making, their single-room houses, their agriculture based on irrigation, and apparently in the entire organization of their society, the Hohokam, at A.D. 1000, were living a kind of life which was quite different from that of any other group of people in the Southwest, and it is very difficult to understand why there is so little evidence of intercourse and exchange of knowledge between the various peoples on the Plateau and the Hohokam in the desert of southern Arizona. A few ball-courts have been found in the Verde and around Flagstaff, but nowhere else on the Plateau. We have a number of copper bells which have come out of Gila Pueblo, and several have been found in the *casas grandes* of northern Chihuahua, but otherwise a single and occasional bell is a rare occurrence. Slate palettes are known to have reached the Mimbres, but are unknown on the Plateau. Three-quarter grooved axes are common below the Mogollon Rim, but are rare on the Plateau, and when found do not compare in workmanship with those which were made by the Hohokam. Tripod and tetrapod trays have not been reported from any other culture in the Southwest, and a small chip from a room in Pueblo Bonito is the only recorded instance of a mosaic plaque from outside of the Hohokam area. Strangest of all, in a country where water adequate for the growth of crops was always a gamble, and among people who were largely dependent upon agriculture, there are few, if any, certain instances of canal irrigation in any other section of the Southwest, although it would seem that diversion dams could have been built on the Puerco, the Little Colorado, the Rio Grande, and probably other streams, without too much trouble. On the other hand, the Hohokam were even less receptive to foreign ideas, and I do not know of a single Puebloan trait which they adopted, even though the Pueblos could at least have taught them the advantages of masonry construction for permanence and the protection of their harvested crops, if for nothing else.

Of the Hohokam at A.D. 1000 it might well be said:

> Far from the madding crowd's ignoble strife
> Their sober wishes never learn'd to stray;
> Along the cool (?) sequestered vale of life
> They kept the noiseless tenor of their way.

As WE TURN NORTH from the Hohokam in the Gila Basin, there is little to record from the Verde Valley during the tenth century, other than to say that the people of the Prescott Branch had withdrawn a few miles westward to Skull Valley and that their black-on-gray pottery was becoming more Kayenta-like. This was undoubtedly due to an increase in the number of people from Flagstaff who were attracted to the warmth and quiet of the Verde after cold winters in pit-houses. The drift of Kayenta people into the Verde continued and grew as the years passed, and it is possible, but by no means certain, that some of the small masonry-walled cliff-dwellings, such as Honanki and Palatki in Oak Creek Canyon, may hark back to the late 900's. There is also a small masonry house in the side of Montezuma's Well, in Beaver Canyon, which may have been built at about the same time. The black-on-white pottery is typical of the Kayenta Branch, but it is accompanied by an abundance of polished red-ware which points clearly to the Red strain in Kayenta ancestry. As a guess, the date was more probably in the early 1000's, but there are no tree-ring dates to support the guess.

CLIMBING UP out of the Verde to the western Plateau, we find conditions near Flagstaff during the tenth century somewhat confused. It seems, however, to be fairly clear that people were building and living in small surface houses of

Verde: 1:5, a small cliff-dwelling in the upper Verde Valley

Montezuma's Well, Verde Valley

which the walls, if not carried up to their full height in masonry, were at least outlined by masonry foundations.

The local black-on-white pottery leaves no doubt that the Flagstaff and Kayenta potters were akin, and the profusion of polished redware points just as clearly to the Red factor in this kinship.

NORTH FROM FLAGSTAFF, up the eastern border of the Coconino Plateau and along the south rim of the Grand Canyon, some of the sites marked by broad-line decoration on their pottery were undoubtedly built during the ninth century, but it is highly probable that a good many of the small ruins outlined by masonry foundations were occupied well up into the tenth century. At present, knowledge is limited to the evidence of the survey we made in 1930, and we shall have to wait for the excavation of a series of sites before being more definite as to details and dates.

IN THE MARSH PASS DISTRICT the situation is a little better in that there are half a dozen sites which have been excavated by Kidder, Guernsey, and Beals. These sites look as if they might fall in the tenth century, but there are no tree-ring dates, so one cannot be sure. Ruins I, II, VII, and VIII, dug by Kidder and Guernsey, and RB 551 by Beals, were all described as having kivas, but whether this means that they were therefore later than the sites in Medicine Valley—where nothing suggestive of a kiva has been found—is open to serious doubt. No great kivas have yet been reported from any part of the Kayenta range, and from the remarks of Kidder and Guernsey it is clear that the kiva complex in the Marsh Pass district was very erratic at the same time that great kivas were being built and small kivas were becoming standardized in the Chaco and Mesa Verde Branches. In other words, judging by the work of Morris, Roberts, Martin, and Brew, all of the available evidence points to the fact that true kivas originated in the Four Corners area; that they evolved and reached their greatest specialization in the Chaco and Mesa Verde Cultures; and that standardized ceremonial structures were not an inherent characteristic of the Reds in any of their cultures or subdivisions. At their first appearance in southeastern Arizona—at Cave Creek, Cameron Creek, and San Simon—there is no evidence of a Red ceremonial structure which differed in size or accessories from their typical dwellings. Later —at the Harris, Mogollon, S. U., Starkweather, Luna, and Bluff villages—great lodges appeared at the same time with pottery and other traits which were diffused from the Hohokam, and it would consequently be fair to suppose that the idea of building great lodges was also borrowed from the Hohokam who are known to have built such structures when they first arrived in southern Arizona. Other groups in which the Reds were a prominent or dominating force, such as the early Prescott, Flagstaff, Grand Canyon, and Nevada subcultures have shown no evidence of great lodges, great kivas, or recognizable small kivas, and it was not until the Reds penetrated deep into Basket Maker territory, in Marsh

Pass, that varieties of kivas show up which give every indication of experimentation with a recently acquired idea. Much the same is true of the later so-called kivas in the Cibola, Salado, and Mimbres Branches, in each of which the Reds were strongly represented and in none of which is it possible to find a typical kiva equipped with the conventional accessories.

An understanding of the cultural significance of kiva specialization involves the relatively simple task of tracing the spread of this type of building throughout the area in which it has been found to occur. Among the people of the Chaco and Mesa Verde Branches, for example, the emphasis on kivas implies that ceremonies played a leading part in their society, and this will become more marked as time goes on. In the case of the Reds, however, the archaeological evidence indicates a form of society in which there was no emphasis on ceremonial structures, other than local and erratic attempts to experiment with those of neighboring tribes.

THE CONTRAST between the haphazard kivas of the Kayenta Branch and the standardized type which was being built by the Mesa Verde people is very marked as soon as one crosses the San Juan. The tenth century in the Mesa Verde region was the period during which the unit-type of house became the prevailing style of architecture. According to Kidder's description "the house consists of a single or double row of one story rooms. Sometimes there are also short right-angled wings extending outward from either end. Directly south of the house lies a kiva." It is significant, in the light of what has just been said above, that Kidder also found that "far from being primitive the kivas are as uniform in plan, and as highly specialized in details, as any kivas known; while the pottery bears a strong resemblance to that of the great ruins of the Mesa Verde."

Another point which is of interest in connection with the unit-type is that although architecture in the Southwest is usually regarded as having developed from small houses to large pueblos, the progression north of the San Juan, from the seventh to the tenth centuries, shows a reversal of such a trend—from the large settlements on Blue Mesa and Alkali Ridge, containing as many as three hundred rooms, to the six or eight-room unit-types which were said by Prudden to have been "very abundant in the northern San Juan country between the Mesa Verde in Colorado and Comb Wash in Utah."

WHEN ONE DROPS down from Mesa Verde to the region occupied by the Chaco people, the architectural series from A.D. 750 to 1000 affords an interesting comparison with that of Mesa Verde during the same period. At A.D. 750, Shabik'eshchee differed in many respects from the contemporaneous villages north of the San Juan. At A.D. 850, the Red Mesa Ruin of the Chaco Branch bore a fairly close resemblance to Site 1 at Ackmen, of the Mesa Verde Branch,

Red Mesa Valley: the Wingate Ruin

and also to Site RB 551 in Marsh Pass, of the Kayenta Branch—in that all three sites show a row of four or five surface contiguous rectangular rooms facing a kiva, and it might be said that these three sites, in their respective areas, all contain the germ of the unit-type plan.

At A.D. 950, the Wingate Ruin in the Red Mesa Valley contained a solid block of two or three living rooms and three or four storerooms arranged in a double row fronting a kiva—so showing a continuation and an accentuation toward the Mesa Verde style of architecture. The direction of this trend is clearly brought out by the greater specialization of the dwelling and kiva of the Mesa Verde unit, and it is important to note, therefore, that Chaco builders were following the lead of Mesa Verde architects at A.D. 950 rather than vice versa. But at the same time that Chaco architecture was converging toward Mesa Verde, it is significant to find that in Marsh Pass the trend toward the unit-type, which was implicit in Site RB 551, did not follow through. Ruins I, II, VII and VIII, which were excavated by Kidder and Guernsey, all show random clusters of rooms with kivas scattered in haphazard fashion, and out of not less than ten kivas, no two are alike.

The convergence of Chaco toward Mesa Verde during the tenth century, however, was not limited to architecture. The northward drift of groups from the Red Mesa Valley, which had begun at about A.D. 850, continued and increased in volume. By A.D. 1000, all of those families which had established themselves in the Red Mesa Valley and eastward to Mount Taylor had abandoned their

The Wingate Ruin: pottery types

Cibola: black-on-white pottery of the tenth century

homesteads and withdrawn to join their compatriots in their northward trek, and it was probably during the late 900's that Chaco Canyon itself was densely populated for the first time. This, however, was an episode which can be discussed more appropriately in the next chapter as a part of the account of the eleventh century.

To OBTAIN SOME IDEA of the Cibola Branch at this time one must cast back to the late 800's when there was a steady southward shift of people from the Rio Puerco and the Zuni district down toward the Upper Gila. These people were originally of Basket Maker extraction and so allied to the people of the Chaco, and in the Puerco-Zuni region they were represented by such sites as Whitewater, Kiatuthlanna, and small villages which have turned up in our survey.

By A.D. 900, this infiltration from the north into the last stage of the Mogollon Culture in the upper San Francisco Valley, represented by red-on-white pottery and rectangular pit-houses, had resulted locally in the transformation of the Mogollon Culture, as such, into the Cibola Branch as a distinct entity.

Early black-on-white Cibola pottery was decorated with balanced designs of solids and longitudinal hatching. Scrolls, which were rare or absent on the red-on-white of late Mogollon pottery, were common on all Cibola decorated ware, increasing from early to late, and it looks as if some Cibola families had week-ended in the Gila Basin to warm up, or some Hohokam had visited the upper San Francisco to cool off. Polished brownware, the bowls of which show highly burnished black interiors, was made in large quantities and was essentially the same as the earlier polished redware, the only difference being that the brownware resulted from firing at lower temperatures—a fairly good indication that northern potters had taken over the controls. Northern influence is also to be found in the increasing use of coils and indenting as forms of decoration on the necks and shoulders of polished brown pots—a process which reached its peak in the Tularosa Valley during the eleventh century.

One cannot be definite about the beginning of Cibola architecture, as no pure early sites have been excavated. It seems probable, however, that the people had given up pit-houses as dwellings and had begun building surface houses with masonry walls by about A.D. 950, since, at the Starkweather Ruin near Reserve they had built a small masonry-walled pueblo containing ten or more rooms soon after A.D. 1000. The Cibola men have always had the reputation of having been poor masons, but while it is true that when they came to building pueblos these were usually agglomerations of living rooms and storerooms and show no particular care in planning, this was the rule rather than the exception in all of those cultures in which the Reds were prominent. The poor quality of the masonry itself may have been partly due to the difficulty of working with lava, which was the only building material locally available. In the Chaco, for instance, the masons were able to use flat sandstone slabs, ideal for laying up in courses and easily trimmed to a square face. But down in southwestern New Mexico, the Cibola masons were reduced to lumps of lava, irregular in size, and almost impossible to shape to uniform thickness, and it is therefore not surprising that their buildings do not compare favorably with those farther north—which is the most that I can say in their defense.

THE SAME COMMENTS apply to the architecture in the Mimbres Branch, about one hundred miles to the southeast. Lava again was the principal building material, and the local ruins show combinations of living rooms and storerooms, but nothing that could properly be called a kiva, judging by northern standards. In the Mimbres, as in the Cibola Branch, the shift from pit-houses, as dwellings, to surface rooms outlined by boulder foundations took place during the late 900's.

The red-on-white pottery of the last days of the Mogollon Culture in the Mimbres area had changed to black-on-white soon after A.D. 900, four broken bowls having been found on the floor of House 2 at the Mogollon village which was built in A.D. 899. In early Mimbres black-on-white bowls, the decoration was carried up to the rim and was usually severely geometric, and rarely ran to naturalistic designs, but toward the end of the tenth century, this gave way to a style in which a band of lines was drawn parallel to the rim of the bowl. Designs of balanced solid and hatched elements became common and were carried out with remarkable precision, but this classic type of Mimbres pottery did not reach its greatest perfection until the eleventh century.

a   b

c   d

Early Mimbres Black-on-white Designs
Mimbres potters are known for the unusual complexity of their designs and the accuracy of their line-work. Decoration covered the entire interior surface of bowls with various treatments of folds, quarters, panels, triangles, pennons, fine parallel lines, wavy hatching, and interlocking scrolls.
    (a. Cosgrove, H. S. & C. B. 1932, Pl. 110 e
    b. Ibid, Pl. 118 d
    c. Ibid, Pl. 117 e
    d. Bradfield, W. 1929, Pl. XXXV)

To THE WEST of the San Francisco Valley there is a wide stretch of country, reaching as far as the Verde, bounded on the north by the Mogollon Rim and on the south by the Gila. This great area was later to become the domain of the Salado people, and it would be natural to suppose that the early stages of this culture were forming during the tenth century, or even earlier, as in other sections of the Southwest. This is true to the extent that there were undoubtedly small groups scattered about in favorable locations, such as that in the Forestdale Valley and others along the Rim and in Tonto Basin, but the real settlement of this area did not take place until the twelfth century. Little or nothing is known about these small pockets of people which were hidden away in the network of canyons and valleys which drain the region, and as they all lost their identity when the new tide flowed in during the 1100's, it is enough now to say that they were probably Reds, leavened with a sprinkling of Basket Makers or Foragers.

THIS COVERS MOST of what is known about what was happening during the tenth century. Archaeologically, the situation at A.D. 1000 is clear. The Mesa Verde, Chaco, Kayenta, Cibola, Mimbres, Mogollon, and Hohokam peoples were all making characteristic types of pottery and they were all living in houses which can be mapped, drawn, and assigned to their respective cultures. As far as the tangible evidence is concerned, most of us should have no difficulty in combining the pottery and architecture at any given site of this period, classifying it as Early Pueblo III, and writing one more report to add to the record.

Historically—by which I mean the interpretation of the tangible evidence—the conditions at A.D. 1000 cannot so easily be described. Collectively, it is customary to refer to the various tribes on the Plateau as the Pueblos, and the stages of their cultural progress have been classified as Pueblo I to V—yet I think it is very doubtful if there was such a thing as an actual pueblo housing more than one family anywhere in the Southwest during the tenth century. From about A.D. 600 up to 900, the villages north of the San Juan could qualify as pueblos in the sense that they were communities in which many families were living together in rows of contiguous one-story rooms and sharing a number of small kivas and an occasional great kiva. This was typical of the villages on Alkali Ridge, in Montezuma Valley, on Mesa Verde, around Durango, and along the La Plata, but there is no recorded instance of such a village south of the San Juan. Whether such villages can properly be said to have been pueblos depends upon what is meant by the term. They were certainly large communities, but it is equally certain that they were not the compact multi-storied communal buildings which is what one usually means when one speaks of a pueblo, but which were unknown in the Southwest prior to A.D. 1000.

Elsewhere in the Southwest, up to A.D. 1000, a village consisted of an assemblage of single separate units, none of which was large enough to house more than one family. Regardless of whether pit-houses were used as dwellings or kivas, or whether surface masonry outlines were once storerooms or living rooms, the fact remains that each of these structures was built for the use of a family. There is no evidence whatever, prior to A.D. 1000, of a communal building that was intended to provide living quarters for more than one family in the Chaco, Kayenta, Cibola, Mimbres, Mogollon, or Hohokam areas. And, to emphasize further this aspect of life in the Southwest at this time, it seems that even the people of the Mesa Verde Branch, north of the San Juan, were turning to the single family unit-type during the tenth century.

It is extremely important to try to understand what all of this means. To me, the tangible archaeological evidence of the eighth, ninth, and tenth centuries is chiefly significant in providing us with a clear exposition of intangible human relationships. During the eighth century, the western section of the Southwest, from the Gila in the south to the San Juan in the north, was overrun by a Red migration which had come up from Mexico. We know that the Reds differed physically from Basket Makers or Farmers. We know that Red culture, as represented by pottery and architecture, was unlike that of the Foragers, Basket

Makers, or Farmers. And it is to be supposed that the language of the Reds was unintelligible to anyone in the Southwest at A.D. 700. Nevertheless, these Reds moved across southern Arizona and up onto the Plateau, meeting and merging with Cochise Foragers, Hohokam, Yuman Foragers, Basket Makers, and Farmers. Nowhere is there to be found any indication whatever of defensive works which would imply resistance by the residents, or any other signs of warfare. On the contrary, it appears that by A.D. 800 the migration had run its course, the Reds had been absorbed, and out of the various resulting combinations it is possible at A.D. 900 to perceive incipient cultures beginning to form. We can see each of these seven cultures—Mesa Verde, Chaco, Kayenta, Cibola, Mimbres, Mogollon, Hohokam—as distinct entities at A.D. 1000, and we can say with assurance that up to this point, their cultures show no evidence of having been affected by fear of enemies from within or without the boundaries of the Southwest.

This is the most important point to make, but a second which deserves to be stressed is that during the tenth century life throughout the Southwest appears to have been based on the family as a unit. It may be that the Hohokam recognized some sort of overlord in the direction of their communal projects, and the great kivas north of the San Juan make one suspect that the priests may have wielded a good deal of power in the Mesa Verde Branch. Otherwise it seems that each family was free to come or go where it pleased, to make its own decisions as to how, where, and when its house should be built, and to exercise its own choice in regard to those arts, crafts, and customs which, collectively, we call private enterprise.

In the midst of this idyllic scene there is only one discordant note. For reasons which will become increasingly clear as time goes on, some of the families in the Red Mesa Valley began to leave their homes in the late 800's and move north to the San Juan. During the tenth century the exodus continued to such an extent that by A.D. 1000 the valley had been completely abandoned. To the west, in the valley of the Puerco, families were also moving out, but in this case, southward to the Upper Gila where they were absorbed into the Cibola villages which showed a phenomenal increase at this time, particularly in the Tularosa Valley and the upper San Francisco.

The area affected covers some two thousand square miles of good arable land, well watered and well timbered, and had supported as dense a population as any other area of like size in any section of the Southwest. There is no evidence, past or present, to suggest that the evacuation of the region was due to soil-exhaustion, erosion, floods, or drought, and the only reasonable explanation seems to be that a powerful but hitherto unrecognized human force was making itself felt. From the fact that the evacuation began and was more complete in the Red Mesa Valley than in the Puerco to the west, there can be little doubt that the force which caused these dislocations was being exerted from the east, presumably in the form of nomadic raids from the western plains.

Rio Grande Branch forming

Chama

Rio Grande

Nomadic Raiders

San Jose

San Augustin Plains

Red Mesa Valley

San Juan

Mesa Verde Branch

Chaco Branch

Rio Puerco

Cibola Branch

Mimbres Branch

Kayenta Branch

Gila River

San ... Mogollon

Mogollon Rim

San Pe...

Flagstaff

Hohokam

Tucson

Prescott Branch

Yuman Foragers

THE SOUTHWEST AT A.D. 1000

In many respects the tenth century was the Golden Age of the Southwest. It was a period of small one-family houses and it is very doubtful if there was a pueblo or communal house anywhere in the Southwest at A.D. 1000.

The Mesa Verde, Chaco, Kayenta, Cibola, Mimbres, and Hohokam peoples had developed their cultures to a degree of specialization which rendered each distinct from all others. The nucleus of the Rio Grande Branch was being formed by Mesa Verde families moving down from southern Colorado. The Prescott Culture was losing its individuality as Kayenta people continued to move down into the Verde Valley, and the Mogollon Culture was increasingly dominated by the Hohokam. All of these relationships and developments were peaceable, and there is nothing to suggest that houses were built or located for defensive purposes.

The shadow of coming trouble was cast when the people who had settled in the Red Mesa Valley abandoned their homes and moved northward to Chaco Canyon, at the same time that other families in the valley of the Rio Puerco pulled out and moved down to the Upper Gila country. The cause of this exodus appears to have been the onset of nomadic raiders, thrusting into the Southwest from the western plains.

The White House, Canyon de Chelly

X I I I

The Enemy at the Gates: A.D. 1000 to 1100

FOR EACH OF THE THREE centuries from A.D. 700 up to 1000, this tale has followed more or less the same course by starting in southeastern Arizona and circling clockwise around the Southwest. So far this has served well enough, as the seven cultures we have been watching as they grew up have come along together and there has been no reason to emphasize one more than another. We have now reached the time, however, when events which took place in one area were widespread in their effects, and it will be easier to understand the outermost ripples if we begin with the center of the splash, and at A.D. 1000 this leads us straight to the Chaco Basin.

I have suggested that beginning in the ninth and continuing through the tenth century the people who had been living in the small one-family houses in the Red Mesa Valley and along the eastern foothills of the Chuskas were pulling out and moving northward. To be more specific, in the Red Mesa Valley we have found ninety-seven sites which show the same pottery types and the same style of architecture as the Red Mesa Ruin, covering the period from A.D. 850 to 930. In the same valley, we have also found sixty-nine sites which show the same pottery and architecture as the Wingate Ruin, covering the years from A.D. 930 to 1000. But within the area lying between Gallup to the west, Mount Taylor to the east, Mount Powell to the north, and the Zuni

Mountains to the south, we have never found a house with more than three living rooms, three or four storerooms and one kiva, or a tree-ring date later than A.D. 1000. Yet as soon as one goes north through Satan's Pass to the Hosta Butte district, the ruins increase in size to as many as twenty rooms, with two or more kivas.

With clear evidence that cultural stages later than the Wingate Ruin should be sought to the north, we turned in 1936 to Chaco Canyon itself where, up to that time, it had always been believed that the Chaco Culture had originated and developed. The results of our survey were very surprising.

Shabik'eshchee turned out to be the only site which could safely be said to have been occupied during the eighth century, and we were unable to find any other indication of a Basket Maker settlement anywhere else in the Canyon.

For the early half of the ninth century, the two pit-houses excavated by Judd were the sole local representatives.

We failed to find a single site in the Canyon which could be said to represent the culture of the Red Mesa Ruin from A.D. 850 to 930, nor were we able to find even one site to cover the time of the Wingate Ruin, from A.D. 930 to 1000.

This dearth of evidence for all the years leading up to A.D. 1000 is all the more remarkable because there was a continuous chain of at least fifty later and larger sites strung along the south side of the Canyon. These were real pueblos, up to thirty rooms in size, two stories high, with as many as five kivas, and they have sometimes been called the Talus Pueblos as they were built on the hummocks which form the talus along the cliff on the south side of the Canyon. Tree-ring dates show that they were built, occupied, and had undergone repairs during the years from about A.D. 1010 to 1080.

And finally, across the Canyon on the north side are the great ruins, such as Pueblo Bonito and Chetro Ketl, which have made Chaco Canyon famous, each with five hundred rooms or more, fifteen to thirty kivas, and great kivas up to 60 feet in diameter.

It is quite possible that early pit-houses have been covered by sands and silts carried down by floods during the last thousand years, and it is quite probable that some of the Talus Pueblos were built over the remains of smaller, earlier ruins. But, even so, the greater number of rooms in the larger pueblos makes it clear that there was a sudden and marked increase in the population of Chaco Canyon beginning at about A.D. 1000.

Our failure to find evidence that the early stages of the Chaco Culture had developed in the Canyon, and the positive evidence that sweeping social and cultural changes had occurred between life in the Red Mesa Valley prior to A.D. 1000 and the later stages in Chaco Canyon after A.D. 1000, cannot be explained by any current theory of Southwestern history. An entirely new approach is demanded, and at this point we make an abrupt break with prevailing ideas.

THE DATE OF A.D. 1000 marks the end of an era. When one looks discerningly at the trends which had been developing during the tenth century, it is clear that a new force was making itself felt, and the actions of the groups which were being affected leave no doubt as to the direction from which this new force was being exerted. Seen through our eyes, this force was intangible. We are given none of its material evidence in the form of new houses, new pottery, new stone implements, or new skulls. The only way we have of judging its onset and magnitude is by the behavior of the people who were compelled to meet it. Lacking concrete evidence which would permit positive identification, it is difficult to give substance to a shadow of this kind, so I am going to hark back to certain incidents which are suggestive of the changing order and for which adequate explanations have not as yet been advanced.

BEGINNING SOME TIME about A.D. 800, a considerable number of people moved into the Red Mesa Valley, apparently as an eastward extension of the earlier settlements in the valley of the Rio Puerco. Their establishments were small, consisting of a few living rooms and storerooms with a pit-house or kiva, and it looks as if each such site represented a single family unit. At about A.D. 850, a few families pulled up stakes and moved northward, thereby starting an exodus which continued and grew until, by A.D. 1000, the entire region from Gallup east to Mount Taylor had been evacuated. To offset any thought that this movement to the north might have been due to a sudden improvement in conditions north of the San Juan, it should also be noted that families in the Zuni-Puerco district, west and south of the Red Mesa Valley, were moving down to the Cibola villages in the Upper Gila at this same time.

THE NEXT INCIDENT took place in Chaco Canyon soon after A.D. 1000. A farming population made up of small family units spread out through the Red Mesa Valley and along the eastern foothills of the Chuskas suddenly decided to abandon this way of life, and crowded into Chaco Canyon where, at intervals of a few yards, they built Talus Pueblos of thirty or more rooms, two stories high, with five or more kivas.

A THIRD INCIDENT occurred at about A.D. 1080 when the people in Chaco Canyon gave up their Talus Pueblos and gathered together in great pueblos of five hundred rooms or more, up to four stories in height, having twenty to thirty kivas, great kivas up to 60 feet in diameter—the whole protected by massive defense walls, of which nothing of the kind is known from any earlier sites anywhere in the Southwest.

THESE THREE EPISODES in the history of the Chaco people give some idea of the nature of the problem with which we have to deal. One must try to decide what the motives were which caused these people to act as they did, and from my point of view, there can be only one answer—fear of enemies, the desire to protect themselves by assembling in great masonry pueblos and building walls for defense.

This raises the question of who these enemies could have been, and to answer this a good beginning can be made by saying that they were not any of the tribes in the Southwest amongst whom the Chaco people had grown up. The fact that groups of Chaco people had been able to settle peaceably in Mesa Verde and Cibola villages, together with the absence of crowding and of fortified sites before A.D. 1000, affords convincing evidence that the relationships of the various Plateau tribes had been friendly.

This narrows the field, and we are left with the reasonable certainty that these enemies must have appeared from somewhere outside the boundaries of the Southwest, and since they brought no additions to any of the existing cultures, it looks as if they were probably nomadic. To be satisfied with this, however, is merely another way of dodging the issue, and there can be very little doubt who these nomads were, even though our only means of identifying them are the effects of their arrival upon the various peoples of the Southwest and their distribution in recent times.

I believe that these nomadic enemies were almost certainly Athabascans—the Navajo and the Apache tribes of our day. They came down from western Canada, where many of their blood brothers are still living in the area lying between British Columbia and Hudson Bay, and it looks as if those who reached the Southwest were merely a southward extension of a migration which came over from eastern Asia in fairly recent times.

From western Canada they came down along the eastern side of the Rockies, and assuming that a movement of this kind would have avoided the forests above 6,000 feet, their route would have led them down through the western plains by way of western Nebraska—where they picked up knowledge of pottery making—eastern Colorado, eastern New Mexico, and so down to the Staked Plains. From the fact that the Farmer villages which had been forming in the upper Rio Grande Valley during the ninth and tenth centuries were not disturbed, there is nothing to suggest that any Athabascans had worked their way westward over passes through the Rockies before the latitude of Albuquerque, at 35° N, was reached. A glance at a contour map will make it clear that for a people launched on the long trek down from Canada through the western plains, this was the first time that the country had opened out to the west, and it was at about this point that the migration appears to have split into two divisions. Many of the Athabascans followed the Pecos southward from the Staked Plains and on down to the Big Bend of Texas and northeastern Chihuahua, where they later became known as Lipan Apache—whom we shall meet again. The division with which we are now concerned are those bands which turned to the west around the southern end of the Manzanos, crossed the Rio Grande, followed the Rio Puerco of the east to the San Jose, past Mount Taylor, and so directly to the eastern end of the Red Mesa Valley—exactly the same course as that followed today by Highway 66 and the Santa Fe Railroad.

With the help of a little hindsight, gained from subsequent history and the distribution of modern tribes, it seems that on or before reaching the Continental

Divide near Mount Taylor, the western division of the Athabascan migration split again into two parts—a northern group which moved up west of the Jemez Mountains to become the Navajo, and a southern group which pushed down to the Upper Gila country, later to become famous as the White Mountain and Chiricahua Apache.

This is an outline based on some guided guesses. We are guided, first, by knowing the recent distribution of the various Athabascan tribes and, second, by the knowledge that they came down from western Canada and were the last people to reach the Southwest before the Spanish invasion. Besides these guide-posts, we can also be quite certain that the arrival of these virile aggressive nomads in the Southwest would have profoundly affected the lives of people already there. I think it can be shown that such a disruption of society occurred at about A.D. 1000 and continued for several centuries; thus our guessing really is reduced to attributing to the Athabascans a series of upheavals for which no other explanation satisfies all of the requirements.

As I try to visualize the conditions prior to A.D. 1000, it seems to me that in a migration of such magnitude, the first warning of impending trouble would come in the form of relatively small nomadic bands, scouting ahead to look over the lay of the land. It was probably the first appearance of such hostile bands in the middle 800's which caused some families in the Red Mesa Valley to pull out and move northward to the San Juan. During the 900's, with increasing numbers of Athabascans reaching the general neighborhood of Mount Taylor, the resulting pressure was the cause of the complete evacuation of the Red Mesa Valley and also of the southward exodus of families from the Zuni-Puerco district. The same explanation would account for the sudden decision of people who had formerly been widely scattered to assemble in Chaco Canyon as a refuge area and build their Talus Pueblos in the early 1000's. By A.D. 1075, the increasing threat imposed by raiding bands is all that is needed to explain the shift from Talus to great pueblos. And, finally, I think that the surprisingly short period during which the great pueblos in Chaco Canyon were occupied was probably due to the relentless pressure exerted by these Athabascan raiders. It is undoubtedly true that a great masonry building, such as Pueblo Bonito, would have provided adequate protection against marauding nomads, equipped only with bows and arrows, but this is not the way that Indians fought. We can be reasonably certain that there was no attempt to storm Pueblo Bonito by massed assault, and we can be equally sure that there was no deliberate siege. Such methods of organized warfare were not practiced by any Indian tribe in North America, and in the case of Pueblo Bonito, they would have been unnecessary. Although their buildings may have been impregnable, the Chaco men and women had to leave the protection of their pueblos when they tilled their fields and harvested their crops, and it was at such times that men were killed from ambush and women and children were captured and carried off. Cornfields were robbed of their grain, but if the Chaco men, driven to desperation, pursued their elusive enemies and left their pueblos unguarded, they would probably find

Mesa Verde: Square Tower House

on their return little left but a smouldering ruin. It was a war of attrition, waged by nomads with nothing to lose, against property owners who, handicapped by their possessions, were unable to retaliate. The fate of the great Chaco pueblos, however, belongs to the history of the twelfth century, and I only mention them here, as most of them were begun late in the eleventh century and the character of their construction lends strong emphasis to the crisis which had been developing.

IN THE MESA VERDE DISTRICT one response of the people to the threat of Athabascan aggression took the form of bigger and better unit-type pueblos. But it was also at this time that the men on Mesa Verde first began to build cliff-dwellings, an innovation which they probably acquired from their Kayenta neighbors to the south. Those ruins which have given dates in the eleventh century all began as relatively small buildings, and depending on their isolation and defensive qualities, they were later enlarged or abandoned. It also seems that it was at about A.D. 1050 that the Mesa Verde Farmers who had settled along the southern border of Colorado began to pull up stakes and leave the district. Some withdrew westward to the protection afforded by the large communities which were forming on and near Mesa Verde, others worked their

Mesa Verde: Balcony House

way eastward to join their compatriots in the upper Rio Grande Valley. Here, the villages which had been founded by eastbound Farmer colonies as long ago as the ninth century showed pronounced growth during the latter half of the eleventh century—a trend that was to develop rapidly in the years that lay ahead.

IN THE MARSH PASS DISTRICT, although the Kayenta architects had never been able to agree on how a kiva should be built, they were of one mind in taking advantage of the features which the country had to offer. The Kayenta people deserve the credit for being the only tribe in the entire Southwest who from their earliest days appreciated the value of an overarching cave as a protection for the mud roofs of their houses. While other peoples were building their houses in the open, exposed to the elements, I think it could be shown that some Kayenta families had used caves as shelters for their houses from Basket Maker times continuously up to the end of Kiet Siel, late in the thirteenth century.

In Canyon del Muerto, for example, Mummy Cave was continuously occupied from A.D. 295 to 701. Tse-ya-tso raised this a few years with dates up to A.D. 739. Next came a cave one mile south of Tse-ya-tso with A.D. 656, 760, 763; then a long string of dates from a cave three hundred yards southeast of Mummy

Cave with a range from A.D. 689 to 792. After this there is a gap of thirty-three years, until Sliding Ruin came through with ten dates from A.D. 825 to 926. Turning to Marsh Pass, we found that Turkey House overlapped Sliding Ruin with seven dates from A.D. 892 to 983. Two small cliff-houses in Canyon de Chelly gave us dates at A.D. 1009, 1027, 1072, and these were backed up by the White House, also in the Canyon de Chelly, with a good series from A.D. 1066 to 1080. Inscription House, in the Marsh Pass area, gave five dates from A.D. 1057 to 1102; and this carries us up to the period of the great cliff-dwellings of the twelfth and thirteenth centuries.

This list leaves one gap between A.D. 792 and 825, and another from A.D. 986 to 1009, but these could almost certainly be spanned by beams from a few more sites, and I think it would be fair to say that caves in northeastern Arizona were continuously occupied from A.D. 295, in Mummy Cave, to Kiet Siel in 1286, the latest date from Tsegi Canyon.

On Mesa Verde, some people lived in Step House Cave from A.D. 593 to 626, but then there is a gap until the eleventh century when several small cliff-dwellings were begun. In the Chaco Branch there are no records of any cliff-dwellings at any time, and none are known from below the Mogollon Rim before the middle of the thirteenth century.

From all of this it would seem that while the Basket Makers were the first Cave Dwellers in the Southwest, it was their mixture with Reds—resulting in the Kayenta Branch—which really was responsible for the origin of the Cliff Dwellers.

ABOUT ONE HUNDRED MILES southwest of Marsh Pass, the Tusayan Ruin stands on the south rim of the Grand Canyon in the midst of a pinyon and juniper forest. We excavated the site in 1930, uncovering a small pueblo which formed three sides of a square, open to the southeast. The central section consisted of four living rooms on the ground floor, and measurements of the volume of rocks and dirt in the mound covering the ruin and its estimated replacement in the form of floors, walls, and roof made it seem probable that this part of the building had originally consisted of two stories. The east and west wings were made up of storerooms too small to serve as living quarters, and a shallow circular kiva with a ventilator had been built as a part of the main house-block in the northwest corner of the plaza. This kiva was destroyed by fire, and two charcoal fragments gave us dates at A.D. 1054 and 1069. It was replaced by another kiva off the southern tip of the east wing, from which we obtained dates running from A.D. 1069 to 1073.

When we were excavating the Tusayan Ruin, we supposed that it was merely one of a number of sites of the same kind, vaguely suggestive of a development from the unit-type which had become popular in the Mesa Verde and Chaco Branches. Our survey, however, failed to reveal any other site which resembled the Tusayan Ruin in size or plan, and one wonders whether here, as in some

The Tusayan Ruin on the south rim of the Grand Canyon

other areas, this small pueblo was the response of a few local families to the threat which was being raised in the east.

SOUTH OF THE GRAND CANYON, around Flagstaff and down into the Verde Valley, the conditions were, if possible, even more confused than in earlier times.

I have already said that Flagstaff, at the head of the Verde Valley, was a crossroads for all of the traffic that flowed between the Gila Basin and the Plateau, and if anything more is needed to show how ideas can get all fouled up at a crossroads, it is to be found in the local conditions during the eleventh century. In one small village near Winona, about fifteen miles east of Flagstaff, Colton reported the finding of a masonry building with three square rooms, and a wide range of original styles in pit-houses. All of these houses contained broadline black-on-white. All were dated within the range from A.D. 1070 to 1125. With the exception of an elliptical house which conformed to Sedentary Hohokam specifications, no one of these houses resembled any type found elsewhere in the Southwest, and to cap the climax, a ball-court and a volcanic eruption were added for good measure.

To the north of Flagstaff, the people in Medicine Valley were badly in need of some of the independent invention that seems to have got out of control at Winona. Here, it has been said, people had been living in the same subterranean plank-lined pit-houses for over two hundred and fifty years. Maybe so, but anyone who has lived in a subterranean plank-lined dugout for only a hundred, or even a mere fifty years, will probably agree it is more likely that

> A young man in the Medicine area,
> Found life growing damper and drearier,
> So he burst from his cell—
> Which was smelling like hell—
> In spite of the tree-ring criteria.

Thereupon he and his friends released their pent-up energy by building a large surface structure, known as Medicine Fort, which was unlike anything else known in any other part of the Southwest. The walls were built of masonry, 4 feet thick, and surrounded a court or patio, but aside from its defensive implications, we shall never know how it was used, as Sunset Crater followed the example of the pit-dwellers and erupted in A.D. 1066.

WHETHER THE PEOPLE in Medicine Valley were actually living in plank-lined pit-houses or some other sort of small family dwellings, the sudden decision to build a large fort with masonry walls 4 feet thick is not the kind of thing that people do without good and sufficient reasons. And whatever these reasons were, they were also effective in the Verde Valley.

I do not think it would be possible to find a pure site of the Prescott Culture dating from the eleventh century. The drift of Kayenta people into the Verde Valley had continued and spread to such an extent that the only remains of the earlier Prescott Culture were a few sherds of black-on-gray pottery mixed with the typical black-on-white of Kayenta potters and the polished redware which covers the floor of the valley.

The fear which may have inspired the building of Medicine Fort, northeast of Flagstaff, may also have resulted, in the Verde, in the construction of Montezuma's Castle, a five-story cliff-dwelling at the mouth of Beaver Creek. The Castle is now a National Monument, and the Park Service has provided us with modern ladders, instead of the notched poles of the old days, so that climbing today is relatively safe and easy. But for anyone who still doubts that fear was abroad in the land during the eleventh century, I think a quick sprint up to the fifth floor on a hot day in July will suggest that the Kayenta builders were concerned with something more than the view.

IN THE GILA BASIN, no one has yet been able to detect any change in the culture of the Hohokam between the tenth and eleventh centuries. For those of us who have been accustomed to the rapid spread and exchange of traits among the various Pueblo tribes on the Plateau, the slowness of change among the Hohokam comes as a pleasant relief from the turmoil of the north. They had found a way of life which gave them ample and secure sustenance, and the heat of their long

Montezuma's Castle, Beaver Creek, Verde Valley
(Reproduced through the courtesy of Southwestern National Monuments)

summer days was unattractive to people who had not been bred to it. During the three centuries from A.D. 750 to 1050, they changed the shape of their houses twice—from square to rectangular, and from rectangular to elliptical. They also made a few changes in their pottery, from the Colonial to Sedentary styles, but these are often difficult to detect. There was no definite progress to which one can point, and in such things as stone-carving and slate palettes, for example, there was actually a decline in both quality and quantity after the Colonial Period.

To THE EAST OF THE HOHOKAM, in southeastern Arizona, a few Mogollon survivors at the San Simon village were having their last fling before disappearing from the local stage. That some of them had lasted until the eleventh century is shown by a number of late Mimbres decorated sherds which were found in their rubbish, but the population had almost dwindled away, as we were able to find only two houses of this last stage in the village. These houses were long and narrow, the length about twice the breadth, and again similar to earlier Hohokam houses, indicating that San Simon architecture was always one lap behind the prevailing Hohokam style. Unless there were a great many more of these late Mogollon houses which have disappeared without leaving any trace, it looks as if the ball-court at the San Simon village must have been built before

A.D. 1000, as otherwise there would not have been enough men to make up two teams, much less to have built the court.

By A.D. 1050, or soon after, the eastern Mogollon settlements, represented by the San Simon village and possibly others of the same kind, had died out, been absorbed into adjacent Mimbres villages, or moved west into the Sulphur Spring Valley. In 1938, Fulton described a site in Texas Canyon, near Dragoon, which seems to have been contemporaneous with the last days at the San Simon village, although showing more of a leaning toward the Hohokam. The actual presence of some Hohokam was shown by several whole pieces of pottery of the Sedentary Period, and also by the fact that cremations and inhumations were about evenly divided. I speak of these people at Dragoon as "Mogollon," but this is one of those times when it would be impossible to draw a line between Mogollon and Red. In a short time we shall be reaching the point where it will be necessary to link prehistoric cultures to modern tribes, and when that time comes, these Dragoon people will turn out to have been prominent in the ancestry of the Sobaipuri Pimas, which should help to identify them.

FROM SOUTHEASTERN ARIZONA this circuit of the Southwest now leads to the Mimbres and San Francisco valleys of southwestern New Mexico.

At A.D. 1000 the people in the Mimbres district were living in masonry-outlined surface houses, often arranged in small groups of three or four contiguous rooms. During the 1000's these groups increased in size, but I doubt if a true terraced pueblo of two or more stories was ever built in the Mimbres Valley. There are numerous examples of rooms which had been built on the collapsed remains of earlier structures. When excavated, these superimposed floors might give the appearance of a two-story building, but I do not think that Mimbres masonry was ever good enough to permit the safe construction of more than one tier of rooms.

The poor quality of Mimbres architecture was more than offset by the decorated black-on-white pottery. This was in a class by itself when compared to other Southwestern types, both in regard to the accuracy of line and the designs themselves. In straight linework the patterns are often so involved as to make one wonder if the bursting point of geometric complexity had not been reached, but it is for their fantastic conceptions of natural history that the Mimbres women are justly famous. Many of the birds, animals, and insects which they drew on their pottery were locally familiar, but some were purely phantoms of their imagination. This, however, could not have been true of the fish which are so common in Mimbres designs. The Mimbres River heads in the mountains about fifteen miles north of Mimbres P. O. and dies out in the sands around Deming about forty miles to the south, and as the stream sometimes almost disappears, it is rather doubtful if there are any fish at all in it. Queerly enough, most of the drawings give the impression of salt-water fish, yet the distance to

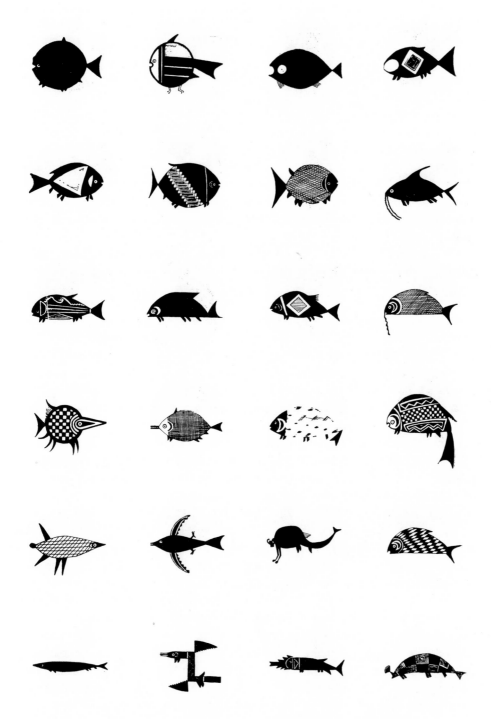

Mimbres Nature Studies: fish, flesh, fowl, or red herring?
(Cosgrove, C. B., 1932. Plates 204-208; 231
Bradfield, W., 1929. Plate LXXII
Gila Pueblo Collections)

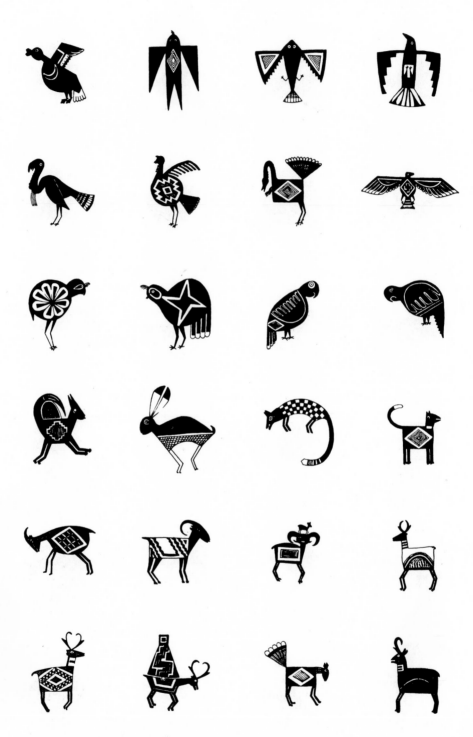

Mimbres Nature Studies: birds and animals
(Cosgrove, C. B., 1932. Plates 192; 210; 211; 214-19; 221; 224; 230; 231
Bradfield, W., 1929. LXVIII; LXXI; LXXV
Gila Pueblo Collections)

Mimbres Nature Studies: reptiles and insects
(Cosgrove, C. B., 1932. Plates 192; 196-99; 201-04; 214
Gila Pueblo Collections)

Mimbres Character Studies

    a.   Masked burglar, armed with a sword
                            (Bradfield, W., 1929. LXXIX : 138)
    b.   A glamor-boy, with mask, ear-bobs, rain sash, bow-guard, shin guards, and swagger-stick
                            (Bradfield, W., 1929. LXXIX : 364)

    c.   A beam-scale
                            (Cosgrove, C. B., 1932. 228 e)
    d.   A stuffed shirt, with quilted armor, shield, quiver, and shin-guards.
                            (Cosgrove, C. B., 1932. 227 e)

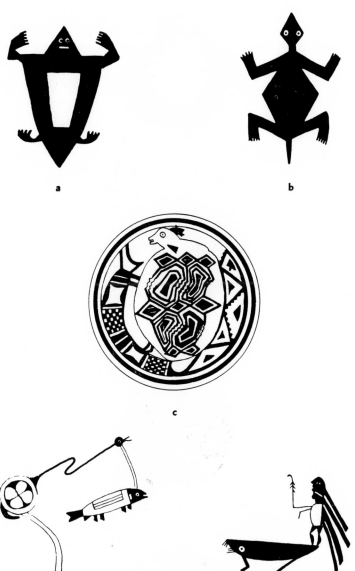

Mimbres Objects

a. Heeby

b. Jeeby

c. Anatomical chart

d. Fly fishing in the Mimbres

e. Circus stunt?

(Gila Pueblo Collections)

(Cosgrove, C. B., 1932. 200 a)

(Cosgrove, C. B., 1932. 232 b)

(Cosgrove, C. B., 1932. 209 c)

(Cosgrove, C. B., 1932. 229 b)

d

c

b

a

Nuclear Fission in the Mimbres
  a. The Mimbres atom
  b. The initial reaction
  c. Nearing the bursting point   (a. Bradfield, W., 1929
  d. ! * ! !   b, c, d. Cosgrove, C. B., 1932)

the Gulf of California is over three hundred and fifty airline miles and to the Gulf of Mexico, over seven hundred. I have therefore given a number of drawings taken from Mimbres bowls in the hope that someone may be able to recognize a face, a shape, or a tail and give us some hint as to how and where the Mimbres women got their icthyological ideas.

FROM A RELATIVELY UNIMPORTANT POSITION, defined by the rather hazy features it had inherited from its Red-Basket Maker ancestry, the Cibola Branch grew rapidly in size during the eleventh century as families moved down from the Puerco-Zuni district to swell the villages on the Tularosa and in the upper drainage of the San Francisco.

The century was begun modestly with small masonry-walled pueblos, such as the Starkweather Ruin near Reserve, in the upper San Francisco Valley. The pueblo here was small, consisting in all of twelve rectangular rooms, of which three were storerooms and one was a large ceremonial room, 23 x 14 feet, built entirely aboveground, with a roof entrance, and equipped with a ventilator.

Most of the decorated pottery was an early local type of black-on-white carrying balanced patterns of solids and longitudinal hatching, but there were also a few pieces of a later form of black-on-white, characteristic of decorated pottery from the Tularosa Valley during the eleventh century. This was unusually fine, running largely to pitchers with rather squat globular bodies, cylindrical necks, and handles which were sometimes braided, sometimes a flat strap, but more often an animal's head protruding from the neck. The favorite design was an interlocking scroll—one element hatched, the other solid—combined with stepped figures. Keys, frets, and panels of parallel lines were used to decorate the necks of pitchers.

Bowls, while not as common as pitchers, were sometimes made, and these were often decorated with an exterior design in white. In some cases, this consisted merely of finger dotting with white paint, but rectilinear figures were occasionally drawn which appear to have been the forerunners of the exterior white designs on various types of Cibola polychromes which later became very popular. Ticked rims, consisting of rows of black dots evenly spaced around the rim, were also characteristic of local black-on-white bowls, and it is worth noting that this quirk was earlier in the Tularosa district than in the Mesa Verde and Salado Branches where the same sort of ticking was in fashion during the 1200's.

Although it was not as spectacular as their black-on-white ware, the Tularosa potters also made great quantities of polished brownware, with black, highly burnished interiors, which was the best of its kind in any culture at any period. Several methods were employed in finishing the exteriors of jars and bowls. Sometimes an unusual kind of coiling was used in which the exposed bands were wiped,

a

b

c

d

e

Cibola Pottery of the Eleventh Century

    a, b.   Bowls of St. Johns polychrome

    c.   Black-on-white pottery

    d.   Coiled and indented

    e.   A bowl showing sixteen coils to an inch

or even polished. In other instances the bands or coils were indented, and the impressions were so carefully spaced that one can often see where an imprint has been added or subtracted to allow for the change in vessel shape, just as stitches are added or subtracted in knitting. Combinations of coiling and indenting were common, particularly the so-called fillet rims, in which two or three rows of indenting were applied just below the outside of the rim.

One of the most remarkable examples of coiled pottery that I have ever seen is a bowl at Gila Pueblo which came from a site on the Spur Ranch, north of Luna on the upper San Francisco. This bowl shows sixteen coils to an inch, and it looks as if the woman who made it must have used strips of clay of about the size and thickness of baby ribbon, yet even with such flimsy material, she was able to build these ribbons of clay into a symmetrically shaped bowl, 8 inches in diameter, with each coil clearly shown.

Toward the end of the eleventh century, the Cibola women in the Tularosa and upper San Francisco valleys began to make the red-black-and-white pottery, known as St. Johns polychrome, by which their fame was carried far and wide. This new combination of colors evidently made a deep impression on other people, as sherds of this ware were quickly carried to the farthest corners of the Southwest. We have found them in sites of the twelfth century or later from Mesa Verde to Chihuahua, and from the Rio Grande to Flagstaff, so providing us with an easily recognized and extremely valuable common denominator for dating equations.

It is highly probable that the Salado Branch began to take shape during the eleventh century. In and around Pleasant Valley, northeast of the Sierra Ancha, there are some sites which are known only from our survey. They are fairly large, up to twenty rooms in size, with masonry walls and one or more patios outlined by rocks.

Black-on-white pottery is scarce and what there is looks as if it were related to some of the decorated ware in the San Francisco Valley, about fifty miles to the east. There are no whole pieces of pottery for comparison, however, and lack of tree-ring dates makes correlation uncertain. The most abundant kind of pottery is an indented ware covered with a maroon paint, which is one of the mysteries of the Southwest. It is never polished but, nevertheless, was carefully made. Vessel walls are thin; interiors are always black, but not burnished; exteriors show an unusual sort of oblique indenting and are covered with a coating of maroon paint which is partly "fugitive," as it can be removed by scrubbing. This type of pottery shows an unusually wide range of vessel shapes, including animal and human effigies, and a further peculiarity is that its sequence is the reverse of that usually found. The earliest type is often decorated over the red paint with chevrons of fine white lines, parallel lines, sometimes with dotted borders or small pendant triangles—all suggestive of Red derivation. Later it was

THE SOUTHWEST AT A.D. 1100

The history of the Southwest during the eleventh century revolved around the effects of the invasion of the eastern provinces by raiding bands of Athabascan nomads.

The people of the Chaco Branch were the first to bear the brunt of these attacks and by A.D. *1100, as their resistance weakened, some groups fled north to the Mesa Verde settlements, others south to the Cibola pueblos.*

On Mesa Verde, the people prepared to meet the Athabascan threat by building their first cliff-dwellings and enlarging their unit-type houses into true pueblos, capable of sheltering large numbers of people, and well situated for defense. The Mesa Verde farming communities along the southern border of Colorado were beginning to break up at A.D. *1100 as the Navajo occupied Canyons Largo and Gobernador, some of the farmers moving down to join their compatriots in the upper Rio Grande Valley, others withdrawing westward to the protection of Mesa Verde.*

In southwestern New Mexico at A.D. *1100 the Mimbres people were being called upon to meet the thrust of the southern section of the Athabascan migration, later known as Apaches.*

To the west of the Mimbres, at this time, the Cibola people in the upper San Francisco drainage were beginning to abandon their villages in the face of the Athabascan threat. Some families went north to the Cibola pueblos in the Zuni district, but most of the people moved westward to Tonto Basin, where with the help of miscellaneous resident groups, they were the principal factor in forming the Salado Branch.

merely indented and turned out in great quantity, and in its final stage—in the 1300's—the surfaces were smoothed.

The range of this type of redware was restricted to the country bounded on the east by the Blue, on the south by the Gila, on the west by the Verde, and on the north by the Mogollon Rim. It poses a very pretty problem for which I think the solution demands the presence of a strong Red (not Mogollon) factor. The indenting, the lack of polishing, and the fugitive quality of the red slip, all indicate that Plateau potters of Basket Maker ancestry had played an important part when this type of pottery was created.

THIS BRINGS MY STORY of the Southwest up to A.D. 1100, and the date marks the end of what might be called the era of free enterprise.

Those days are gone. From here on, it is going to be a tale of how each group responded to the challenge of Athabascan tribes coming down through the western plains, attracted by the granaries of the Southwest, and seeking an entry by every weak or unguarded channel. It will be the same old story of the Haves and the Have-nots, with the Puebloan peoples cast for the role of the Haves—tied to their fields, their houses, and stored food, unable to retaliate by adopting the hit-and-run tactics of their nomadic persecutors. It has been customary to regard the thirteenth century as the Classic Period of the Southwest, but from my point of view, the Golden Age came to an end soon after A.D. 1000. This, I think, was about the time when the carefree life of earlier days gave way to a society governed by fear, and progress was measured by Chamber of Commerce standards that anything bigger must be better and that a thing which is complex must be worth more than something simple.

XIV

The Quick or the Dead: A.D. 1100 to 1200

AT A.D. 1100 the peoples of the Southwest were faced with a rapidly developing crisis, and for us to understand the seriousness of their plight and the steps they took to try to save themselves, there are a few points that need to be considered.

From the over-all point of view, the factor which, more than any other, was responsible for most of their misfortunes was lack of leadership. Here were seven tribes—Chaco, Mesa Verde, Kayenta, Cibola, Mimbres, Salado, and Hohokam—each of which was well established in country of its own choosing; each of which was on friendly terms with its neighbors; all of which were faced with the same threat; but at A.D. 1100, it was a clear case of every group for itself and the devil take the hindmost. Not only was there no cooperation between tribes, but lacking any sort of central control, there was no way of holding any one tribe together. As a result, when danger threatened, some families simply moved elsewhere and weakened the resistance of those who remained.

Another factor which was largely responsible for the downfall of the people in Chaco Canyon, in particular, was their ignorance of cause and effect when one changes the face of nature. In the eighth century, for example, when Basket Makers moved in and built Shabik', Chaco Canyon probably had a good deal to offer to an agricultural housebuilding people who were foot-loose and fancy free. At that time the Southwest was not crowded. People were not being shoved off into refuge areas, but could choose the sort of surroundings which best

Chaco Canyon: black-on-white pottery of the twelfth century

suited their needs. Some Basket Makers chose to settle in Chaco Canyon and the fact that they did so should be sufficient evidence that the environment in the eighth century was favorable as regards their essential requirements.

Shabik' was followed fifty years later by the people who built the two Chaco pit-houses; but there is nothing to warrant the belief that the population in the Canyon had increased over the level of Shabik', and consequently there was no deterioration of the environment.

This appears also to have held true during the ninth and tenth centuries. The Canyon was probably a pleasant enough place in which to live, but even so, it must have been an oasis in the middle of a barren and exposed stretch of country, and the evidence is clear that collateral branches of the Chaco family preferred to live around the southern and western borders of the Basin. At A.D. 850, some of these families from the Red Mesa Valley and the foothills of the Chuskas started to move northward, and many of them actually crossed the San Juan and filtered into the Mesa Verde villages where they can be identified by their characteristic pottery. A few may also have drifted across to Chaco Canyon at this same time, but if they did, their remains have been covered by later buildings.

This northward movement continued and increased in volume during the 900's, until by A.D. 1000, the Red Mesa and southern Chuska villages had been completely abandoned. At just about this same time, there was the first influx of people into Chaco Canyon on a large scale, and it is important to realize that when these people chose this location for their pueblos their choice was largely governed by the fact that the Canyon afforded them those things which were necessary to their way of life—water, arable land, timber, and building stone. If these things had not been locally available at A.D. 1000, it is self-evident that the Chaco people could not have built their Talus Pueblos in the Canyon and would have gone elsewhere. But while Chaco Canyon at A.D. 1000 may have

Chaco Canyon: Pueblo Bonito

been an oasis in a barren land, and although the Talus Pueblos undoubtedly provided greater protection against the Navajo than the small one-family houses in the Red Mesa Valley, the Chaco people were sowing seeds of disaster when they built their Talus Pueblos in Chaco Canyon.

In 1936 we found fifty Talus Pueblos along the south side of the Canyon, and there were many more which we did not visit. As far as the present discussion is concerned, it would make no difference whether these pueblos were started from scratch or were enlarged from smaller, earlier buildings. In either case, it is quite certain that a sudden building boom at about A.D. 1000, resulting in the construction of fifty pueblos with a total of more than one thousand rooms and over one hundred kivas, would have demanded the felling of many hundreds of trees. There does not appear to be any alternative. Trees, which probably were never plentiful in the immediate vicinity of the Canyon, were cut down for the new buildings, and with the removal of the ground cover, an erosion problem was created which was to become rapidly and progressively more acute as time went on.

At A.D. 1080, the Chaco people were consequently called upon to meet a crisis which was accelerating as Navajo raids increased in strength and frequency, while at the same time their resources were diminishing as their crops failed with the lowering of the water table due to erosion.

The response of the Chaco people to these challenges was to build still larger pueblos, and it was at this time that the great pueblos were begun or enlarged. Any trees which had survived the construction of the Talus Pueblos were cut down, so accounting for a number of dates in the early 1100's, and when these had been exhausted, posts and beams were removed from the Talus Pueblos and

a

b

Aztec
a. Part of main ruin
b. Detail of wall-construction

used over again in building the great pueblos. From having once been an oasis, Chaco Canyon at about A.D. 1100 was rapidly reaching its present state—a barren, sandy, wind-swept scar across the face of nature.

For a few years after A.D. 1100 the concentration of the population in the great pueblos enabled the Chaco people to stand off the attacks of Navajo raiders, but the piling of themselves and their troubles on top of one another aggravated the problem of diminishing food supplies. It was at about this time that the Chaco people brought their great kivas up to their highest degree of specialization, but in any case, the end was near. One family after another had been pulling out and moving northward to seek protection in the Mesa Verde settlements or southward to Cibola. A large group left Chaco Canyon at A.D. 1110 and moved up into Mesa Verde territory, where they built the Aztec Pueblo, a large site of over two hundred rooms, on the Animas River, a few miles north of the San Juan. The fact that there are only eight published tree-ring dates later than A.D. 1110 from all of the great pueblos in Chaco Canyon strongly suggests that the local population had dwindled to a small remnant by this time. During the next few years, this remnant died out, was killed off, or left the Canyon and by A.D. 1130, or a few years later, Chaco Canyon had been abandoned.

At Aztec, the refugees from the Chaco wasted no time on vain regrets, and during the years from A.D. 1110 to 1115, they managed to build a great kiva, several smaller standard kivas, and over two hundred rooms arranged around three sides of a court with a heavy defense wall enclosing the fourth side. Here they did not have to contend with deficiencies of food or water, but even so, they were able to hold out against the Navajo for only a few years. The latest date of the Chaco occupation of Aztec was A.D. 1121, and the Chaco Branch, as an identifiable culture, disappeared from the Southwestern stage not later than about A.D. 1140.

While the Navajo had been primarily concerned with the destruction of the exposed and weakening settlements in Chaco Canyon, the steady stream of refugees from the south had given the people on Mesa Verde ample warning of what lay ahead.

Having experimented with a few small cliff-dwellings in the eleventh century, the Mesa Verde architects had come to appreciate the defensive value of this type of building, and construction was in full swing. All of the smaller cliff-dwellings which had been begun in the 1000's were continued and enlarged, and a number of the larger and better known strongholds, such as Cliff Palace, were built or started during the twelfth century. In addition to the protection provided by these cliff-dwellings in their inaccessible locations, the Mesa Verde people were favored by the great difference between the environment of Chaco Canyon and that of Mesa Verde. Chaco Canyon was little better than a desert and there were no physical barriers to serve as a natural protection. On Mesa Verde, however, the deep canyons, sheer escarpments, and forested mesas

a

b

Mesa Verde
   a.   Square Tower House
   b.   Balcony House

provided a strongly protected refuge area so that the people there were among the last to succumb.

Besides the cliff-dwellings, several large pueblos, such as Far View House, had been built on prominent sites affording a wide range of vision. It may have been as a result of this concentration of large numbers of people in a few large buildings and the consequent interchange of ideas that the culture of Mesa Verde reached its peak during the twelfth and early thirteenth centuries. Furthermore, it also looks as if the population of the Mesa Verde Branch at A.D. 1200 was considerably larger than that of any other Southwestern tribe and this, in itself, was a potent factor in their struggle for survival.

What I think can best be regarded, for the moment, as a subdivision of the Mesa Verde Branch were the colonies in the upper Rio Grande Valley which had been developing rapidly since the late 1000's. It would not be at all surprising to learn that as far back as the 700's, when the Farmers were moving out of their Durango villages and settling along the southern border of Colorado, some groups had followed the Chama southeastward and had settled in the upper Rio Grande Valley. Whether this drift had begun before A.D. 800 is still uncertain, but it is fairly clear that such a movement was under way during the 800's and was gaining momentum in the 900's. From the fact that the evacuation of farms in southern Colorado was taking place at just the same time that the Red Mesa Valley was being abandoned, it seems fairly safe to say that both events were due to the same cause and that as the Navajo began to move into Canyons Largo and Gobernador, the Mesa Verde Farmers along the southern border of Colorado, a few miles to the north, began to move away—many of them heading eastward into the northern Rio Grande drainage. By A.D. 1100, a number of the settlements in the upper Rio Grande Valley had grown to the point where they were capable of serving as havens of refuge, and during the twelfth century, the population in some of the local pueblos showed a marked increase—partly due to the arrival of more refugees from the northwest, partly as a result of greater concentration in sites that were favorably situated for defense.

According to this version of early history in the northern Rio Grande area, the culture at A.D. 1200 was still predominantly the product of people who had moved into the district from southern Colorado. In fact, one might say that if the Athabascans entered the Southwest at the time and by the route which has been suggested, it would have been extremely difficult and dangerous for any other Southwestern people to have reached the upper Rio Grande settlements between, say, A.D. 1000 and 1200, *except* through southern Colorado. This will help to explain the suggestion made above that the colonies in the upper Rio Grande at A.D. 1200 can best be regarded as a subdivision of the Mesa Verde Branch.

THE CONDITIONS WHICH had been developing in the Southwest up to A.D. 1100 are also clearly reflected in the actions of the Kayenta people in the Marsh Pass district. Although Mesa Verde served them as a buffer to the northeast, and the

Mesa Verde: black-on-white pottery of the twelfth century

Chuskas provided a barrier between them and the Chaco Basin to the east, many Kayenta families had decided during the twelfth century that discretion was the better part of valor and had moved away from Marsh Pass. One indication of this exodus is to be found in the falling off of building activity. Though they lived in caves at all stages of their career, the only signs of local cliff-dwelling construction during this period are the dates from Ladder House, A.D. 1067; Kiet Siel, A.D. 1116; Twin Caves, A.D. 1110; and Inscription House, A.D. 1057 to 1102.

The record of sites in the open in the Marsh Pass district is also significant. Beals ran across a ruin which he named RB 564, containing six rooms, and which he classified as late Pueblo II or early Pueblo III, and about seven miles northwest of Kayenta, he also found RB 568 which he classified as early to middle Pueblo III—so indicating a close continuity. But whereas RB 564 had only six rooms, RB 568 ran up to over a hundred with "several surface rooms on the bluff, including two on the summit, which rose fifty feet above the main ground level of the village and one hundred feet above the floor of the neighboring canyon. These two rooms may well have served as a lookout."

There are no tree-ring dates from these sites, but Beals' estimate that RB 568 covered the span from early to middle Pueblo III should set the beginning of the occupation in the 1100's and carry it well up into the 1200's. The comparison of RB 568 to RB 564 is chiefly important as it emphasizes the rush to shift from small to large communities which took place at this time and also the adoption of defensive measures, such as lookouts, which were unknown in Kayenta sites of earlier periods.

Let us turn to the trail of the Kayenta families who were deserting Marsh Pass. Some joined the communities around the Hopi towns and in the Ganado area which were just starting their growth, while others moved on to Flagstaff. Here their progress is marked by such ruins as Wupatki, the Citadel, Turkey Hill, and Elden pueblos, all of which were built or under construction during the twelfth century. Either as a result of the impetus of the movement, or due to repercussions, some of the groups in this southward exodus of Kayenta people overshot the Flagstaff region and ended up in the Walnut Canyon cliff-dwellings at dates of A.D. 1120 to 1200, while others pushed even farther south and down into the Verde Valley to Tuzigoot, a large pueblo near Clarkdale, and Montezuma's Castle which has already been mentioned as having been begun in the eleventh century.

UP TO THIS POINT it has been the Navajo who have been scorching the earth. We come now to the Apache branch of the Athabascan family, and if anything more is needed to show that their invasion of the Southwest in the eleventh and twelfth centuries was real and not fanciful, it will be found in the events about to be described.

It has been suggested above that when the Athabascans who had been moving down through the western plains reached the latitude of Albuquerque, a large number turned to the west following the course of the Rio Puerco of the east, thence by way of the San Jose to Mount Taylor where the Southwest lay open to them. Straight ahead to the west was the Red Mesa Valley with its scattered unprotected farms. To the north was the San Mateo Valley opening up to big country west of the Jemez Mountains where Canyons Largo and Gobernador offered ideal bases for raids against the Chaco and Mesa Verde settlements. And to the south of the Puerco and the San Jose were the San Augustin Plains leading down to the villages in the drainage of the Upper Gila, wide open to attack.

This appraisal of the situation on the eastern frontier of the Southwest at about A.D. 1000 gains a good deal of support from the archaeological conditions within the area around Mount Taylor. These show that there is remarkable scarcity of ruins which could be dated in the eleventh or twelfth centuries throughout the region bounded by the Colorado state line on the north, the Jemez Mountains on the east, the San Augustin Plains in the south, and the Chaco settlements to the west, or an over-all area of about twelve thousand square miles. Ever since this part of the country has been known to Europeans, the section north of Mount Taylor has been the exclusive domain of the Navajo, while the southern half has been the stamping ground of various Apache bands. Unless this was the territory through which the Athabascans were circulating in the eleventh and twelfth centuries, I know of no explanation to account for this cultural vacuum on the eastern border of the Southwest.

As far as the people in the Mimbres and San Francisco valleys were concerned, it made no difference whether the Apaches came down from the north, leaving the Navajo behind to attend to the farmers on the Plateau, or in from the east, leaving the Lipan to clean up western Texas. In any case, I am quite sure that if a public opinion poll could have been held in the Mimbres and Cibola villages at A.D. 1100, the vote would have been unanimous that the Apaches had come straight up from hell.

At a date which can be set at about A.D. 1050, the people of the Mimbres Branch were still flourishing in their small farming villages, scattered among the valleys in the foothills of the mountains of the Upper Gila. As described in the last chapter, the women were turning out large quantities of pottery, the black-on-white ware decorated with great exactness and covering most of the known—and many unknown—species of local animals, birds, and insects, besides various kinds of fish which almost certainly were not local. While the women were giving vent to their artistic leanings through the medium of pottery, the men were building one-story houses in groups of a few rooms. These scattered aggregations possessed no defensive value whatever, and there were a great many of them throughout the Mimbres Valley, but at A.D. 1050, it does not seem to have occurred to anyone that defense was needed. I say that the date was about A.D. 1050, but one cannot be exact. There are no tree-ring dates from any late Mimbres sites, and the best guide we have to the chronology of the area is a type of polychrome, black-on-red with white exterior decoration, a few sherds of which were just beginning to find their way into some of the latest ruins. This kind of pottery originated in the Cibola Branch, adjoining the Mimbres on the west, at some time between A.D. 1050 and 1075, and it is fairly safe to say that it reached the Mimbres sometime between A.D. 1075 and 1100. Whatever the actual date may have been—and it could hardly have been any later than A.D. 1100—the appearance of these few sherds of polychrome marked the beginning of the end of the Mimbres Branch. Shortly thereafter the people and their culture disappeared completely from the Southwestern scene.

This is a case where the environment cannot be blamed. There is plenty of arable land, water, and timber in the Mimbres Valley, and excellent hunting in the mountains near by. Yet a numerous and industrious people vanished, and there is not a trace of them or their easily recognized pottery in any later culture in any section of the Southwest. Granted the invasion, from an Apache point of view the operation was a complete success, as there were no survivors left to spread the warning abroad of what was to be expected when Athabascans appeared on the scene. In fact, since there are no indications that any Mimbres survivors managed to escape and seek refuge in the Cibola villages immediately to the west, it looks as if the Apache raids on the Mimbres settlements must have been staged from base-camps in the mountains of the Upper Gila, so cutting off any chance of escape to the west. This deduction would also agree with the suggestion, made above, that the Apaches came down through the San Augustin Plains. If so, they were probably beginning to raid the Cibola villages on the upper San Francisco at about this same time.

RESERVE, at the junction of the Tularosa and the San Francisco in southwestern New Mexico, was the center of another thriving and densely populated community during the eleventh century. Sites were very numerous, but were small, compact, one-story houses rarely of more than a dozen rooms, and show no signs of having been built for defense, either as regards construction or choice of locations. At A.D. 1050, the polished brownware with fillet rims, the corrugated and black-on-white pottery from the Tularosa villages ranked favorably with that of any other culture, and the local potters were just beginning to turn out their red-black-and-white polychromes which were to become one of the most— if not *the* most—popular types of pottery ever to be produced in the Southwest. It was almost certainly more widely distributed than any other kind, having been found as far north as Mesa Verde, as far south as Casas Grandes, in Chihuahua, as far east as Las Vegas, New Mexico, and as far west as the Verde, or an over-all spread of about 450 by 375 miles, so covering the entire archaeological Southwest.

By A.D. 1100, or a few years thereafter, every village in the Tularosa and San Francisco valleys had been either sacked or abandoned, and it would be hard to find a single site between the San Francisco and the Rio Grande which was occupied at A.D. 1150. An area of about ten thousand square miles, well watered, well timbered, in which every valley had supported a dense population, was suddenly and completely evacuated, or the people killed. There was, however, one great difference between the disaster which overwhelmed the Mimbres and the events which took place in the Tularosa and San Francisco valleys. In the case of the Mimbres, the people passed out of the Southwestern picture, never to return; but in the case of the Cibola people, they abandoned their villages in the Tularosa and San Francisco valleys, some moving northward, most of them westward, and lived to fight again.

Those who took the high road to the north joined their Cibola compatriots in the open country along the Little Colorado from Springerville, north past St. Johns, to the Zuni villages and west along the Rio Puerco to Holbrook. The sites of this period in this area were all considerably larger than any in the Tularosa district, and all show the presence of the red-black-and-white polychrome pottery which had started on the Tularosa and was just beginning to show up in the Mimbres when the curtain fell. It is also significant that these sites in the northern range of the Cibola Branch usually show a strong Chacoan component in their make-up.

An excellent example of a site which was just entering this period is to be found in the pueblo ruin at Kiatuthlanna, about twenty miles north of St. Johns, described by Roberts. His diagrams, illustrating three stages in the growth of the pueblo, give a clear outline of the architectural development, and although no tree-ring dates have been obtained, Roberts' description leaves no doubt as to the place of the site in the Cibola series. He mentioned one instance of a design on the exterior of a black-on-white bowl, similar to that of some Tularosa bowls, and he also found that black-on-red bowls with exterior white decoration were just coming into fashion, so making the Kiatuthlanna pueblo approximately contemporaneous with the last days of the Mimbres, or about A.D. 1100. Roberts' description of two earlier stages in the growth of the pueblo, however, indicates that it must have been begun in the 1000's and that it only reached its greatest size after a small indigenous population had been swelled by refugees fleeing south from Chaco Canyon and north from the Tularosa Valley.

Another ruin which helps to round out the Cibola picture is the village of the Great Kivas, in Nutria Canyon, seventeen miles northeast of Zuni, which was also excavated by Roberts. The site consisted of three pueblos, the largest running up to sixty-four rooms, and two great kivas similar in all respects to those which had been built in Chaco Canyon and at Aztec. Roberts found that the early occupation of the village, including the two great kivas, had been predominantly Chacoan in character. Then he recognized an influx of people from the Upper Gila, and the addition of black-on-red pottery with exterior white decoration stamps the late period as about A.D. 1100—all of which requires no comment, as it fits perfectly into the outline as it has been drawn.

WHEN THE APACHES came down like wolves on the fold of the Tularosa villages, some of the settlers took the high road north to the Zuni country, but many, if not most, of them took the low road west through the upper Salt River drainage to Tonto Basin. Herein lies one of the most convincing illustrations of the effects of the Athabascan invasion, not only of the menace which it conveyed to a sedentary people but also the direction from which it came. Black-on-white and polychrome pottery, typical of the Tularosa villages, was suddenly transported 125 miles westward, and most of us would find it impossible to tell the difference between a pot which came from a late site in the upper San Francisco Valley and one from an early site in Tonto Basin. The decorated pottery identifies the people in their new setting, but there were three significant changes from their earlier carefree life. Instead of homesteads in the forested valleys of the Upper Gila, the people now decided to settle on the mesas which border the Salt

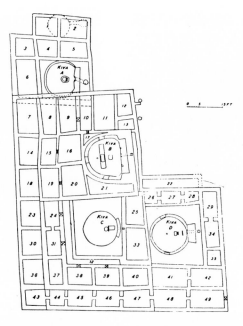

Kiatuthlanna Pueblo: plan of complete pueblo ruin
(Roberts, F. H. H., Jr. 1931)

River, from which a wide range of country was visible. Instead of small un-protected clusters of a few rooms, they now surrounded their houses and patios with a defense wall, forming an enclosed rectangle which Dr. J. W. Fewkes very aptly called a *compound*. The third difference was in their plain pottery which from a polished brownware became a polished redware with black interior, a change in color which may have been partly due to differences in the quality of the clay in Tonto Basin, but more probably to higher firing tem-peratures. They also adopted the dull magenta redware mentioned in the last chapter, so indicating that they had swept up some of the earlier residents in the Salt drainage as they moved westward.

After a long delay and many uncertainties, the influx of a large number of people from the upper San Francisco district, combined with whoever and what-ever was on the ground before their arrival, has finally resulted in the formation of the Salado Branch—so called from the Rio Salado, the old Spanish name for the Salt River.

In the Salado Branch we have no tree-ring dates prior to the late 1200's—the period of the Sierra Ancha cliff-dwellings—but it is safe to set the beginning of the culture in Tonto Basin in the first half of the twelfth century on the evidence of the black-on-white and polychrome pottery. Features of the early local black-on-white which were shared with late Tularosa ware included pitchers of the same squat globular shape with cylindrical necks; a habit of starting the design on a pot by drawing a line around the shoulder, another around the bottom, and

a

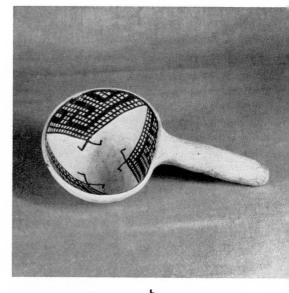

b

c

d

Comparisons
  a & c. Salado
  b & d. Cibola

then filling the space with geometric patterns; leaving the shoulders of their pots undecorated, and applying panels of a few vertical lines, or sometimes crosses, to the cylindrical necks of their pitchers. We used to think that some of these quirks were peculiar to the black-on-white pottery in Tonto Basin, but

An Early Salado Site in Pleasant Valley
The wall outlines suggest the beginning of the compound style of architecture.

our excavation of the Gallo Pueblo in the Tularosa drainage in 1949 showed a large number of pots with exactly the same sort of treatment, and for the Gallo Ruin we have a number of tree-ring dates in the late 1000's, so indicating that the settlement of Tonto Basin took place at about A.D. 1100, or soon after. Designs of keys, frets, and woven patterns are common to both Tonto and Tularosa wares, but animal head handles and hatched designs are rare in Tonto Basin, where there is a greater emphasis on rather heavy parallel lines. A short time after the Salado Branch became established in Tonto Basin and on the mesas bordering the Salt River in what is now Roosevelt Lake, a local type of poly- chrome appeared. It was the forerunner of the later Salado polychromes which were almost as widely distributed as the Cibola polychromes. The base color of this new type was a good clear red, but the interior of bowls was covered with white paint on which hatched and solid designs of interlocking scrolls and stepped figures were drawn, covering the entire field and carrying right up to the rim. The type and its designs are remarkably uniform, and we gave it the name of Pinto polychrome, but it is strange that hatched scrolls should be rare on local black-on-white pottery although consistently present on the new polychrome. The date of its appearance was about A.D. 1150, and it lasted until about A.D. 1200 when it merged into a later and more widespread type known as Gila polychrome.

Pinto polychrome

During the twelfth century the compounds of the Salado people increased in numbers, but there was no noticeable growth in size and they rarely enclosed more than twelve rooms or houses. A few compounds have been found during the course of our survey in the Verde Valley and several in the eastern section of the Gila Basin, at or near Casa Grande, marking the earliest incursion of Salado people into the territory of the Hohokam—a trickle which was to become a flood during the next hundred years as Apache pressure in the east increased and spread.

IN THE LAST CHAPTER, in discussion of the last days of the Mogollon survivors at the San Simon village, it was suggested that they had either died out by A.D. 1050 or had withdrawn westward to Dragoon. No mention was made of the Athabascans as a possible cause of the end of the San Simon villagers, as to do so would have been premature. Now that the subject has been broached, however, and with the examples of the Mimbres and Cibola disasters on record, it seems highly probable that it was the arrival of some advanced Apache bands which were responsible for the blotting out of the San Simon village and any other Mogollon settlements in the eastern sector of their range.

At A.D. 1100 the Mogollon people were reduced to a few villages along the western edge of the Sulphur Spring Valley, from Dragoon south to Bisbee.

Compounds in the Gila Basin near Casa Grande

Fulton and Tuthill have described what seems to have been one of the latest sites in the area, but as late Mimbres black-on-white was the most recent type of intrusive pottery, it looks as if even these western Mogollon villages had died out soon after A.D. 1100. Architecturally, some of the pit-houses at the Gleeson site were said to resemble Mogollon dwellings—which is all as it should be. Most of the houses, however, were typically Hohokam, and Fulton and Tuthill also recognized a strong Hohokam factor in the local decorated pottery, so pointing to the presence of Hohokam in the population and raising some doubt as to whether these western villages should still be regarded as representative of what has been known as Mogollon.

At Tucson, the situation can be covered by saying that the local culture continued to reflect its joint inheritance from Reds and Hohokam. In this southwestern corner of the Southwest the rumors of battle, murder, and sudden death which were filtering through from the east lost a good deal of their force and do not appear to have brought about any significant changes in the way of life in these sequestered settlements.

DURING THE TWELFTH CENTURY an important event took place in the Gila Basin when the spearhead of the Salado migration reached the eastern Hohokam villages. This meeting was most clearly illustrated at sites on or near the Casa Grande National Monument, and as there are several facts which bear on later developments that need to be considered, it will be well to have some knowledge of the local conditions and the surroundings where these events occurred.

The Casa Grande ruins are situated on the flat flood-plain of the Gila, about one and a half miles south of the river in the middle of the desert of southern Arizona. The settlement was originally founded by the Hohokam in the early days of their Colonial Period, and it is important to realize that a site so far from water could only have been chosen by a people who were already familiar

Compound defense walls in Tonto Basin

with the planning and construction of irrigation canals. In 1927, when we were
digging at Casa Grande, the remains of the old canal could still be seen at Adamsville, midway between Florence and Casa Grande.

Compound defense walls in the Verde Valley

The Casa Grande National Monument covers 480 acres and includes not less than ten separate compounds, no two of which are the same as regards either size or plan. There are at least two ball-courts, a great number of rubbish mounds,

Middle Gila: compound defense walls

Sulphur Spring Valley: compound defense walls

and in all probability several other ruins which have not yet been found. It may seem strange to suggest that on a stretch of ground as well known as a national monument, there could be any ruins which have not yet been discovered, but the local conditions are very peculiar. There are no rocks and very few stones near Casa Grande, so all of the old houses and walls were built of the local hardpan—a form of adobe known as *caliche*. As long as walls of this kind are standing they will last indefinitely, but when they fall due to erosion at ground level, they gradually melt away and return to the desert from which they were made. In March, 1928, while working at Casa Grande, I was walking one day with Frank Pinkley, the Custodian of the Monument. It had been a very wet winter and the floor of the desert was covered with scattered tufts of grass and wild flowers. We were about a mile east of the Monument when Pinkley stopped and pointed to a straight line of grass, about 4 feet long, and said that it might indicate a wall of an old house. The ground was perfectly flat and as there were no other indications of a buried ruin, I tied a handkerchief to a creosote bush near by, for otherwise I should never have been able to find the spot again. The next morning, I took one of our Pimas and asked him to dig along the wall and left him to outline the room. I returned after a couple of hours and thought the man must be crazy when I saw that he had opened up a trench over fifty feet long. Nevertheless, he was right, and the 4-foot strip of grass eventually turned out to be a part of the south wall of a compound which measured 120 x 60 feet, with several rooms scattered about within the enclosure—but I can vouch for it that there were no surface signs of a ruin, other than the few sherds which are sprinkled all over the desert in the vicinity of large sites.

Seven of the compounds at Casa Grande consist of clusters of one-story rooms or houses, variously arranged within rectangular defense walls, but I am now concerned only with the three ruins which were wholly or partly excavated by Dr. J. W. Fewkes in 1906-1908 for the Smithsonian Institution, and which he designated as Compound A, Compound B, and Clan-house 1.

Compound A

COMPOUND A is the most important ruin of the local group since it is the largest and also includes the Casa Grande from which the Monument derives its name. The over-all dimensions of the compound were about 420 x 220 feet, the enclosing wall being said to have been originally 7 feet high. Only about half of the area lying within the compound was excavated, but this revealed a number of buildings in addition to the Casa Grande itself. All of the walls in Compound A were made of solid *caliche*, their thickness ranging from 15 to 54 inches, depending upon the height of the building. For the Casa Grande and the other structures in Compound A, I think that illustrations will give a better idea of scale and arrangement than pages of description. There are, however, one or two things about the main building that should be mentioned.

Sacaton: 9:6
    The only surface indication of this compound wall was a strip of grass four feet
long.

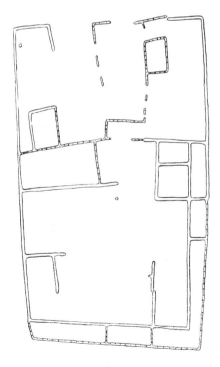

Sacaton: 9:6

Casa Grande

(From Mindeleff, C. 1896)

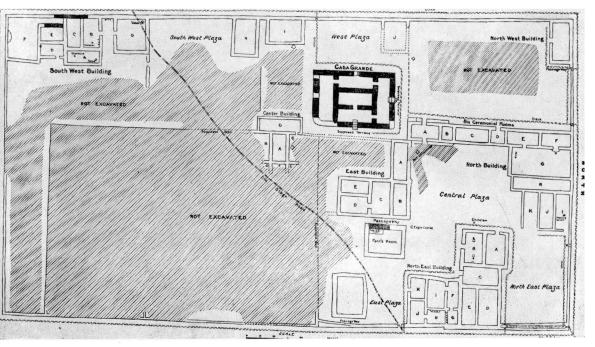

Casa Grande: Compound A

(From Fewkes, J. W. 1912)

On March 7th, 1927, when we were camped at the Monument, everyone was up before dawn and gathered together in the east and central rooms of the Casa Grande. There is a small hole, about 2 inches in diameter, which runs through the outer eastern wall of the building which is 48 inches thick at this point, and lines up with a similar hole in the eastern wall of the central room, which is 44 inches thick. At sunrise on March 7th and September 7th, the sun shines through the outer hole and strikes within one quarter inch of the hole through the inner wall. It was evidently the original intention that the sun should shine through both holes to the west wall of the central room and so, presumably, establish the dates for semiannual ceremonies, such as seedtime and harvest. The description sounds simple, but actually, the making of two such holes in perfect alignment through walls 4 feet thick was an extremely difficult operation. Frank Pinkley thought that the holes no longer lined up because the building had settled during the last seven hundred years. He was probably right and the sun once shone through as planned, but I am curious to know how an old Salado priest managed the job when the straight rib of a sahuaro cactus was the best and possibly the only available tool.

Another feature on one of the walls of the Casa Grande is even more difficult to explain. This is a pictograph on the wall of a second-story room which has been said to represent the "House of Tcuhu," a symbol of Pima mythology. Whatever its origin or meaning, it has been shown by Dr. Harold Colton that "this diagram appears on the reverse of a silver coin of Cnossus in Crete of the Greek Period (B.C. 200-67). In this case the figure represents the Minoan Labyrinth. . . . A comparison of this Greek coin, with the House of Tcuhu when inverted, shows that the two are identical in every respect"—all of which provides food for thought and futile argument.

Compound B

COMPOUND B lies about three hundred yards north and slightly east of Compound A, with a ball-court situated about halfway between the two ruins.

Aside from the fact that both ruins were contained within compound walls, the size, shape, and methods of construction in Compound B were entirely different from those in A. On the one hand, the Casa Grande and all of the subordinate buildings in Compound A had been built with massive walls of solid *caliche*, and some of the houses were two or more stories in height. In Compound B, on the other hand, all of the houses were single units of only one story, and with few exceptions, the walls were relatively flimsy, having been made by daubing *caliche* on a framework of poles.

Judged by themselves without considering any other evidence, these two radically different styles of architecture could be regarded as the contemporaneous dwellings of two different peoples, or they could be interpreted as representing two different periods or classes of the same people. Up to 1927 the latter idea prevailed, but the work which has been done since then has shown

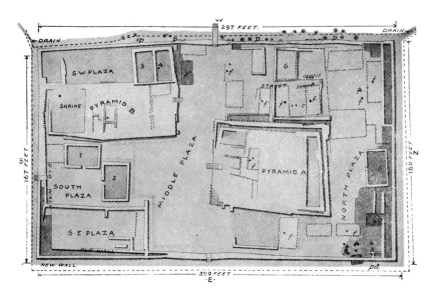

Casa Grande: Compound B

that, actually, two distinct peoples were involved—Hohokam and Salado. We now know enough about each of these peoples before they became associated for us to be able to distinguish their respective crafts and customs when these are found to have been mixed together in the same site, as at Casa Grande.

First, there were the Hohokam who settled in the Gila Basin soon after A.D. 700, and whose culture is known from the Roosevelt village, the Grewe site, and Snaketown, at dates from about A.D. 750 up to 1100, before there was any taint of Salado influence. Among those traits which have been found at these

Casa Grande: Gila polychrome

sites, but which have not been found in Salado sites in Tonto Basin, the following can be listed:

> Red-on-buff pottery
> Canal irrigation
> Ball-courts
> Single family dwellings
> Adobe-on-brush construction (wattle-and-daub)

a

b

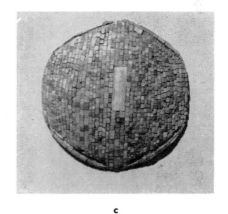

c

Casa Grande
   a. Carved shell. Is this a Masonic emblem?
   b & c. Turquoise mosaic on shell
                    (Excavated by Frank Pinkley, Custodian of the
                    Monument: Reproduced through the courtesy
                    of the Southwestern Monuments Association)

Side entrances
Great lodges
Slate palettes
Carved stone bowls
Etched shell
Earplugs
Mosaic plaques, or mirrors
Modelled clay heads
Rubbish mounds
Cremation

Second, there were the Salado people in Tonto Basin, to whom the following traits can be attributed:

Black-on-white pottery
Black-and-white-on-red pottery
Polished redware
Corrugated plainware
Pueblo architecture
Coursed masonry or solid adobe construction
Compound or defense walls
Cliff-dwellings
Storage pits
Sheet rubbish (broadcast, no mounds)
Inhumation

There are several other things, such as copper bells and three-quarter grooved axes, which might be added to the Hohokam list, but these have also been found in Salado sites. In making these lists, I have erred on the safe side since no padding is needed to show that the two cultures were distinct.

From this evidence three deductions may be drawn: First, that Compound B had originally been occupied by the Hohokam with a thin and late veneer of Salado; second, that Compound A was almost exclusively Salado; third, that the Hohokam—as known from the Roosevelt village, the Grewe site, and Snaketown —had nothing whatever to do with building the Casa Grande in the Gila Basin.

Clan-house 1

IN SOME RESPECTS, the ruin which Fewkes called Clan-house 1 is one of the most remarkable buildings of the Casa Grande group. It lies about 250 yards east of Compound A and was described as consisting of eleven rooms enclosing a court, with an annex of two rooms which Fewkes believed to have been added as a sort of tomb for the former owner—presumably a chief. The walls were solid *caliche*, 4 feet thick, and the measurements of the main building were about 50 x 115 feet. For the rest of the description, I quote from Fewkes' report:

In the middle of the centrally placed of the 11 rooms above mentioned was found a seat facing the south, made of a great block of natural cement. . . .

Perhaps the most remarkable of the several rooms in Clan-house 1 are two massive-walled inclosures on the north side, which have been designated 'the annex.' One of these seems to have been merely an open space surrounded by thick walls formerly higher than at present. In this inclosure were found the remains of a walled-up cyst of natural cement, one side of which was built continuous with the south wall; the other sides of this cyst, visible from the room, were decorated with figures of birds and other animals, painted red.

In the interior of this cyst, or rude sarcophagus, was found a human skeleton extended at full length with the head directed to the east; near the head was a receptacle for mortuary offerings. From the nature of the objects associated with this skeleton and the special receptacle apparently

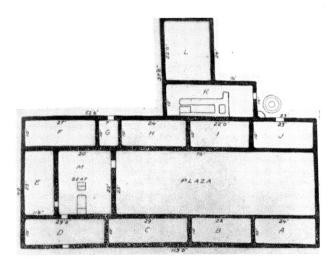

Casa Grande: Clan-house I ruin and ground plan

(From Fewkes, J. W. 1912)

made for them, it is supposed that the remains were those of an old priest, possibly of a chief, who once occupied these rooms. . . . All the facts gathered show that this burial chamber was built after the main building was constructed, but its age, as compared with that of other compounds, is unknown.

THESE DESCRIPTIONS and comments cover the three most important ruins on the Casa Grande National Monument. The rest is mainly a question of interpretation and this brings me to the problems which were raised when the Salado people moved into the Gila Basin and settled down amongst the Hohokam. These events fall into three consecutive archaeological periods, a pure Hohokam period, prior to A.D. 1100; an early period of Hohokam-Salado association which lasted until about A.D. 1200; and a late period, chiefly Salado, which belongs in the history of the thirteenth and fourteenth centuries.

The Hohokam Period at Casa Grande
Compound B, Pre-A.D. 1100

THE EVIDENCE for a pure Hohokam occupation of the Compound B area is to be found, first, in Fewkes' description of the conditions which he found under the surface of what he called "Pyramid A"—seven successive layers of super-imposed floors—fragile walls, reinforced with posts; rectangular rooms, length double the width; side entrances; and fireplaces opposite the doorways. These houses appear to have been identical to those of the Middle and Late Periods at Snaketown, and from the fact that the bulk of Pyramid A was formed of "the accumulations of earth resulting from the decay of these habitations," there is no reason to suppose that while this mound was thus forming it either looked like or served as a pyramid. Nor is there any evidence to suggest that the massive wall enclosing Compound B had been built during the Hohokam period, since there was no connection between it and the houses with reinforced walls— in fact, the compound wall was described by Fewkes as having been built directly over some earlier pit-rooms which appear to have been Hohokam houses. To help further in defining this period, it can be added that there were no indications of compound walls or of the massive type of wall construction at the Roosevelt village, the Grewe site, or Snaketown, and I do not know of an instance of this kind of architecture or of this method of construction having been found in any pure Hohokam settlement prior to A.D. 1100.

The evidence of pottery is even more conclusive in showing that there had once been a pure Hohokam occupation in the area now covered by Compound B. In 1927, when we cut a trench down to desert level through the rubbish mound immediately east of Compound B, we found only a thin film of poly-chrome on the surface of the mound. All the rest of the rubbish had been laid down during the years when red-on-buff was the only type of decorated pottery being made locally, and judging by the vessel shapes and designs, this period overlapped on the occupation at Snaketown and the Grewe site and reached back to the late Colonial Period of the Hohokam, or to about A.D. 900.

To this same pure Hohokam period at Casa Grande one can also attribute the ball-court, a few yards southwest of Compound B, burial by cremation, and at least a part of the irrigation system described by Fewkes.

To emphasize further the distinction between this pure Hohokam period in the Compound B area and any later stage at Casa Grande, one could also add that at this time there were no houses with massive walls, no two-story houses, no compound walls, no pyramids, no polychrome, no polished red pottery, no inhumations; and as a final note, Compound A and Clan-house 1 had not been begun.

The Early Period of Salado-Hohokam Association
The Sacaton Village, Compound B, A.D. 1100 to 1200

IT WAS PROBABLY at about A.D. 1150 that the vanguard of the Salado migration moved into the eastern section of the Gila Basin, and the Hohokam villages near Casa Grande were therefore among the first to be affected by this movement. The advent of these strangers from the east was marked by the first appearance of compounds in this area; by the construction of houses with massive walls, sometimes contiguous to the compound wall, but rarely, if ever, of more than one story; by polished red pottery; and by inhumations. The compound at the Sacaton village, about one mile east of Compound B, probably represents one of the earliest instances of the entry of a Salado group into a Hohokam community. When we excavated the site in 1928, we found a few black-on-white sherds, plenty of polished redware, but no polychrome pottery, and from this I should estimate the date to have been pre-A.D. 1200, and probably not far from A.D. 1150. Most of the house and compound walls were of solid *caliche*, but not much over a foot in width, from which it would seem that they were not wide enough to support a second story. A feature found here which I have not seen or heard of at any other site is that the south and part of the east walls of the compound were of the fragile Hohokam type, reinforced with posts, making a wall about 8 inches thick. This suggests, I think, an early stage in the association of these two peoples wherein the Salado men had not yet begun the building of great massive walls 4 feet thick and correspondingly high, but in which they had convinced the Hohokam men of the necessity of protecting themselves with defense walls against Apache raids.

There is no evidence of this stage in Compound B, but from the fact that these were the only fragile reinforced compound walls found and that narrow solid walls are rare, it would seem that this type of construction was soon discarded and that massive-type compound walls, 4 feet wide and up to 7 feet in height, were being made by or before A.D. 1200. I think, therefore, that the massive wall which enclosed Compound B was probably built late in the twelfth century and that it was at about this time, or possibly a few years later, that thick solid walls were built to retain the mounds of demolished house floors known as Pyramids A and B. To Dr. Fewkes these two mounds suggested "a style of architecture common in Mexico," but it is important to note that they differed from one another as regards height, size, and shape, and that in each case they were surmounted by houses, some of which had walls of solid *caliche*, while in others the walls were thin, fragile, and reinforced with posts. There is nothing to suggest that either of these mounds had served as a base for a temple, and in my opinion, they were nothing more nor less than raised platforms to provide a wider range of visibility.

In both Compound B and at the Sacaton village, houses with walls of solid *caliche*, which I attribute to Salado builders, have been found side by side with houses of fragile walls reinforced with posts, which are typically Hohokam. This close association of the two peoples is further confirmed in the rubbish mound of Compound B, where, in the top layer, Salado polychrome pottery has been found mixed with Hohokam red-on-buff. The date was probably within a few years of A.D. 1200, although some of the buildings in Compound B were undoubtedly somewhat later. It is quite possible—one might say probable—that construction of the surrounding wall and of some of the smaller buildings in Compound A had been begun by A.D. 1200, but I do not believe that Clan-house 1 had yet been started.

THE ARCHAEOLOGICAL EVIDENCE at Casa Grande provides us with a clear and extremely significant record of local history during the twelfth, thirteenth, and fourteenth centuries. It is clear in showing a pre-Salado stage of pure Hohokam culture in Compound B which compares well with other pure Hohokam sites; a stage which covers the meeting and association of Hohokam and Salado groups during the twelfth century; and a late stage in Compound A and Clan-house 1— still to be discussed—which will show a post-Hohokam brand of relatively pure Salado culture. While this, I think, is clear, it seems to me to be one of those cases where the intangible considerations are more significant than the sherds, stone tools, and demolished walls.

Judging by what is known of the Hohokam up to A.D. 1000, one is justified in saying that they were docile, hard-working, and almost exclusively concerned with their own affairs. In their irrigation systems, ball-courts, and domestic establishments, they had built up a capital investment which assured them of a relatively high standard of living, which could not be moved, and which could not be adapted to the mountainous country to the north and east of the Gila Basin. Into this fixed and self-sufficient society there came, during the twelfth century, a horde of Salado people from the east—men, women, and children of an unrelated tribe, with a totally different cultural background, who had been terrified and displaced by the Apaches, and who had overshot Tonto Basin in their anxiety to put as much distance as possible between themselves and their enemies.

By A.D. 1150, or possibly a few years earlier, these two peoples—Hohokam and Salado—were meeting in the eastern Hohokam villages around Casa Grande. For a short time the Hohokam appear to have agreed to a Salado partnership in their enterprises—particularly in the large settlements, such as Casa Grande— but by A.D. 1200, the Hohokam had started an exodus from the Gila Basin and were moving down to the Papagueria.

THIS BRINGS MY TALE up to A.D. 1200, and the best part of Southwestern archaeology is behind us. Chaco is gone. Mogollon is gone. Mimbres is gone. Those people north of the San Juan and those in western New Mexico who can still walk are crowding into cliff-dwellings, gathering together in larger and ever larger pueblos, or trekking west. One great concentration is forming west of the Chuskas, from the Hopi towns over to Ganado; another south of the Zuni Mountains, where the fabled Seven Cities of Cibola are beginning to grow; and in the upper Rio Grande Valley the foundations have been laid for some of the largest communities in the Southwest. Otherwise, the whole region from the Rio Grande to the Arizona line, and from the San Juan to the Mexican Border, has been abandoned to the Athabascan invaders.

The archaeology of the Southwest is no longer a story of peaceful cultural development. From here on, it will be an account of how the Pueblo peoples reacted to fear—cowering in inaccessible locations and gradually dwindling away, or restlessly shifting and herding together to seek protection in numbers. In every village in the Southwest at A.D. 1200, the same questions are being asked: Where to go? What to do? to obtain relief from the ceaseless persecution of the marauding Athabascans.

THE SOUTHWEST AT A.D. 1200

During the early part of the twelfth century the Chaco Branch in the north and the Mimbres in the south were overwhelmed by Athabascans, and their peoples disappeared from the Southwestern stage.

As the Mimbres villages were being destroyed on their eastern border, the people who had been living on the Tularosa and in the upper San Francisco Valley abandoned their homes. Some fled north to the growing communities in the Cibola district. Others moved west into the drainage of the Salt River, resulting in the formation of the Salado Branch.

North of the San Juan the outlying eastern settlements of the Mesa Verde Branch were being withdrawn and there was a marked drift to the west.

In northeastern Arizona, by A.D. 1200, the evacuation of the Marsh Pass district had begun, and Kayenta people were moving southward to Antelope Mesa, southwestward to Flagstaff, and down into the Verde Valley.

As Kayenta and Salado people pressed down from the north and northeast, some Hohokam families started to leave the Gila Basin and moved down into northern Sonora.

a

b

Mesa Verde
   a. Cliff Palace
   b. Sun Temple

X V

The Gathering of the Clans: A.D. 1200 to 1300

At A.D. 1200, the Navajo had been in touch with Mesa Verde people for two hundred years or more and were fully aware that these northern highlanders were more numerous than the lowland Chaco people whom they had recently destroyed. The people on Mesa Verde also had the advantage of living in broken rugged country, more easily defended than the exposed settlements in Chaco Canyon. And in addition, they had been warned of the danger which was building up in the east and had had more time to prepare. In consequence, Mesa Verde was seething with building activity at A.D. 1200. The outlying farms off to the east, along the southern border of Colorado, had been or were being abandoned—the evacuees moving down to join their relatives in the upper Rio Grande Valley, where the villages showed phenomenal growth at this time, or else seeking safety to the west by crowding into the large pueblos and cliff-dwellings on Mesa Verde. Those already begun were enlarged, and many new ones were started. And to play safe, the great ceremonial center, known as Sun Temple, was built to placate whatever Powers there might be who were sufficiently interested to help them through their time of trouble.

Beams from the cliff-dwellings tell an interesting although incomplete story:

Hoot Owl House	A.D. 1091 to 1106	
Kodak House		1132
Hemenway House	1110	1184

Oak Tree House	A.D. 1055	to	1184
Bone Awl House	958		1196
Pipe Shrine House	989		1214
Sun Point Cliff-dwelling	1236		1252
Square Tower House	1066		1259
Mug House	1032		1262
Cliff Palace	1073		1273
Spring House	1064		1273
Buzzard House	1273		1274
Spruce Tree House	1020		1274
Long House	1184		1277
Balcony House	1096		1279

This series indicates that most of the smaller and more isolated cliff-dwellings had been abandoned by about A.D. 1250, and that their former occupants had followed the usual Pueblo custom of pulling up and out when danger threatened —a custom which was responsible for most of their troubles. This, in turn, suggests that at A.D. 1250 the defense of Mesa Verde was falling apart, and even though the tree-ring evidence is incomplete—since many beams must have been destroyed during the last seven hundred years—nevertheless, it is well backed up by information from other sources.

In the upper Rio Grande Valley, for example, the large communities which had been forming during the eleventh and twelfth centuries were made up principally of people of the Mesa Verde Branch, and so afford clear evidence that the exodus of these people from southern Colorado was on a grand scale.

The same thing is shown at Aztec, where, after presumably standing empty since about A.D. 1120, the site was reoccupied by refugees from Mesa Verde. Repairs and renewals were made with beams that have given dates from A.D. 1225 to 1252, indicating that the movement was in sufficient force to provide an adequate defense for at least twenty-seven years. It will also give some idea of the magnitude and severity of the threat to which Mesa Verde was being subjected in the early 1200's when it is realized that this was the first time in over a thousand years that any group of the Farmer-Mesa Verde stock had been induced to settle anywhere south of the San Juan.

Weakened by the defections to the Rio Grande and Aztec, many of the people who were left in the Mesa Verde district at A.D. 1250 sought safety to the west, in the southwestern corner of Colorado and southeastern Utah. Here, on the mesas and promontories along and between the McElmo, Yellow Jacket, and Ruin canyons, they built watchtowers and pueblos fortified by sheer blank walls which could only be scaled with the help of ladders. All tree-ring dates from these western Mesa Verde sites fall in the middle of the thirteenth century, showing that this exodus occurred at about the same time as the withdrawals to Aztec and the Rio Grande Valley.

On Mesa Verde itself, the tree-ring dates indicate that some groups may have held out in some of the large cliff-dwellings until about A.D. 1280, but it also looks as if they had fought to the last man, and there is nothing to suggest that any of these last die-hards had succeeded in extricating themselves in order to fight again. The main exodus from Mesa Verde took place during the early half of the thirteenth century, and of the people who shared in this movement, the only survivors were those who succeeded in reaching the Rio Grande pueblos, and possibly a few who may have reached and lost their identity in the great communities which had been forming in the Hopi district.

Before the thirteenth century had come to an end, the Mesa Verde Branch had gone the way of the Chaco, Mimbres, and Mogollon Branches, and the Navajo had succeeded in completely destroying what was probably the richest and most powerful culture in the Southwest.

IN MARSH PASS, the conditions at about A.D. 1200 were somewhat better, or at any rate less desperate, than in the regions to the east and northeast. The Kayenta settlements were over 125 tough miles southwest of Mesa Verde, and at A.D. 1200 the people of the Mesa Verde Branch were still numerous enough and strong enough to serve as an effective barrier between the villages in Marsh Pass and the raiding bands of the Navajo. In addition, the Kayenta people were further protected along their eastern frontier by the Carrizo, Lukachukai, and Chuska Mountains.

It was at about this time, roughly in the early 1200's, that the Kayenta potters reached the zenith of their art with the production of a type of decorated black-on-white ware which was probably the finest ever made in the Southwest. The designs were almost invariably suggestive of textile patterns, usually as four overlapping folds, drawn in negative, and often tied together by interlocking scrolls. It is a far cry from Marsh Pass to the Gila Basin, but I sometimes wonder if the inspiration for this style of decoration may not have come up from the Hohokam whose pottery during the eleventh, twelfth, and thirteenth centuries often shows much the same kind of designs. If so, it throws an interesting side-light on prehistoric intercourse up and down the Verde Valley.

This is one side of the Kayenta picture, but the other is not so bright. For some years prior to A.D. 1200, refugees from the east had been spreading tales of Navajo depredations against the Chaco and Mesa Verde settlements and it had become increasingly clear that trouble was looming on the eastern horizon. With the overrunning of the Chaco in the middle of the twelfth century, the way was open for occasional Navajo bands to thrust westward through Red Rock Valley and raid isolated Kayenta outposts along the western foothills of the Lukachukais. Some of these, such as the White House in Canyon de Chelly and Mummy Cave in Canyon del Muerto, although founded and built by Kayenta people during the eleventh and twelfth centuries, had provided a haven to refugees from both Chaco Canyon and Mesa Verde. Soon after A.D. 1200 these mixed colonies were either wiped out or the people moved away and were lost in the shuffle of peoples who were gathering on Antelope Mesa, just south of the Hopi towns on the southern edge of Black Mesa. That these eastern outposts

Mesa Verde: black-on-white pottery of the thirteenth century

were the first of the Kayenta settlements to succumb is shown by the scarcity or complete absence of the black-on-white pottery mentioned above, although it occurs in some of the sites on Antelope Mesa and has also been found in some of the late ruins as far west as Flagstaff.

In the face of the Navajo menace which became imminent soon after A.D. 1200, the Kayenta people in the Marsh Pass area reacted in much the same way as those on Mesa Verde. Large numbers left the district altogether and moved south some seventy-five miles to the villages on Antelope Mesa which were rapidly developing into some of the largest communities ever to be known in the Southwest. Some chose to remain, however, and it was during the third quarter of the thirteenth century that the cliff-dwellings in Tsegi Canyon reached their greatest size, as shown by the range of their dates:

Swallow's Nest	1 date at	A.D.	1249
Bat Woman House	6 dates from	A.D. 1245 to	1275
Calamity Cave	1 date at	A.D.	1275
Betatakin	13 dates from	A.D. 1242 to	1277
Scaffold House	12 dates from	A.D. 1267 to	1278
Loloma-Ki	1 date at	A.D.	1278
Kiet Siel	19 dates from	A.D. 1255 to	1286

This series indicates that in Marsh Pass, as on Mesa Verde, the smaller and isolated cliff-dwellings had been evacuated by the early 1200's and that those Kayenta families who had remained in Marsh Pass were crowding into a few of the larger cliff-dwellings. There is, however, one important and significant difference between the Marsh Pass and Mesa Verde series. On Mesa Verde, the period of greatest building activity was at about A.D. 1246, the average date of ninety-five beams which were cut in the thirteenth century, and there are only sixteen dates at A.D. 1270 or later. In Marsh Pass, the average date of fifty-three beams cut in the thirteenth century was A.D. 1271, and of these, twenty-seven gave dates of A.D. 1270 or later.

From this it seems that the peak of building activity was appreciably later in Marsh Pass than on Mesa Verde, and this tends to support the belief that the resistance to Navajo pressure put up by the defense of Mesa Verde gave the Kayenta people some thirty years of grace before they too were compelled to entrench themselves within the walls of their great cliff-dwellings.

Judging by the tree-ring dates, it looks as if Betatakin, Loloma-Ki, and Scaffold House were among the last of the Kayenta citadels to hold out, with, finally, a last-ditch stand in Kiet Siel. When this fell, the Navajo were in undisputed control of the entire range of country lying between the Jemez Mountains to the east and the Grand Canyon to the west, including all of the Chaco Basin.

WITH THE END of the Kayenta Branch in the Marsh Pass district in the latter half of the thirteenth century, we come to the end of another epoch in the Southwest. Up to this point we have been considering individual cultures, in each of which the various peoples did certain things in certain ways, and their products have usually been so characteristic that it has been possible to trace their movements and the effects of their influence on one another. Those days, however, are past. From now on, our problems will no longer be concerned with individual cultures but with melting pots, and with each year that passes it will become increasingly difficult to select and segregate the quirks of design and the varieties of technique which will be mixed in the brew. For eight hundred years, various forms of black-on-white ware had been the prevailing type of decorated pottery on the Plateau, but by A.D. 1300 it had ceased to be made and was replaced by

Betatakin: Tsegi Canyon, Marsh Pass

a

b

Betatakin
    a.   A wattle-and-daub wall
    b.   There were no circular kivas.

polychromes in combinations of yellow, brown, red, and black, in which white was rarely used except as a border to emphasize a line.

These innovations took place at about the same time, both in the Hopi towns, off the southern edge of Black Mesa, and in the Zuni villages, one hundred miles to the southeast; and within a few years they had also spread to the upper Rio Grande. But while the change occurred in each of these three melting pots within a few years of A.D. 1300, each center soon thereafter began to diverge in terms of pottery—the Hopi toward the yellow types, the Zuni toward the reds, and the Rio Grande toward glazed decoration. In each of these areas great pueblos had grown from smaller, earlier beginnings, and it is not always possible to assign the tree-ring dates which have been obtained to specific stages in their development. One cannot therefore be sure, but I think it would probably be safe to say that the Hopi towns were the first to register these changes, a little before A.D. 1300; then the Zuni villages, at about A.D. 1300; and last, the Rio Grande pueblos, soon after A.D. 1300. So I begin with the Hopi towns.

ANTELOPE MESA is a broad neck of land, pointing in a southwesterly direction, about seventy-five miles south of Marsh Pass and about seventy-five miles west of the Chuskas. It is bounded on the north by the Polacca Wash—which separates it from First Mesa on which the Hopi villages of Walpi, Sichomovi, and Hano are situated—and on the south by the Jeddito Wash. Visibility is limited only by the far horizons, and the mesa-top is flat and barren except for scattered junipers which would provide little cover to an approaching enemy. Crops could be grown on the slopes of the washes where loose sand forms a mulch to retain moisture, but with a record of only 12 inches of annual rainfall at Keams Canyon near by, an adequate water supply for a large population would be, and in the old days must have been, a very serious problem, as water flows in the washes only after heavy rains. At all other times, the beds of the Polacca and Jeddito Washes are loose drifting sand.

People had been living continuously in the general area ever since Basket Maker times, and a large number of sites from Ganado in the east, around the southern edge of Black Mesa and up to the Kaibito Plateau, show that the culture had kept pace with the Kayenta developments in Marsh Pass. These conditions prevailed until well along in the eleventh century, when there was a perceptible increase in the size of the local pueblos and the pottery showed a strong admixture of decorated ware which might have come from the Chaco, but more probably from the Puerco—an estimate based on a number of sites in this area which were excavated by H. H. Scorse, the pottery from which formed the nucleus of the Gila Pueblo collections.

By the middle of the twelfth century, most of the smaller scattered settlements north of the valley of the Puerco and up past Ganado had been abandoned. Some people were moving eastward into the villages which were springing up around Zuni, such as Kiatuthlanna and Nutria Canyon which have already been

a

b

Kintiel, or Wide Ruin
  a. **A kiva**
  b. **Looking east toward the Defiance Plateau**

described. Others were gathering in the large sites along the foothills of the western Chuskas, such as Klagetoh and Kin-Klee-Chee with dates in the early and middle 1100's, closely followed by Kintiel (Wide Ruin), Kokopnyama, and other sites on Antelope, First, and Second mesas which had been founded during the thirteenth century or earlier.

During the years which followed, this trend continued and increased in volume as various peoples poured into the Hopi area in steady streams. They came in from farms and villages near by, over the Chuskas from the Chaco Basin, from Mesa Verde, from Canyons de Chelly and del Muerto, from Marsh Pass, and possibly from even farther afield, since it would often be difficult to trace the traits which showed up in some of these mixtures to a source in the Chaco, Mesa Verde, or Kayenta cultures.

A good example of this abrupt break with the past is to be found in a type of pottery which made its first appearance in the Hopi area sometime in the early 1200's, and which was distinct as regards color, shape, and design from anything made by Chaco, Mesa Verde, or Kayenta potters. The color was a muddy red, often brown, shading into a dark orange—so eliminating Chaco, Mesa Verde, Mimbres, and Hohokam as potential ancestors, as none of these are known to have ever made a red or orange ware. Furthermore the reddish-orange color was not the result of an applied slip, which would rule out the Kayenta and Cibola black-on-reds as a source, since these were invariably slipped with a heavy coating of red paint.

The shape was limited almost exclusively to bowls. These were more shallow than in any type of earlier black-on-white ware, and were further distinguished by incurving sides, topped off with square rims.

The designs are one of the most distinctive features of this kind of pottery, particularly the treatment of the so-called broken life-line. This is a very peculiar quirk of design which harks back to early times in the Southwest. The earliest instances that I have seen occur on a few bowls such as have been found at Kiatuthlanna and the pit-houses in Chaco Canyon. In these cases, the design consists of a black line drawn around the top of the rim of a black-on-white bowl, with a short break, sometimes emphasized by curling the ends of the line down the outside of the bowl. The same treatment of a broken black rim-line is also occasionally found on some later Chaco and northern Cibola bowls, but it was not common, and I have never seen or heard of an example on pottery from Mesa Verde, Kayenta, the Tularosa, Mimbres, Mogollon, or Hohokam.

In this new Hopi ware, the treatment of the broken life-line was quite different from anything known from earlier times. Instead of a narrow rim-line, it was now drawn as a broad black band, about half an inch wide, around the inside of the bowl about an inch or so below the rim. And instead of being a rare occurrence, the idea had such a hold on the Hopi potters of this and later times that it is very unusual to find a piece of their pottery without this form of decoration.

How to account for the changes which began early in the thirteenth century is quite a problem. If I had to guess where the Hopi version of the broken life-line came from I should look to the Rio Grande, where it was also very popular after A.D. 1300, and where it may have started in some earlier but little known culture. The thirteenth century was a period of drastic changes, when human currents were swirling around in all directions, and one cannot always be sure where these currents started, what wreckage they carried, and how far they travelled.

To the southeast of the Hopi area much the same conditions prevailed during the thirteenth century as those already described. The large tract of country lying east of the Little Colorado, from the Puerco in the north to the upper Gila in the south, had been completely evacuated soon after A.D. 1200, and the people were swarming into the large pueblos around Zuni. As in all of the other big communities which were forming at this time, black-on-white pottery was no longer being made, and potters were experimenting with various types of poly-chrome—in this case, usually black-on-reds with white added as an interior slip, an exterior decoration, or to accentuate the black designs. Some of these poly-chromes which were turned out by the Cibola potters are of particular interest, as they were decorated with a true lead-glaze paint in several colors—chiefly black, but sometimes green, purple, or brown, depending upon the thickness and consistency of the paint and the color of the base on which it was applied.

There does not seem to be any doubt that this type of painting was first intentionally employed by the potters of the Cibola Branch since examples of glaze-painting are not uncommon on some of the black-on-white ware from the Tularosa Valley at dates early in the twelfth century. The point is of considerable importance, as the adoption of glaze-painting as the customary method of deco-rating pottery in the Zuni pueblos during the thirteenth century and the reason-able assurance that the technique was originated and developed by the potters of the Cibola Branch provide an extremely valuable clue in attempting to recon-struct the history of the period. To the peculiar qualities of the paint which stand out as an easily recognizable cultural beacon, there can be added several types of polychrome ware which were either being developed locally or were finding their way into the Cibola district from the areas to the south and west. Band designs were employed on most, if not all, of these types, sometimes as unbroken parallel bands which served as borders for fine-lined white patterns on bowl exteriors, and often as a broken life-line in much the same form as on the pottery from the Hopi pueblos.

These traits, singly and in combination, make it possible to trace the route of a migration from the Cibola district, eastward past Acoma, the San Jose, and the Rio Puerco of the east, and so to the upper Rio Grande Valley. The evidence of a building boom afforded by tree-ring dates and also the fact that glaze-painting was well and widely established in the Rio Grande pueblos by A.D. 1350 indicate that the migration from Cibola had occurred by about A.D. 1300.

This movement of a large number of people from the Zuni villages to the Rio Grande Valley at A.D. 1300 is of great importance in its bearing on contempo-rary and also on later Pueblo history. For the period of A.D. 1300, it is very significant that considerable numbers of men, women, and children were able to make the journey from Zuni, past Acoma and Laguna, to the Rio Grande Valley without being massacred. Their way appears to have led along the San Jose to the Rio Puerco of the east, and thence to the Jemez Valley—a route which would have taken them through the heart of the country formerly oc-cupied by the Athabascans. Not only did these people from Cibola make this trek without meeting disaster, but they even left colonies at Acoma and Laguna, in the very midst of earlier enemy territory. This would seem to make it reasonably certain that at A.D. 1300 the Navajo and Apache had parted company—the Navajo concentrating their energies on the communities in northeastern Arizona, the Apache concerned with the settlements below the Rim, so leaving a gap through which the people from Cibola passed to the Rio Grande.

Recognition of the fact that a large number of people had been transplanted from the province of Cibola to the Rio Grande Valley is also of the utmost importance to a reconstruction of the modern history of the Pueblos. It is fair to suppose, for instance, that during the thirteenth century the various groups which constituted the Cibola Branch were able to communicate with one another, even though some were indigenous, some had come down from the Puerco, and others from the Chaco, the Upper Gila, and other points of the compass. Sometime about A.D. 1300—or possibly a little earlier—a number of these groups took off and headed eastward. Colonies were left at Acoma and Laguna—about seventy-five airline miles from Zuni—the main body pressing onward to the junction of the Jemez and the Rio Grande—another seventy-five airline miles beyond Acoma—where, within a radius of about fifteen miles, they are living today in the pueblos of Zia, Santa Ana, San Felipe, Santo Domingo, and Cochiti.

The clue which helps to establish the relationship of these five Rio Grande pueblos to Acoma and Laguna is that the modern inhabitants of all seven towns speak the same language, known as Keresan. This historic intangible evidence is also backed up by the prehistoric tangible evidence of polychrome pottery, designs, and glaze-painting which marked the trail of the migration from Cibola to the Rio Grande. With this in the bag, so to speak, one might then go on to suggest that since these Keresan-speaking people all seem to have come from the province of Cibola, the people of modern Zuni—who at present are rated as linguistic orphans—may, once upon a time, have spoken some dialect of the Keresan tongue.

TURNING NOW to the third of the great concentrations which had been forming during the thirteenth century, it seems that it was the arrival and subsequent interplay of contingents from the Mesa Verde and Cibola districts which made up the sum and substance of the Rio Grande Branch at A.D. 1300.

From an earlier position of relative unimportance the Rio Grande Branch at A.D. 1300 had become one of the most powerful aggregations of people in the Southwest, and to set this development in its proper perspective, it will be well to enlist the help of some of the men who have made special studies of this section of the Southwest.

In his *Pottery of Pecos*, Dr. Kidder reduced the problem of the Rio Grande to its bare essentials when he said, "The Rio Grande seems to have played no part whatever in the origin of the Anasazi Basket Maker-Pueblo ceramic complex; nor did it ever, save possibly in early historic times, contribute materially to cultures in the west. The Rio Grande received but apparently gave nothing in return."

Doctors Mera, Stallings, and Stubbs, working out from the Laboratory of Anthropology at Sante Fe, regarded the early decorated pottery in the upper Rio Grande area as having been "in the 'Chacoan' or 'eastern Pueblo' tradition . . . decorated with mineral paint." But a contrary opinion was expressed when, in referring to examples of "Chacoan" pottery illustrated by Mera, Kidder said, "The pieces which he figures are to my mind not at all Chacoan, from the point of view of decoration. They seem, on the other hand, to resemble more closely a generalized Black-on-white of the northern San Juan."

I mention these two different points of view, as they have a direct bearing on the problem of Rio Grande origins. Mera, Stallings, and Stubbs appear to have been at least partly governed by the fact that some of their local pottery was decorated with mineral paint—as was customary on Chaco pottery, but unusual on that of Mesa Verde. Kidder objected to their classification on the grounds that the decoration on this early pottery was characteristic of the northern San Juan (Mesa Verde), but not of the Chaco.

At the risk of further complicating the problem, it seems to me that a solution might be found by harking back to the events which took place in the eighth century. I have suggested above, in Chapter IX, that when the Reds moved up through Marsh Pass in the 700's, they crossed the San Juan into southeastern Utah and some of them pushed eastward as far as the La Plata Valley. Although this infusion of Red blood was admittedly weak, since it was the fag end of a movement that had already traversed the entire Southwest from south to north, nevertheless one of the results of their arrival was to leave a Red stamp on the local pottery. In 1939, Miss Shepard announced in her section of *Archaeological Studies in the La Plata District*, that whereas 80 per cent of the black-on-white pottery in the northern La Plata Valley was decorated with vegetable paint, the sites in the southern section of the district showed 85 per cent mineral paint on the black-on-white ware. She then added, "Superficially there appears to be no noticeable difference in paste, surface finish or design between the mineral- and the organic-paint groups." In other words, the black-on-white pottery in the southern La Plata Valley carried Mesa Verde designs—so agreeing with Kidder's belief—but the decoration was applied with mineral paint—which might satisfy Mera, Stallings, and Stubbs, although this explanation makes no allowance for a Chacoan element in the mixture.

For the rest, there seems to be general agreement. Kidder's recognition of a northern San Juan (Mesa Verde) factor in the upper Rio Grande has already been mentioned. Stallings, in a summary to accompany a list of dates in the Tree-ring Bulletin, October, 1937, was more specific when he recognized a marked change in the local culture during the early part of the thirteenth century, as a result of "the introduction of new styles, many of which may be attributed to the Mesa Verde complex."

So also with the migration from Cibola bringing the technique of glaze-painting to the upper Rio Grande. Stallings regarded this as "a major flow of culture from the upper Little Colorado" region, whereas Kidder spoke of it as "a wave of pottery making [which] rolled eastward, crossed the Rio Grande, and extended nearly to the Texas border"—all of which comes rather unusually close to a meeting of archaeological minds.

For a time-scale of these various events, I use the recent series of dates published by Smiley, Stubbs, and Bannister in Bulletin 6 of the Laboratory of Tree-ring Research. This is a revision of the list compiled by Stallings in 1937, and includes 1083 dates from forty-five ruins in the northern Rio Grande area. The dates fall as follows:

The earliest recorded date is A.D. 963, followed by one at 968.

Then 2 dates in the quarter century ending at A.D.	975
7	1000
1	1025
3	1050
51	1075
9	1100
69	1125
69	1150
11	1175
61	1200
22	1225
35	1250
80	1275
106	1300
101	1325
86	1350
22	1375
62	1400
41	1425
112	1450
57	1475
15	1500
16	1525
6	1550
36	1575
3	1600

As I read these figures, it looks to me as if:

1. The Rio Grande Branch was late in getting started.
2. The area was only sparsely populated until about A.D. 1050.
3. Beginning in the middle of the eleventh century, there was a marked increase in building activity that lasted up to about A.D. 1250, which I

attribute to the arrival of Mesa Verde immigrants from southern Colorado.

4. Soon after A.D. 1250, the leading groups of the migration from Cibola began to arrive in the Rio Grande Valley, reaching a maximum during the period from A.D. 1276 to 1350.

5. Following A.D. 1350, the population in the Rio Grande pueblos showed no appreciable increase, and building activity fluctuated as some sites were abandoned and others enlarged to accommodate greater concentrations.

SOUTH OF THE HOPI TOWNS and west of the Zuni villages, one runs into another series of mixtures which, in some ways, are even more confused than those we have been considering. This is partly because more is known about what the Hopi and Zuni were doing during the thirteenth century, but I think that most of the uncertainty is due to the fact that the country lying along and below the Mogollon Rim is very broken and the people who lived in this region during the thirteenth century were more scattered than those who congregated on Antelope Mesa, near Zuni, or in the upper Rio Grande. It will be easier to deal with the situation if I break it up into three sections—the southern half of the Little Colorado Basin to the edge of the Rim; an eastern section below the Rim, lying between the Sierra Ancha and the White Mountains; and a western section, from the Rim down to the Gila, which was the domain of the Salado people.

Beginning with the southern half of the Little Colorado Basin, there are several large isolated pueblos most of which had been founded during the thirteenth century—judging by the presence of black-on-white pottery—in each of which the culture was composed of a blend of blends. Near Winslow there is Homolobi, made up chiefly of people who had moved down from the Hopi towns, but also containing a minor representation of southerners from the drainage of the Salt, below the Rim. About twenty-five miles due south of Homolobi, there is the Chevelon Ruin, and here again the Hopi were in the great majority, but there were also contingents from the farms and villages along the Mogollon Rim, with a marked increase in redware over the sites farther north. Some forty miles west of the Chevelon Ruin, in the juniper belt bordering the western margin of the Little Colorado Basin, there are two other large sites, Kinni-Kinik and the Chavez Pass Ruin, both of which were founded by people of the Kayenta Branch at a time when black-on-white pottery was still being made, possibly by groups which had moved down from the Flagstaff district. Most of the later, yellow pottery at these sites is indistinguishable from that of the Hopi towns on Antelope Mesa, but redware and southern polychromes are also present in considerable quantities. The same mixtures, in varying proportions, are also to be found at Tuzigoot and other large ruins in the Verde Valley, and it seems that the earlier liking of Kayenta people for the Verde lasted well up into the fourteenth century.

Going in the opposite direction, there is a very large site near Taylor, Arizona, known as the Four Mile Ruin, which from surface sherds appears to be much the same as the Chevelon Ruin, but when and if these large sites are thoroughly excavated, I doubt if any two of them will show exactly the same combinations. The composition of the population in the Hopi towns was made up primarily of people from the Kayenta Branch with some leavening from Chaco and Mesa Verde, and possibly a few southern refugees. But while some of these combinations were also undoubtedly present in the Four Mile, Chevelon, Kinni-Kinik, and Chavez Pass pueblos, they were themselves still in a state of flux at A.D. 1300, and these more southerly communities were receiving heavy increments from the south.

One of the most significant features about these large southern pueblos—particularly Homolobi, Chevelon, and the Four Mile Ruin—was the choice of location. Up to the time of their founding, the only people who had braved the harsh and arid environment of the Little Colorado Basin had been a small group from the Flagstaff area who had settled around Canyon Diablo in the days when broad-line black-on-white was the fashion, and a few families that had homesteaded in the Petrified Forest without much lasting success. It is all the more remarkable, therefore, that a large number of people should have chosen to build these three large pueblos in the thirteenth century in a section of the Little Colorado Basin where occasional rains were the only source of water supply and the weather record at Winslow, near by, shows only 8 inches of average annual rainfall. The water problem for the large population in the Hopi towns must have been very difficult to meet, but how the people in Homolobi, Chevelon, and the Four Mile Ruin obtained enough water for their bare necessities is a question which would be hard to answer. The only explanation for the selection of such exposed sites would seem to be that visibility was unlimited in all directions, but if this was the primary consideration, it speaks volumes for the fear of the Athabascan raiders that prompted the choice.

THE SCENE shifts, from the Plateau to below the Mogollon Rim. Up to this point, we have been chiefly concerned with tracing the effects of the Navajo invasion of the northern country—the destruction of the Chaco Branch in northwestern New Mexico in the twelfth century; the overwhelming of the Mesa Verde people in southwestern Colorado and southeastern Utah during the thirteenth century; the expulsion of the Kayenta people from the Marsh Pass district in the latter half of the thirteenth century; and the flight of the survivors of these three disasters to the shelter of the Hopi towns, the Zuni villages, and the Rio Grande pueblos. Although many of the units in each of these three refuge areas had been founded in earlier times, their phenomenal growth during the thirteenth century was obviously due to the influx of people who had fled from their former homes, and there can be very little doubt that the absorption of this steady stream of refugees created problems of water supply, sanitation, accommodation, and adjustment which must have been extremely difficult to solve. In the case of the Zuni villages, it may have been these problems which were the cause of migration eastward to the upper Rio Grande, late in the thirteenth century. In the case of the Hopi towns, they may have been responsible for many of the people continuing their trek southward to Homolobi, Chevelon, Four Mile, and southwestward to Kinni-Kinik, Chavez Pass, and down into the Verde Valley. For these poor souls, however, it was a case of out of the frying pan into the fire, since the farther they moved away from the Navajo, the nearer they came to the Apache—and it is with the Apache that we now have to deal.

Four Mile polychrome

The southern division of the Athabascan migration was made up of various bands or tribes of Apaches, some in the Big Bend of western Texas, some in northern Chihuahua, but most of them in the mountains of the Upper Gila and the Chiricahuas, from which they raided the Zuni villages to the north and the White Mountain and Salado settlements to the west, and penetrated westward through every gap that was opened as their victims withdrew.

The reactions of the people below the Rim were much the same as those of the Pueblos on the Plateau. In the eastern section, lying between the Sierra Ancha and the White Mountains, there was a frontier line of defense, stretching from Fort Apache in the north to Point of Pines in the south, all facing eastward to the Upper Gila. This front line was based on a series of large pueblos which had grown from smaller earlier sites, and the herding together of scattered families in these large centers had resulted in the same process of mixing peoples

Kinishba

(Reproduced through the courtesy of Arizona Highways)

and their cultures as had occurred on the Plateau, although the mixtures, of course, were entirely different.

A very good example of one of these eastern frontier posts is provided by Kinishba, a large pueblo four miles west of Fort Apache, which was excavated by Dr. Byron Cummings. Dates for the ruin have been given as covering the period from A.D. 1050 to 1350, so indicating that it was founded during black-on-white pottery times and consequently was contemporaneous with most of the large pueblos on the Plateau—a correlation which is also confirmed by the finding of a number of Hopi yellow-ware bowls associated with the local types. At the peak of its development, at about A.D. 1300, most of the decorated pottery at Kinishba consisted of southern polychromes—some from the Salado Branch to the west, in Tonto Basin, but mainly of local manufacture.

The most fashionable type of decorated pottery at Kinishba was a bright red ware ornamented with black bands, outlined by narrow white borders. One band was drawn around the interior of bowls, just below the rim, and two parallel bands encircled the exterior, serving as a frame for designs of keys, frets, and chevrons, drawn with fine white lines. A pattern, complete in itself, was sometimes drawn to cover the bottom of a bowl, but in most cases, the interiors were left plain below the band at the rim. The jars of this type of polychrome were also characteristic in having white necks and shoulders, usually with a few black crosses or turkey-tracks spaced at intervals, and a band of black geometric design around the body of the pot. It is worth noting, however, that although bands were an invariable feature on this type of polychrome, I have never seen an instance of a broken life-line.

Behind this first line of defense along the eastern frontier, the country is broken up by the mountains and canyons which form the upper drainage of the Salt River. This rugged forested section was not suitable for the establishment of great communities where large numbers of men, women, and children could band together for their mutual protection, and in this secondary zone, the people turned to cliff-dwellings for their salvation, building them in inaccessible locations in the canyons which head under the Rim. It is very significant that at just the time when cliff-dwellings on Mesa Verde and in Tsegi Canyon were being abandoned, some people started building them in eastern central Arizona, in a part of the Southwest where none had been known before. It suggests that some groups from the north may have worked their way down below the Rim, but if so, they must have been men who had left their women behind, as there is no Kayenta or Mesa Verde pottery in the Sierra Ancha cliff-dwellings, and even sherds of Hopi yellow ware are rare or completely absent.

The mixture of southern polychromes in the cliff-dwellings was the same as that in Kinishba, and tree-ring dates also show that the large pueblos and the cliff-dwellings were both functioning during the latter half of the thirteenth and carried over into the early fourteenth century. The following list includes only those cliff-dwellings in the Sierra Ancha which were begun before A.D. 1300:

Center Mountain No. 2, 3 rooms	A.D. 1286 to 1312
Pueblo Canyon, 60 to 70 rooms	1278 to 1324
Workman Creek, 15 rooms	1289 to 1314
Cold Springs Canyon No. 1, 6 rooms	1260 to 1316
Cherry Creek, 12 rooms	1286 to 1308
Cooper Fork, 12 rooms	1283 to 1322

From this it can be seen that construction of the Sierra Ancha cliff-dwellings did not begin until about A.D. 1280, or within a year or two of the last dates from the cliff-dwellings on Mesa Verde and in Tsegi Canyon—so implying some sort of a connection between the northern and southern cliff-dwellers, however indirect it may have been.

DURING THE THIRTEENTH CENTURY the Salado Branch had been developing into one of the most important cultures in the Southwest. Its actual homeland covered about four thousand square miles, bounded on the north by the Mogollon Rim, on the east by the Sierra Ancha, on the south by the Gila, and on the west by the Verde. This, however, was merely the territory which the Salado people could call their own. In addition, they were personally represented in pueblos as far east as Kinishba, as far south as Casas Grandes in northern Chihuahua, as far west as Gila Bend, and as far north as Chevelon. In each of these directions there was enough of their typical pottery to be able to say that if this was the result of "trade," it was the Salado potters themselves, not just their pots, that were traded.

a

b

Sierra Ancha Cliff-dwellings of the Thirteenth Century
a.   A small site in Cold Springs Canyon
b.   The stuff that tree-ring dates are made of

In the last chapter, the origin of the Salado Branch was explained as having been the result of a migration westward of people who had formerly lived in the Tularosa and upper San Francisco valleys in southwestern New Mexico. During the 1100's, these migrants from the southern Cibola district were busily settling themselves in compounds on the mesas which border Tonto Creek and the Middle Salt River, 125 airline miles west of their former homes. Here they were making their black-on-red pottery with outside white decoration, a type of black-on-white ware which was practically identical with that which they used to make in the Tularosa Valley, and a few years before A.D. 1200, they started making their Pinto polychrome as described in the last chapter.

This new polychrome had only a short life, however, as soon after A.D. 1200 the exodus of people from Mesa Verde and Marsh Pass caused shifts and dislocations which were felt all the way down to Tonto Basin. As refugees swarmed down from the north, groups of people from the Hopi area moved south, some to Homolobi, some continuing on to Chevelon, and a considerable number pushing still farther southward, down over the Rim and into Tonto Basin, where they sought refuge in the Salado compounds.

The absorption of these northern groups wrought some drastic changes in the culture of the Salado Branch. Instead of clusters of a few one-story rooms arranged around the inside of the compound walls, pueblos of two or more stories were built in the middle of the compounds, standing clear of the walls. There was also a marked change in the pottery. Black-on-white ware declined rapidly in quantity and ceased to be made by about A.D. 1250. Pinto polychrome was replaced by a new type, known as Gila polychrome, which was made of the same combination of colors—red, white inside slip, and black decoration— but which was decorated with entirely different designs. Instead of interlocking scrolls, hatched and solid, bands now became the fashion, sometimes continuous, but more often as a broken life-line, exactly the same as on the orange and later yellow wares of the Hopi. Fine hatching disappeared and was replaced by rather heavy pennons, keys, solid scrolls, and triangles with scalloped edges.

By A.D. 1250, the Salado people had spread far and wide, but wherever they went their trail is clearly marked by their architecture and distinctive pottery. Partly because of increasing Apache pressure from the east, partly as a result of the crowding in Tonto Basin as more refugees came down from the Plateau, large numbers of Salado people sought to improve their lot by moving out to the south and west. Some groups settled along the Middle Gila and in the Pinal district where, at Bylas, San Carlos, and Gila Pueblo, they managed to stand off the Apaches until well up in the fourteenth century. Other groups moved into the San Pedro Valley where they held out until Father Kino arrived, late in the seventeenth century. A considerable number by-passed the Salado villages which were forming along the Middle Gila and the San Pedro and continued down into northwestern Chihuahua, where they brought about a marked increase in the population and completely changed the complexion of the local culture.

On the one hand, prior to A.D. 1200, small scattered groups of people had been living in the open exposed plains of central Chihuahua in huts built of perishable materials which have dissolved into low mounds, of which during the entire course of our survey we were able to find only twelve sites.

On the other hand, after A.D. 1200, the population showed a phenomenal increase, with the center of density shifting to the Babicora Plateau in western Chihuahua. Here we found forty-four sites, consisting of houses with walls of stone laid up in adobe mortar, up to sixty rooms in size and often divided into house-groups, as in earlier Mimbres times. It was also in this district, during the thirteenth and fourteenth centuries, that cliff-dwellings, with as many as eighty rooms and up to three stories in height, with walls of coursed masonry, and T-shaped doors, were built in defensive locations in the canyon walls of the Sierra Madre.

The change in pottery was just as abrupt as that in architecture. Brown pottery with a red decoration on a white slip ceased to be made and was entirely replaced by two varieties of polychrome—a black and red on a tan-colored surface, and a black and red on a chalky white slip. The two types appear to have been approximately contemporaneous, and the designs in each case were much the same, consisting of balanced elements in black and red, made up of scrolls, keys, triangles, and stepped figures, usually bordered by fine lines forming a maze or meander.

The events which began in the Babicora district during the thirteenth century resulted in transforming a culture which had been locally distinct in central Chihuahua into one which was typically Southwestern in the western section of the state. Black-white-and-red polychrome pottery, three-quarter grooved axes, coursed masonry, T-shaped doors, and cliff-dwellings suddenly appeared in a region where nothing of the kind had been known before. At the same time there was a marked increase in population—from a sprinkling of undefended farming sites in the open plains of central Chihuahua to a dense concentration on the western plateau as people sought protection behind stone walls and in cliff-dwellings in the canyons of the Sierra Madre. None of these innovations had formerly been known in the areas to the south, east, or west. All had been known and used by the Salado people in Tonto Basin, and it is therefore safe to say that the changes which took place in Chihuahua during the thirteenth century were caused primarily by Salado immigrants, aided and abetted by a few survivors of the earlier local culture.

Although it is clear that western Chihuahua was populated during the thirteenth century by people coming down from the north, there is no evidence that this movement included any Hohokam refugees. In addition to those characteristic features of Salado culture which have already been mentioned, the methods of agriculture in the Babicora district were those of the Salado people, not the Hohokam. In canyons and gullies near house ruins, Sayles found check-dams which were the same as those we have found on the lower slopes of the Graham Mountains on the Middle Gila. Nothing like these dams has been reported from any part of the Gila Basin, and as further proof that the Hohokam were not present in Chihuahua, there were no indications of canal irrigation, no cremations, no Hohokam type of house, and not a sherd of red-on-buff pottery.

WE TURN NOW from those who fled south to those who fled west. The steady stream of Salado people into the Gila Basin which had begun in the twelfth century continued and expanded until, soon after A.D. 1200, the Salado people had actually become the dominant force in the Gila Basin. But while this movement undoubtedly involved large numbers of people, the Salado preponderance was at least partly due to the fact that as they poured into the Gila Basin from the east, many of the Hohokam began to move out, southward to the Papagueria and down into northern Sonora.

Some of the Hohokam in the larger settlements chose to remain and fraternize with the incoming Salado families, and it is very remarkable that each of these peoples continued the customs and fashions which they had followed before their meeting took place. There are no signs whatever that any fighting occurred, such as would be indicated by a Salado conquest and the resultant dropping or modification of traits by a vanquished Hohokam. It is also strange that there is nothing in the later culture of the Salado or the Hohokam to suggest that either one was in any way affected by the other. The Salado people continued to build their pueblos, to bury their dead, to make their red and polychrome pottery—indistinguishable from the same types in Tonto Basin, on the Middle Gila, and the San Pedro—and when some of them left the Gila Basin in the fourteenth century they joined their Salado relatives in northwestern Chihuahua. Meanwhile, those Hohokam who had decided to remain continued to live in their one-room houses, to cremate their dead, and to make their brown and red-on-buff pottery which bore no resemblance in color, shape, or designs to the Gila polychrome which was being made next door, at the same time. When they finally left their homes in the Gila Basin, it is again significant that they did not follow their Salado friends into Chihuahua, but joined their Hohokam relatives in the Papagueria.

The dates of these various arrivals and departures cannot as yet be definitely pinned down, but I think that most of them can be bounded within fairly narrow limits. The main trek of Cibola people into Tonto Basin to found the Salado Branch is well established by tree-ring dates up to A.D. 1100 from the upper San Francisco Valley. This date also agrees with the evidence from Snaketown, where the occupation lasted up to about A.D. 1100—an estimate based on dated types of foreign pottery which were found at the site. There was no evidence at Snaketown, however, to indicate that the Salado migration into the Gila Basin had begun during the time the site was occupied. In fact, it is quite possible that the local Hohokam abandoned Snaketown and moved down to the Papagueria at the time and because of the Salado influx. Certain it is that we did not find a sherd of any type of Salado pottery at the site.

THE SOUTHWEST AT A.D. 1300

By the middle of the thirteenth century resistance by Mesa Verde people to Navajo aggression was breaking down. A large number left southwestern Colorado and migrated southeastward to the upper Rio Grande. Some reoccupied Aztec for a few years; some moved west to southeastern Utah; and some held out in the large cliff-dwellings on Mesa Verde, but by A.D. 1300, the only survivors of the Mesa Verde Branch were those who had reached the upper Rio Grande.

Warned by the disasters which had overtaken Chaco and Mesa Verde, most of the Kayenta people saved themselves by assembling in the great communities on Antelope Mesa. Many continued south to the large pueblos along the Mogollon Rim, and some pushed even farther south to the Salado compounds below the Rim.

The Cibola villages increased rapidly in size as outlying farms and settlements were abandoned, and it was possibly due to this crowding that a number of people left the Cibola district at about A.D. 1300 and migrated eastward to the Rio Grande Valley.

During the thirteenth century the Salado people were the dominant force in the drainage of the Salt River, as their numbers were augmented by refugees from the north and east. By A.D. 1300, however, they were beginning to give way to the Apache and there was a well-defined shift westward to the Gila Basin and southward to northwestern Chihuahua.

By the middle of the thirteenth century the Salado people had taken over the controls, as shown by a tree-ring date of A.D. 1241 on a beam from Casa Grande which helps to establish the time when this building was begun.

Between these limits of A.D. 1100 and 1241, we must make allowance for the westward migration of Cibola people into Tonto Basin to found the Salado Branch; the overrunning of Tonto Basin by some of these groups and their penetration as far westward as the eastern section of the Gila Basin; changes in pottery; and the progress in architectural development which led up to the planning and construction of the Casa Grande in A.D. 1241. If this makes it seem that too much has been crowded into too little time, I can only suggest that after A.D. 1100, the tempo of cultural change in the Southwest was greatly accelerated by fears inspired by Athabascan aggression. This is clearly shown by the abandonment of favorable areas, the sudden shifts and crowding of peoples, the selection of defensive locations, and the building of watchtowers, lookouts, defense walls, and elevated structures to give wider range of visibility. Seen from this point of view, the whole series of events—from the evacuation of the Tularosa Valley at about A.D. 1100, up to the building of the Casa Grande in A.D. 1241—were successive steps taken by the Cibola-Salado people to evade the Apaches, or failing escape, to protect themselves by architectural ingenuity. The Casa Grande was the end result of these efforts and the building was actually a citadel, conceived, built, garrisoned, and defended by Salado men—a project in which the Hohokam show no signs of having played a part.

IN CLOSING THIS CHAPTER on the thirteenth century, it is necessary to refer briefly to a theory which has gained wide circulation since it was first broached in 1929. This is the idea which began with the claim that a narrow annual tree-ring should be accepted as reliable evidence of deficiency of moisture for the year during which the ring was formed. From this as a beginning, the claim was then advanced that prehistoric droughts were indicated by certain ancient ring patterns in which some narrow rings were included. The drought theory then was broadened to cover the failure of crops during the period represented by these patterns of tree growth. And finally the theory was applied directly to the reconstruction of Southwestern history when it was used to explain the abandonment, at about A.D. 1300, of the great pueblos and cliff-dwellings on Mesa Verde and in the Marsh Pass district because of a supposedly catastrophic drought which has been said to have lasted from A.D. 1276 to 1299.

The subject was discussed in detail in "Tree-rings and Droughts," *Medallion Papers XXXVII*, and for present purposes, it will be enough merely to list some of the objections to the theory.

First, the suggestion that a narrow annual tree-ring is an invariable indication of deficient moisture has been shown to be mistaken, since comparisons of modern tree growth with climatic records have demonstrated that some of the narrowest rings in living trees have been formed during seasons of excess rainfall and low temperatures.

Second, it has been shown that, as regards moisture, tree growth is primarily dependent upon winter precipitation, and that the thunderstorms of summer have little, if any, effect upon ring-width—so making it evident that the width of an annual ring cannot be relied upon to provide an accurate index of crop conditions, since these were governed chiefly by summer rainfall.

Third, the exodus from the pueblos and cliff-dwellings in the Mesa Verde and Marsh Pass districts had actually started many years before A.D. 1276, as shown by the dates of A.D. 1225 to 1252 for the Mesa Verde reoccupation of Aztec, the dates in the early half of the thirteenth century for the influx of Mesa Verde people into the upper Rio Grande Valley, and the phenomenal increase in the population of the great pueblos on Antelope Mesa which had begun in the twelfth and continued throughout the thirteenth century.

Fourth, it is difficult to understand how the supposedly drought-striken people on Mesa Verde and in Marsh Pass could have hoped to obtain any relief by moving only sixty miles south to Antelope Mesa. Modern weather records show that there is considerably *less* rainfall in the Jeddito district than in the regions which had been abandoned, and there can be no doubt that an adequate water supply for the large and growing communities on Antelope Mesa must have been a very serious problem under the best of conditions.

Fifth, the drought theory originally was based on the inner rings of a single beam from Oraibi, one of the Hopi towns on the southern flank of Black Mesa. These great Hopi pueblos, however, had been founded long before A.D. 1276. They not only were continuously occupied throughout the period of the supposed drought, but also accommodated a stream of refugees from the north. They continued to grow up into the 1400's without any interruption, and in the case of Oraibi, the pueblo has been continuously occupied up to the present day.

Sixth, if people anywhere in the Southwest had been suffering from drought in the last quarter of the thirteenth century, it would be reasonable to suppose that they would have sought relief in an area of heavy rainfall. According to modern weather records, the heaviest rainfall in any section of the Southwest occurs along the eastern end of the Mogollon Rim, the White Mountains, and the Upper Gila drainage—the sources of the Little Colorado, the White, Black, Blue, San Francisco, and Gila rivers. Yet there is no evidence whatever of any movement of Pueblo people into this area during the thirteenth century, and at A.D. 1276 the former inhabitants had virtually disappeared.

Under the circumstances, it would seem that the uncritical acceptance of an unsubstantiated theory of drought to explain the abandonment of the Mesa Verde and Marsh Pass districts in the thirteenth century is not justified by the evidence of tree-ring growth or of archaeology.

The Canyon Creek Ruin

Modern Peoples out of Ancient Cultures: A.D. 1300 to 1450

AT A.D. 1300, the old order, represented by well-known archaeological cultures, was changing into a series of new groupings in which it is often difficult to trace connections between the new and the old. The situation at A.D. 1300 is admittedly hard to appraise, but out of the welter of shifts and combinations, the modern peoples who now occupy the Southwest are beginning to emerge, and we have reached the time when an effort should be made to establish connections between living peoples and their archaeological ancestors.

This transformation began early in the thirteenth century when various Plateau peoples abandoned their former homes, sought security by joining other groups, and in most instances, lost their individuality in the resulting fusion. The process of blending continued through the late thirteenth and early fourteenth centuries, and at about A.D. 1350 the Hopi towns, the Zuni villages, and the Rio Grande pueblos were the three concentrations into which all of the Plateau peoples of the earlier cultures had crowded, and out of which the modern Pueblo peoples have emerged. A new perspective has been opened up, and I think it will be advisable to adjust our sights rather than be governed by conventional classifications. It has been customary, for example, to regard the historic period of the Southwest as having begun at A.D. 1540 with the first written accounts of the chroniclers who accompanied the Spanish expeditions of exploration and conquest. But, as a matter of fact, the arrival of the Spaniards did not bring about any marked changes in native customs or crafts, and as far as the peoples of the Southwest are concerned, the cultures of the so-called historic period were ushered in by the changes which made their first appearance during the thirteenth century. This attitude may seem more reasonable and easier to understand when it is realized that all of the old cultures for which archaeologists have coined such names as Kayenta, Mesa Verde, Chaco, Cibola, and Mimbres have disappeared. We are now dealing with peoples who can more accurately be identified as the ancestors of modern tribes than as the descendants of the people who were responsible for the ancient cultures. A few examples will make this clear.

For five hundred years, from A.D. 700 to 1200, the Province of Tusayan had been the domain of the Kayenta people—a name which Kidder selected some years ago to label the remains which he had found in the Marsh Pass district. During the thirteenth century, however, the culture which has been recognized as distinctively Kayenta disappeared, and from Keams Canyon down to the Mogollon Rim, west to Flagstaff, and down into the Verde Valley, we find people making a reddish-brown pottery which later became orange, then yellow, and which continued without any perceptible break into the pottery of the modern Hopi. There can be no doubt that the Kayenta people were one of the chief components in the population on Antelope Mesa during the thirteenth century, but it is equally certain that the yellow ware which made its appearance in this same area at A.D. 1300 was directly ancestral to modern Hopi pottery. This will explain why the name "Hopi" has been substituted for the archaeologists' label of "Kayenta," and I think it should now also be clear that the era of the modern Hopi began at about A.D. 1300, many years before the first Spaniard set foot in Arizona.

The same is true of the Province of Cibola where the archaeological culture known as the Cibola Branch faded out at about A.D. 1300 to take the name and form of the modern Zuni. Here, as a result of his study of Zuni pottery, Kroeber, in 1916, was able to draw a sharp line of demarcation between the prehistoric period, represented by black-on-white ware, and the later historic Zuni polychromes. Nevertheless, although he recognized that "the separateness of the two is fundamental," Kroeber gave it as his opinion that "they do not represent two different migrations, nationalities, or waves of culture but rather a steady and continuous development on the soil."

The Rio Grande Branch was later in getting started, but during the thirteenth century, the arrival of one migration from Mesa Verde, followed shortly by another from the Cibola district, raised the Rio Grande to full Pueblo status, and since the early 1200's, it has become one of the three important Pueblo centers in the Southwest. Judging by the black-on-white pottery in the lowest levels of some of their sites and also by the location of some of their pueblos, it looks as if it was the influx of Mesa Verde people, early in the thirteenth century, which resulted in the founding of the Tanoan pueblos in the upper Rio Grande Valley. It seems also that it was the migration of people from the Cibola district

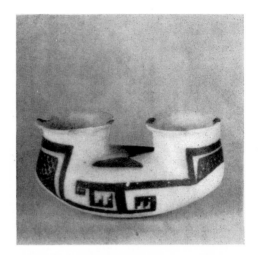

Black-on-yellow ware of the fourteenth century

at about A.D. 1300 which led up to the establishment of the Keresan pueblos near the junction of the Jemez River and the Rio Grande. From a cultural standpoint, the arrival of these people from Cibola, bringing with them their technique of glaze-painting, marked the end of the era of black-on-white pottery and the beginning of the series of Rio Grande glazed wares which lasted through the Spanish invasion and up to recent times.

These examples explain how the *historic cultures* of the present-day peoples of the Southwest had begun to take form by A.D. 1300, and also why the *historic period*, marked by the coming of the Spaniards in A.D. 1540, was merely a date in our calendar and did not inaugurate a definite stage of Southwestern cultural development. The distinction is important, as it has sometimes been re-

a

b

Puye
    a.   The pueblo on top of Puye Mesa
    b.   Cave-rooms at the base of the tufa cliff

a

b

Rito de los Frijoles, Pajarito Plateau
  a. Rooms dug out of the tufa cliff
  b. The ruin of Tyuonyi

The ruins of Pecos Pueblo, New Mexico

garded as rash or unjustifiable to connect modern peoples with ancient cultures. To my mind, however, this is the essence of history, and it is for this reason that I have emphasized the fact that all of our historic cultures had taken recognizable shape in prehistoric times.

WHAT HAS BEEN SAID above applies only to the Pueblo peoples on the Plateau, as in the southern area there were very few people left to span the gap between past and present. Below the Mogollon Rim, from the San Francisco Valley in the east to the Verde in the west, the Apaches were waging a war, chiefly against the Salado people, which was still being fought as late as the eighteenth century. It was a war in which no quarter was asked or given, but it was one-sided and the result was a foregone conclusion. On one hand were Apache bands —here today, gone tomorrow—operating under leadership which in historic times often showed remarkable tactical ability. On the other hand were the Salado people—sitting ducks. It is true that in the fourteenth century the Salado people were very numerous. It is also true that at this time they had many allies—White Mountain Pueblos along the frontier in eastern Arizona; Hopi expatriates along the Rim; Hopi, and possibly some Yuman people in the Verde Valley; Hohokam in the Gila Basin; Hohokam, and a few Mogollon survivors along the Middle Gila and in the San Pedro Valley; and scattered groups in northwestern Chihuahua. The fact that the Salado people had all of these allies, however, is in itself evidence that they were spread all over central and southern Arizona and down into Chihuahua, and it was this dispersion with its lack of hegemony that was mainly the cause of their downfall. When a settlement in Tonto Basin was attacked, the men in another compound a few miles away might know nothing about the fight until it was all over—or if they were near enough to send help, they would probably find their undefended homes had been destroyed during their absence. Concentrations such as those on the Plateau were the only adequate response to the challenge of Athabascan raiders, but with a few exceptions, such as Point of Pines, Gila Pueblo, and the Casas Grandes of the Gila Basin and Chihuahua, the conditions below the Rim were not favorable to the maintenance of large concentrated communities. Lacking centralized authority, the occupants of each Salado compound possessed freedom of action, and when confronted with danger, many of them pulled up stakes and moved away—only to have to fight another day. Each step in the process of a large number of people being divided and conquered is clearly illustrated by the Salado strategy in the Apache wars of the twelfth, thirteenth, and fourteenth centuries.

The first split occurred soon after A.D. 1100 when the upper San Francisco villages were evacuated and many Cibola families went north to Zuni, leaving the Salado Branch to fend for itself. Of those who moved west, the greatest con-

Dr. Kidder talking things over with an ancient Pecan

centration was in Tonto Basin, but at this same time, there was another split when Salado colonies fanned out to the south and west. At A.D. 1300, I think it would be possible to distinguish not less than nine different alliances into which the Salado people had entered in varying degrees.

There were evidently large contingents of Salado people in the White Mountain pueblos at Kinishba and Point of Pines. They were even more prominent in the Sierra Ancha cliff-dwellings. Their home grounds were in Tonto Basin, but we have found them on the Middle Gila mixed with Hohokam. On the San Pedro they had combined with Hohokam and Mogollon; in the Pinal pueblos, with Mogollon but no Hohokam. In the Verde they built their compounds among Kayenta people. In the Gila Basin they may actually have outnumbered the Hohokam, and there was very little in Chihuahua before the Salado people moved in and took over the controls.

The Apaches disposed of their Salado problems by picking them off one by one, so I will follow their example.

To BEGIN, on the eastern frontier, Kinishba came through into the fourteenth century with its latest tree-ring date at A.D. 1320, and it would be fair to suppose that the pueblo was occupied for some time after this tree was felled. There is nothing in the pottery or other archaeological evidence, however, to indicate that Kinishba had lasted later than A.D. 1350.

About thirty or forty miles of very rough country to the southeast of Kinishba, there was another very large community at Point of Pines which had been founded back in Mogollon times and which had served as a rallying point for all the scattered groups in the lower San Francisco and the drainage of the Blue in eastern Arizona. The site is now being excavated by the University of Arizona, and Haury, who is directing the work, thinks that it may have lasted until A.D. 1400. Owing to its size and location, Point of Pines would have been a hard nut for the Apaches to crack, and it well may be that the estimate of A.D. 1400 will turn out to be right. My own guess would be nearer A.D. 1350, as I doubt if the people at Point of Pines could have held out for fifty years after their neighbors at Kinishba had succumbed. In either case, they appear to have fought to the last man, as there is no sign of any survivors in any later site or culture.

THERE IS NO DOUBT about the next line of defense having been overwhelmed by about A.D. 1350. This consisted of the cliff-dwellings in the canyons which head under the Mogollon Rim and on the eastern face of the Sierra Ancha, about fifty of the roughest miles in the Southwest west of Kinishba. Here the dates from a big collection of beams show that only two of the largest cliff-dwellings, in Canyon Creek, can surely be said to have held out for a few years after A.D. 1340.

a

b

The Canyon Creek Ruin
  a. Chinked masonry
  b. Clay-covered storage basket

After visiting these ruins and obtaining a general idea of the culture, we selected the Canyon Creek Ruin for excavation. We found a number of interesting things, especially various kinds of textiles, but the feature which provided an unusual sense of reality was that each room contained datable timbers which made it possible to trace the progress of construction from its beginning in A.D. 1326 up to the final date at 1348. It also aroused a feeling of intimacy, not often associated with archaeology, when we found the burial of an old lady, still wearing her string skirt, wrapped in the cotton blanket which she had woven, with the spindle and workbasket filled with partly spun yarn which her children had placed by her side to accompany her on her long journey.

The life of the Canyon Creek cliff-dwelling, from A.D. 1326 to 1348, was surprisingly short, considering the amount of labor that went into the building of its fifty-eight rooms. The ruggedness of the country, the choice of location, and the abrupt ending of the episode, all help to give the explanation—the inevitable failure of a small group of farmers to withstand the ceaseless pressure of nomadic raiders. By A.D. 1350, the entire region from the Rim to the Gila and west to the Sierra Ancha had been cleared of Puebloan people, and the Apaches were ready to test the resistance of the settlements to the west.

ABOUT FIFTY MILES WEST of the Canyon Creek cliff-dwelling there was once a large settlement on the west bank of Rye Creek, a tributary of upper Tonto Creek. We excavated the site in 1930, and besides the usual run-of-the-mill pottery and architecture, we found some conditions suggestive of a practice not usually associated with Southwestern peoples.

The Rye Creek Ruin was a large site of over two hundred rooms, built in an arc, with a defense wall joining the ends of the arc to enclose a large court. The central section of the pueblo was at least two stories high. All of the rooms were square or rectangular, with walls of river boulders laid up in mud. There were no indications of circular kivas, and none of the rooms in the main building contained any evidence—either as regards size or accessories—which suggested ceremonial use. On the floor in one of the rooms we found the impression of one of the enormous coiled storage baskets, such as are used today by the Pima, but otherwise there was nothing worthy of note in any of the rooms in the pueblo. Many slab-lined storage cists were scattered around in the plaza, some of them not much bigger than flowerpots.

The pottery was a mixture. There was a good deal of black-on-yellow, apparently identical with that made in the Hopi towns. Gila polychrome was the same as that found in all Salado sites, and there was a large amount of redware, some dull magenta, some polished orange-red. The decorated types were distinct, and neither one showed any signs of having been influenced by the other although both were made on the spot. Counting the redware as Salado, it and the Gila polychrome outnumbered the products from the north, and the Rye

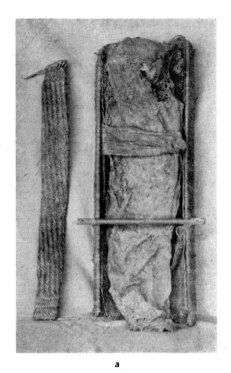

a

b

c

The Canyon Creek Ruin
  a.   A cradle
  b.   One-piece needles and threads of yucca spines
  c.   An old lady's work basket

a

b

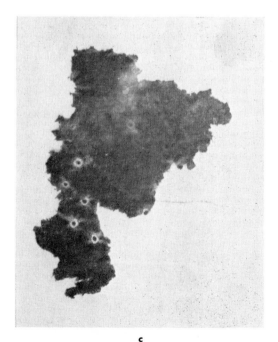

c

The Canyon Creek Ruin
  a. An old lady's cotton blanket
  b. Weft-wrap open work
  c. An example of tie-dying

a

b

The Rye Creek Ruin
   a.   Looking across the site to the Mazatzal Range
   b.   The mound of rooms from the plaza

a

b

The Rye Creek Ruin
   a.   Storage cists
   b.   Sherd-mosaic floor

Creek Ruin can safely be listed as a Salado settlement where some Hopi refugees had sought shelter.

I come now to a queer situation which we uncovered at the south end of the plaza, and I am probably wrong in my suspicions of what it may mean. For the benefit of those who are not familiar with the Southwest, I should begin by drawing attention to the fact that everything that has been said about South-western archaeology up to this point should have made it clear that the Basket Makers, the Hohokam and the various Pueblo tribes were well-mannered, in-dustrious, and peaceable. It is true that one occasionally finds the burial of a body without a head, or a head without a body, but when this happens most of us mutter something about rodents, erosion, or secondary burial, and I know of no references in Southwestern literature to head-hunting, torture, or human sacrifice.

At the south end of the plaza there was a mound about 9 feet high, covered with loose boulders, which, before excavation, we had supposed was merely an extension of living rooms around the southern side of the court. A trench was run in from the court, but it was not until the middle of the mound was reached that we struck a wall—showing that the talus through which we had been trenching represented the debris of a structure which originally had been considerably higher than the present mound. When the face of the wall was cleared, we found that it was actually double—a substantial wall of boulders about 8 feet high, plastered, with another wall of boulders, also plastered, in immediate contact with the inner wall. The queerest feature of this double wall, however, is that it seems to have been built to retain a sort of platform, rather than to bound a room. Unfortunately, the top of the mound had crumbled badly and the east and west sides could not be defined, but instead of a room filled with debris behind the wall, we came upon what looked like a platform of boulders about 5 feet wide, although it is quite possible that it may have been an upper wall which had fallen more or less intact. South of this pavement of rocks, we came to a room, but it was unlike any other room that I have ever seen in a Southwestern ruin. It was 9 feet deep, with sheer, well-plastered walls in which there were no indications of rafter holes or other signs of a floor at the customary level of 6 to 7 feet in a two-story building. The floor had been tamped to a hard flat surface, then a covering of 2 inches of mud had been poured on, and in this mud, while it was still soft, a mosaic of plain sherds had been laid with their edges fitted closely together.

The mound was little more than a heap of mud and boulders. The sides had fallen away, and what was left was poorly defined. The evidence was admittedly vague, and I should probably have passed off the incident as queer but unintelli-gible had it not been that we later found a flint blade about 8 inches long which bore a most suggestive resemblance to the sacrificial knives which were used in Mexico. The knife may have had no connection whatever with the mound, but the combination in the same site of a platform which *may* have been an altar; a deep room with a sherd-mosaic floor which *could* have been a sort of dungeon;

Tonto cliff-dwellings

and a flint blade which *might* have been a sacrificial knife has made me wonder if human sacrifice may not have been practiced at the Rye Creek Ruin. I hope I have been sufficiently vague as not to have brought discredit on my Salado friends. My suspicions are probably ill-founded and probably a more pleasant and satisfying explanation could be advanced.

To THE SOUTH of Rye Creek, and scattered at intervals along Tonto Creek down to its junction with the Salt River at what is now Roosevelt Dam, there are a number of other late Salado sites. These all show the presence of black-on-yellow pottery which appears to be the same as that from the Hopi towns, but also contain a late type of Salado polychrome, which we called Tonto polychrome, on which red, black, and white paints were used to decorate an otherwise red vessel. Architecturally, the sites are pueblos of two stories or more, with courts enclosed by defense walls. None have been dated by tree-rings, but judging by similar ruins to the south which contain the same types of pottery, they lasted up to about the middle of the fourteenth century. The pottery from the two cliff-dwellings which are now included in the Tonto National Monument falls in this same class, and a beam from the upper ruin has given a date of A.D. 1346. This suggests that the Salado occupation of Tonto Basin came to an end at about the same time as the cliff-dwellings in the Sierra Ancha. If this is right— and I think it is—then by A.D. 1400 the Apaches were in control of the entire region from the Rim down to the Gila and west to the Verde.

WHEN THE CIBOLA people decided, in the early twelfth century, to abandon their villages in the upper San Francisco Valley to the Apaches, many of them moved west to Tonto Basin by way of the White and Black rivers which join to form the Salt River. At this same time and as a part of the same exodus, some groups moved into Kinishba and some into Point of Pines, but a considerable number followed the Valley of the Blue southward and settled along the Gila in the open plain from Safford west to the San Carlos Dam. This section of the river, known as the Middle Gila, runs between the Gila Mountains on the north and the Grahams to the south. On his way from Fort Apache to Casa Grande in May, 1883, Adolph Bandelier passed through the valley and mentioned several ruins which he visited. One near Fort Thomas was described as having a large mound, 48 x 43 feet, within an enclosure 74 feet long, which clearly was the same as the ruins in Tonto Basin that I have been calling compounds. About eight miles east of Fort Thomas, Bandelier visited another ruin of the same type and of about the same size. There was also a compound at the point where the Fort Apache road crossed the Gila, near San Carlos, and another about five miles west of San Carlos, both of which belonged in the same class as those already mentioned. The only architectural feature in which these ruins differed from the compounds in Tonto Basin was in having large basins near by which Bandelier regarded as

Middle Gila: prehistoric check dams

tanks. At Fort Thomas the measurements of the basin were given as 190 x 48 feet, and at the site five miles west of San Carlos the basin was said to measure 76 feet across, and was "encased by a rim of stones."

In our survey of the Middle Gila, we found that here, as in Tonto Basin, the ruins represented two periods. The earlier of these two stages was defined by one-story houses inside a compound wall, and black-on-white pottery. The later stage included pueblos of two or more stories standing clear of the surrounding wall, with Gila polychrome as the characteristic type of decorated pottery. But although both stages were typical of the Salado people, we also found that a considerable amount of red-on-buff pottery was present in all of these compounds. I do not know of any pure Hohokam sites along the Middle Gila, and as the local red-on-buff pottery seems to have been later than that of the Colonial Period, it looks as if these Hohokam groups had not arrived until about A.D. 1200, after the villages had been founded. The great basins which Bandelier regarded as tanks can safely be said to have been ball-courts of the same shape and size as those at Snaketown and other Hohokam sites in the Gila Basin.

One other feature of interest was the custom of building a low stone and earth-filled dam across a swale or shallow gulch. Silts washed down from higher ground backed up against the dam and formed a patch of fine friable soil which was ideal for the growing of small crops. We have found that the same practice was followed in the eastern foothills of the Sierra Madre by the people of the *casas grandes* in northwestern Chihuahua. It is interesting to realize that in a few years it will be impossible to distinguish between these prehistoric check-dams and those which have recently been built by the Soil Erosion Service.

At about A.D. 1350, with the fall of the Sierra Ancha cliff-dwellings and the overwhelming of the Salado compounds in Tonto Basin, the Apaches were free to attend to the settlements along the Middle Gila, and for the first time in this southern area, the archaeological record is backed up by the traditions of modern people.

Grenville Goodwin, who made an intimate study of the San Carlos Apache with whom he often lived, has told me some of the tales he learned from the old men. Among these were accounts of the fighting which took place between the San Carlos Apaches and the people who once lived in the now ruined pueblos which stand on Dewey Flat, near Bylas, and at the junction of the San Carlos and the Gila, mentioned by Bandelier. It is the same old story and the same old sequel—Pueblo farmers staying to be killed, or moving away to seek a corner of the world where there were no Apaches. In this case, the Salado survivors, with any who were left of their Hohokam allies, abandoned their farms and pueblos on the Middle Gila and crossed the Galiuro Mountains into the San Pedro Valley.

ASIDE FROM a few Cochise Foragers in the early days of the Southwest, the San Pedro Valley does not seem to have attracted an appreciable number of people

The San Pedro Valley

Ruins and cactus

until well along in the twelfth or early in the thirteenth century. It was at this time, judging by the underlying black-on-white pottery which looks as if it might have been made by a Cibola potter, that the Salado occupation of the valley began—possibly at a site at the mouth of Arivaipa Creek which harks back to early times.

During the fourteenth century, Salado refugees from the country to the north and northeast poured into the San Pedro Valley and built pueblos surrounded by defense walls, leaving us their typical polychromes by which to identify them. Sites of this kind, containing Gila and Tonto polychromes, red-on-buff, and red-on-brown with black polished interiors, have been found on promontories above the river, all the way from Winkelman, at the junction of the San Pedro and the Gila, up to Benson, seventy-five miles to the south.

To ANYONE who has climbed these steep bluffs and visited the sites along the San Pedro, the thing which will always be remembered is the extraordinary growth of cactus. Every ruin is thickly overgrown with tree-cholla, staghorn, and prickly pear, and the slopes and tops of the mesas are literally covered with a carpet of spines which stick to one's shoes and make it difficult to find and pick up sherds. To make things worse, I have never seen so many rattlesnakes and Gila monsters—and, Bandelier to the contrary notwithstanding, a Gila monster is not regarded as harmless in our part of Arizona. Bandelier did not visit the San Pedro, but if he had I am sure that his distaste for southern Arizona would have been even more pronounced than it was.

The pottery and architecture of the San Pedro ruins are sufficiently well known to be able to say that the influx of Salado people into the valley took place during the fourteenth century. It seems, however, that these people may have carried on their fourteenth century brand of culture for quite a long time after A.D. 1400, but for how long it would be hard to say. Some of these villages were still occupied when Father Kino passed through the San Pedro Valley late in the seventeenth century. There is nothing to show, however, that the people originated any new types of pottery or changed their style of architecture after A.D. 1400, and it was probably at about this time that they ceased to make decorated pottery of any kind. Those sites, such as that at Quiburi, which were occupied in Kino's time show only a rather coarse redware mixed with sherds of Spanish glass and china.

The San Pedro joins the Gila at Winkelman, due south of the Pinal Mountains, and the trail we are following now leads north to Gila Pueblo and other Salado strongholds in the foothills of the Pinals.

THE SALADO OCCUPATION of the Pinal district began at about A.D. 1150 when some families from eastern Arizona moved in and settled along Pinal Creek and its tributaries. At this time they were living in one-story clusters of five or six rooms, outlined by rows of stones, with walls of mud which have completely disintegrated. Pottery on the surface of such sites is chiefly plain brown or red, and the small amount of black-on-white has a distinctly eastern look. A site of this kind lies about four hundred yards north of Gila Pueblo; there are three or four more in Six Shooter Canyon, below the Pueblo; and they are scattered at intervals along Pinal Creek all the way down to its junction with the Salt River in Tonto Basin.

This stage was followed, at about A.D. 1250, by small pueblos up to about twenty rooms, with walls of boulders laid up in mud, and small courts enclosed by defense walls. The pottery was brown or red, or black-and-white-on-red polychrome, but black-on-white was no longer made. There is a twenty-room unit two hundred yards south of Gila Pueblo, and another of about fifteen rooms four hundred yards still farther south. There are probably at least twenty such sites in the canyon within two miles of Gila Pueblo.

The last stage began around A.D. 1300 and is marked by the abandonment of the small sites and the concentration of the population in two large pueblos. One of these, known to the San Carlos Apache as Besh-ba-gowah, is situated on the west bank of Pinal Creek, about a mile and a half north of Gila Pueblo. Here there was a progressive increase from a small farming community to a small pueblo, and finally up to a large pueblo of one hundred rooms, with the pottery running the gamut from black-on-white up to late polychrome.

The other was Gila Pueblo, which was a very considerable mound of rocks and dirt when we first saw it in 1928, during the course of our survey. Excavation has uncovered two hundred rooms, and there are still about twenty-five rooms at the south end of the pueblo that have not been touched. In this case, it looks as if construction had not begun until after A.D. 1300. We have never found any black-on-white pottery, and if there ever was the nucleus of a small pueblo, we

Six Shooter Canyon: small early Salado sites near Gila Pueblo

Besh-ba-gowah, one mile north of Gila Pueblo. Excavated and partly restored by the city of Globe.

have not been able to distinguish it from later rooms. The posts in one of the rooms gave us a date of A.D. 1345, and a large pine beam in another room was cut in A.D. 1385, but most of the posts and beams were juniper and therefore useless for dating purposes. All of the rooms were much the same, 12 to 15 feet square.

with walls of boulders and mud, plastered with mud. There was usually a fire-place about the shape and size of a soup plate near the middle of each room, and rooms were sometimes connected by doorways, which in some cases had later been sealed with rocks and mud. We found no indications whatever that any room in the pueblo had been used for ceremonial purposes, and it looks as if the old Saladins of Gila Pueblo had either carried their religion in their heads or had danced and sung their way to glory out of doors.

In several of the rooms we found burials under the floors, but we were unable to detect any difference, as regards age or offerings, between these room-burials and those in the two cemeteries—one to the southeast, the other to the southwest of the pueblo. In the rooms, the floors were packed and smoothed over the graves, and life appears to have gone on as usual. In the cemeteries, the graves were sometimes covered with slabs of mica-schist, and one is apt to jump at the conclusion that this was intended to protect the grave from coyotes or other animals, but I am not at all sure. Some years ago, near Santa Barbara, I found the burial of an old man whose body had been covered by six large milling stones. My first impression was that his relatives had shown unusual reverence and care in tucking him away, but when the milling stones were removed, it turned out that every bone in his body had been smashed. I may be wrong, but I think that the stones were dropped on him to make assurance doubly sure that he would stay where he was planted and not come back to haunt his relatives.

The burial of a man who I think must have been a chief or medicine man was found in one of the small houses south of Gila Pueblo. The grave was over 6 feet deep, which in itself was unusual, as the ground is very hard. The body had been laid flat on its back, and at the knees and also at the shoulders, a pair of notched stones had been driven into the ground at the sides of the grave. Crossbars had then been set in the notches and poles laid lengthwise above the body, making a sort of sarcophagus. Six bowls had been placed in the grave, and although I am sure that these offerings had been made with the best of intentions, it was rather suggestive to find two large lumps of asbestos in one of the bowls.

During the fourteenth century, the Pinal pueblos had served as the western anchor for the line of Salado settlements along the Middle Gila. One by one these villages had been wiped out or abandoned, any possible survivors fleeing west to the Pinals, or southwest to the San Pedro. By about A.D. 1400, all of the country off to the east had been cleared of Salado people, and the Apaches were able to give their undivided attention to Gila Pueblo. Every room shows that it was burned. Bodies were thrown into the rooms at random angles without any pretense of burial, some on their heads, some doubled up, no offerings, covered by the debris of fallen walls and roofs. It is possible, but I am afraid it is mostly wishful thinking, that some of our old friends at Gila Pueblo may have escaped over the shoulder of the Pinals and found refuge in some of the San Pedro pueblos. If they did, their descendants may still be found among the Papago near Tucson, but I do not press the point, other than to tell a story about Jones Williams, a Papago who lived with us at Gila Pueblo.

a

b

Gila Pueblo: The Grave of a VIP
   a.   When this man died it looks as if his relatives took no chances on his
        returning to haunt the Pueblo.
   b.   But they made sure that he was well provided for on his journey.

a

b

Gila Pueblo
  a.   The first room excavated, October, 1928
  b.   Jones Williams and his grandfather

Jones had worked with us in 1927 when we trenched the rubbish mounds at Casa Grande, and as we started to excavate Gila Pueblo in 1928, he turned the first shovelful of dirt. Several years later, Governor Phillips and some friends

Verde Valley: Tuzigoot
(Reproduced through the courtesy of the Southwestern Monuments Association)

visited the Pueblo and after lunch we were standing on top of one of the pottery halls, watching Jones as he was excavating a room below us. The Governor became interested and called down, asking Jones what he was digging up. "My grandfather," said Jones, without cracking a grin, and we like to think that if he had added a few generations, it is just barely possible that he might have been right.

At about A.D. 1350, as Salado resistance in Tonto Basin was breaking down, a few groups of evacuees worked their way westward to the Verde Valley, probably by way of the East Verde and Fossil Creek. The movement does not seem to have involved a large number of people as I do not know of any pure late Salado sites in the valley. The situation is of interest chiefly because the Verde was literally the last ditch for any Puebloan refugees from the east, as the Yuman Yavapai, west of the Verde, strongly objected to any invasion of their domain.

Tuzigoot, at the mouth of Oak Creek, appears to have been one of the last strongholds in the valley. It is a beautiful site, covering the top of a rounded hill and obviously situated for visibility and defense. No tree-ring dates have been obtained, but the black-on-white pottery in some of the early rooms seems to be the same as that at Montezuma's Castle, so it was probably begun at about the same time and by the same people—the southern branch of the Kayenta tribe in which the Red strain predominated. During the twelfth and thirteenth centuries, as smaller outlying sites in the Verde were abandoned, Tuzigoot served as a rallying point until it numbered well over one hundred rooms and at A.D. 1300 was the largest pueblo in the valley. The latest type of decorated pottery was the black-on-yellow which was the handiwork of Hopi potters wherever found. A small amount of Gila polychrome, however, suggests that Tuzigoot had afforded asylum to some Salado refugees after they had left their farms and pueblos in Tonto Basin, across the Mazatzal Range to the east.

Tuzigoot may have lasted until about A.D. 1350, but not much after this date, as none of the later types of Hopi decorated pottery have been found at the site. As conditions deteriorated and the end was approaching, most of the defenders pulled out and moved northeastward to join their compatriots in the Hopi towns, so accounting for the Hopi tradition that some of their clans had come up from the Verde Valley. With this dwindling of the population, a few non-Hopi families—apparently the Salado remnant—sought refuge in Beaver Creek. Here they dug burrows at the base of the lava escarpment, not high enough to permit a man to stand erect, often too short to allow a person to lie at full length, and 1,000 feet or more above the nearest water in the bed of Beaver Creek. When one looks into these shelters, the first impression is that human beings could not have lived in them. But when the pack rats' nests have been cleared away, one

Beaver Creek: a rock-shelter

Beaver Creek, Verde Valley: a refuge site of the fourteenth century

can find sherds of crude redware, sandals, shreds of basketry, and quantities of yucca quids—representing the debris of the daily life of a few individuals clinging to existence on the ragged edge of utter destitution.

On the north side of Beaver Creek, near the top of the talus where it breaks down from the lava escarpment, there are several places where pinnacles of rock rise 50 to 75 feet above the slope. In each case, stones and boulders have been carried up to the top and arranged in piles and rows, to form a sort of combined defense wall and ammunition dump. These crags appear to have been the ultimate refuge for the local troglodytes when danger threatened—a condition which might be said to have been chronic.

We found a bowl of late Salado polychrome in one of these shelters, but it is very doubtful if it was made there. It seems much more probable that it was carried up when the shelters were first occupied. Its chief interest is in showing that the Beaver Creek outcasts were not Hopi, and that the date was not far from A.D. 1350.

FROM THE VERDE VALLEY we are going to follow the old trail down to the Gila Basin where, during the fourteenth century, the Salado people were putting up a desperate but losing fight against the Apaches.

Under the Salado regime, up to about A.D. 1300, projects were undertaken and carried out which established a standard of living that may have been more advanced than anything theretofore known in the Southwest. Pueblos of several stories made their first appearance on the local stage during the thirteenth century, but while I think it proper to speak of these great houses as pueblos, they did not attain their size by accretion, in the hit or miss fashion of most of the large pueblos on the Plateau. The Casa Grande, for example, was symmetrical, built according to a preconceived plan, and its construction demanded a knowledge of engineering which has rarely been claimed or credited to any of the Indian tribes elsewhere in the Southwest. The Salado idea of a compound was retained and each pueblo was surrounded by a high defense wall which could only be scaled by means of ladders. It was also at this time, in the 1200's, that the irrigation systems in the Gila Basin were brought to their peak of development, but while the Hohokam residue may have helped with their labor and technical knowledge, I think that these great projects were conducted under Salado leadership. In fact, it seems highly probable that during the thirteenth century, as the Salado influx increased, there was a steady exodus of Hohokam families down into the Papagueria and northern Sonora. By A.D. 1300, as the Apaches swept westward, it looks as if most, if not all, of the Hohokam population had evacuated the Gila Basin and moved southward, leaving the Salado people to defend their compounds and pueblos. There was certainly a marked decline in the output of red-on-buff pottery and other characteristic Hohokam products, and I do not know of a ball-court which could surely be said to have been built after A.D. 1250.

Soon after A.D. 1300 some Salado groups pulled up stakes and moved down into northwestern Chihuahua where they introduced the idea of building great houses. For those who remained at Casa Grande and other strongholds in the Gila Basin there was safety as long as they could fight behind the protection of their buildings and defense walls. Unfortunately for them, however, they had to till their fields, harvest whatever crops they had been able to save, and haul water, and it was at such times that men were lost and women captured. At Casa Grande the defenders were peculiarly vulnerable, as the compounds were a mile and a half south of the Gila and it would have been simple for a raiding Apache band to destroy a diversion dam or divert an irrigation canal, then ambush the men who would have been compelled to leave the shelter of their compounds to repair the damage. There is no reason to suppose that organized warfare was waged on a large scale, since there was no need for the Apaches to run the risk of defeat. It was rather a relentless strategy of hit and run, a remorseless whittling away of the defenders until they were so reduced in numbers that they were unable to offer effective resistance—then massacre and the torch. It was an episode which took place time and time again in the history of the Southwest, but how long the ordeal lasted at Casa Grande there is no way of knowing. Under such conditions, men were not cutting down trees for us to date their rings, and women were not originating new pottery types for us to compare. With the same kinds of pottery and a tree-ring date of A.D. 1385 at Gila Pueblo, seventy miles to the east, it seems probable that Casa Grande was still functioning as a Salado stronghold at A.D. 1400, but doubtless not much later than A.D. 1450.

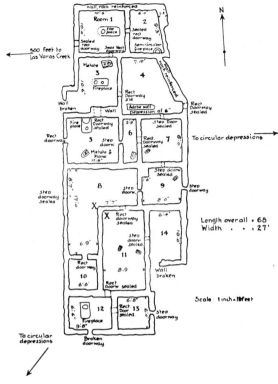

A masonry-walled pueblo in the Babicora district

(From Carey, H. A. 1931)

AT A.D. 1400, below the Rim, sound archaeological evidence becomes increasingly hard to find and in this brillig of uncertainty the slithy toves of pet theories are apt to gyre and gimble in the wabe until they become established dogma and it would take more than a mimsy borogrove to outgrabe them. This is particularly true of Chihuahua where lack of knowledge plus the fact that it was the southernmost cultural province of the Southwest could easily lead to the idea that Chihuahua might also have been a northernmost outpost of Mexico.

There can be no doubt that Mexican influence was present in Chihuahua, but I would qualify this by adding that it was more apparent in early than in late times. In Chapters VII and VIII an outline was drawn of the migration which came up from the south along the Gulf Coast, bringing polished red pottery, a house-type, beans, and the custom of deforming broad skulls. In Chapter X an attempt was made to show how a culture which had developed from this source in southern New Mexico had affected the hunting and foraging groups in central Chihuahua during the eleventh century or later. In Chapter XV the suggestion was made that this small, early, and local culture in the central basin had been absorbed by groups of Salado people moving down from southern Arizona who introduced black-white-and-red polychrome pottery, cliff-dwellings, pueblos with walls of coursed masonry, T-shaped doors, the three-quarter grooved axe,

Casas Grandes, northwestern Chihuahua

(From Bartlett, J. R. 1854)

trough-shaped milling stones, and check-dams—none of which were known in Chihuahua before the Salado people arrived. At the same time, during the thirteenth century, there was a phenomenal increase in population and a shift in the center of density from the open plains of central Chihuahua to the plateaux and canyons in the western section of the state.

Against this background we come now to the last stage—the Casas Grandes culture in northwestern Chihuahua which has made the local archaeology famous. It would be a serious mistake, however, to regard the culture of this period as having been represented throughout Chihuahua. In a state which measured four hundred miles from north to south and over three hundred miles from east to west, the ruins of the Casas Grandes period were clustered in the north-western corner within an area little more than fifty miles square. Furthermore, while the typical pottery has frequently been found as far north as Tonto Basin, the culture was practically unknown in other parts of Chihuahua outside of the Casas Grandes district.

Because of the spectacular quality of the pottery and some of the larger ruins, it is easy to exaggerate their importance and it is well to realize that although this was the only period when great houses were built, it is by no means true that all the buildings of the period were *casas grandes*. The great majority of sites consist of house-groups, sometimes only three or four rooms in a group, with walls of stone and adobe and only one story in height. Pottery shows a greater degree of refinement as regards finish and accuracy of line. Effigy vessels were many and varied, including human figures—mostly women—animals, birds, frogs, fish, and snakes. Designs were drawn with great accuracy—suggesting some Mimbres mothers in the pedigree—and were made up of balanced elements of red and black steps, scrolls, pennons, and fine lines forming mazes and meanders in an endless variety of combinations.

Two features of Casas Grandes pottery—the plumed serpent design and polished blackware—look as if they had come up from Mexico in late times, possibly A.D. 1300 or later. Both are typically Mexican, and as neither one has been reported from Texas or the Mogollon area, it seems probable that they came north through Durango. Both of these traits later found their way up into the upper Rio Grande Valley, but were not accepted by Hopi or Zuni potters.

It has sometimes been said that the idea of effigy vessels, which were so popular among Casas Grandes potters, may also have been diffused northward from Mexico. This is probably true, but I think that the idea harks back to times long before the Casas Grandes period. Carey thought that recumbent pottery figures might indicate a link with Chacmool, the reclining god of Central Mexico, but as he said, the same figures have been found in the Mississippi Valley, so implying traffic along the Gulf Coast rather than direct contact through Durango.

The other types of effigy vessels are just one more legacy from the Salado Culture. Squatting human figures, animal, duck, and bird effigies in red and black-on-white ware have been found in the Salado compounds in Tonto Basin, and also in polychrome at Gila Pueblo and near Casa Grande. Parrot heads in polychrome have turned up in the rooms at Gila Pueblo, and we found one in black-on-yellow at the Rye Creek Ruin. In the Salado redware which was confined principally to Tonto Basin, effigies appeared earlier and their proportion to other vessel shapes was as high, or higher, than in Chihuahua.

The gist of all this is that there were a number of things in the pottery of Chihuahua which looked as if they had come up from Mexico, but with the exception of blackware and the plumed serpent design, each of these features can be traced back to an earlier source in the Mogollon, Mimbres, or Salado Cultures and beyond these to the earlier Red strain which they shared. To this extent the culture of Chihuahua shows affinities with Mexico, but I see little to indicate diffusion from the south during the thirteenth, fourteenth, or fifteenth centuries. With a series of tree-ring dates from A.D. 1362 to 1393 from some of the late cliff-dwellings, it is fairly safe to say that the great houses in northwestern Chihuahua were not built until late in the fourteenth or early in the fifteenth century. It is very doubtful if the period lasted later than about A.D. 1450, and when the curtain fell it must have been suddenly, as there are no signs of deterioration in the pottery, such as one would expect in the event of a long-drawn period of gradual exhaustion. In all probability the Lipan Apache were chiefly responsible for the obliteration of the Casas Grandes people, but the Chiricahua and Mimbreno Apache might also claim some of the credit for introducing their brand of democracy to Chihuahua.

a

b

c

d

e

Casas Grandes
a. Polished redware
b & c. Polished blackware
d. White-slipped polychrome
e. Self-slipped polychrome

Gila Polychrome from Casas Grandes, a typical Salado product

Casas Grandes: local adaptations of Gila Polychrome

MODERN PEOPLES OUT OF ANCIENT CULTURES: A.D. 1300 TO 1450

a

b

c

d

e

f

Casas Grandes
    a & b. **The plumed serpent**   c. A duck
    d.   A parrot head   e. An owl   f. A tattooed human face

Rio Grande Pueblos

Salado Casas Grandes in Northern Chihuahua.

Navajo

Zuni Villages

Apaches.

Hopi Towns

Apaches

Salado Villages

Yuman Foragers.

Hohokam settlements in Northern Sonora.

Yuman Farmers

THE SOUTHWEST AT A.D. 1400

At A.D. 1400, the survivors of the archaeological cultures on the Plateau were grouped in three concentrations—the Hopi Towns at the southern edge of Black Mesa; the Zuni Villages in the Province of Cibola; and the Tanoan and Keresan pueblos in the upper Rio Grande Valley.

To the south, at A.D. 1400, there were also three main concentrations—one in the valley of the San Pedro, chiefly Salado with a few Mogollon and Hohokam remnants; a second in northern Sonora, made up of Hohokam groups which had moved down from the Gila Basin; and a third in northwestern Chihuahua, consisting chiefly of Salado refugees from southern Arizona who had combined with a resident mixture of Reds and Foragers.

To the west were the Yuman tribes, foragers for the most part, but becoming farmers through contact with the Hohokam along the Gila.

Otherwise the Southwest, from the Rio Grande to the Verde, from the Four Corners to the Mexican Border, was in the power of the Navajo and Apache.

Sikyatki polychrome with a design that looks like an airplane propeller

X V I I

Then and There, Here and Now: A.D. 1450 to Today

IT WOULD BE natural to expect that, having brought this story of the Southwest up to A.D. 1450, we could carry the remainder of the tale up to the present day with a detailed account of the last five hundred years, for most of which the records of Spanish historians are available. There are several reasons, however, why this cannot be done, or to be more accurate, why I am not the man to do it.

The first and foremost of these reasons is that this version of the archaeology of the Southwest has been mainly an attempt to translate the architecture, pottery, stones, and bones that have been uncovered into something resembling a history of the peoples who left these things behind them. My ideas of what these things may mean in terms of human history may be all wrong, in which case it will only be necessary for someone else to take the same sticks and stones, pots and bones, and show wherein I have been mistaken, but the evidence itself will not change. Strange as it may seem, however, there is very little archaeological evidence to cover the years since A.D. 1400 in the Southwest.

In the upper Rio Grande Valley, the glaze-paint wares showed a marked deterioration after Spanish contact, both as regards accuracy of line and control of the lead glaze. To the west, this was partly offset by some of the Hopi polychromes, although, to my mind, the designs are too complicated and confused to compare favorably with their prehistoric pottery. We have one of these Hopi jars at Gila Pueblo which was made in Sikyatki at about A.D. 1600 and comes nearer to a duplicate independent invention than anything else I have ever seen. The woman who decorated this pot had come far enough along in aerodynamics to be able to draw a perfect reproduction of an aeroplane propeller, but unfortunately the rest of the machine appears to have been too much for her.

Otherwise I do not know of anything which an archaeologist might regard as significant, and I suspect that one reason for this may be that several of the best-known pueblos—such as Acoma, Zuni, Walpi, and Oraibi—have been occupied continuously since before the days of the Spaniards. Distrust of Europeans is therefore still latent, and the people show an unscientific lack of cooperation in their refusal to surrender their clothes and household effects, or to permit archaeologists to dig up their relatives and take their houses apart.

From a strictly archaeological standpoint, there is another factor which I think has been largely responsible for much of the uncertainty since the eleventh century when the arrival of the Athabascans changed the course of Southwestern development. Prior to about A.D. 1000, there was a period when small houses of from two to five rooms were the rule, and these houses were of such a size and spaced far enough apart as to leave no doubt that life in the Southwest during this period revolved around the family as a unit. In the course of our survey we have found hundreds of such sites in all sections of the Southwest—from Mesa Verde to the Gila and from the Rio Grande to the Verde. Wherever excavations have been made, it has been found that each unit was complete and self-contained; that the dead were carefully buried, usually in the loose soil of adjacent rubbish mounds where it was easy to dig the graves; that implements and pots containing food were placed beside the body to accompany the departing spirit on its long journey to the Happy Hunting Grounds. In such cases one can connect a specific type of pottery with a certain kind of architecture, and can then relate not only the pottery and architecture but also the household paraphernalia to the physical type of the individuals in the graves. Any tree-ring dates that may be obtained can be applied to this particular unit. It was all wrapped up in one package, so to speak, and the discovery of the same kinds of evidence in site after site within a given area established a definite model which was of the utmost value when it came to building cultural sequences and drawing comparisons between conditions in different areas.

Soon after A.D. 1000, however, these burial customs began to change, first in Chaco Cayon, and later, on Mesa Verde and in Marsh Pass. As Kidder has said,

> One of the many mysteries of the Chaco is the fact that in spite of persistent search the cemeteries of the large ruins have never been found. The burial mounds of the smaller and apparently earlier sites are obvious and can easily be located; but the rubbish-heaps of Bonito, Chettro Kettle, and the other great communities contain no graves whatever. Although a few bodies have been taken from rooms, these do not represent a hundredth part of the number of individuals that must have died during the occupancy of the towns. There is no hint of cremation, and so one can only suppose that the Chacones differed from all other Pueblos of

whom we have knowledge in that they buried their dead at a distance from their houses. When the cemeteries are eventually discovered, they should yield a marvellously rich harvest of pottery, ornaments, and utensils.

Since 1924, when this was written, the only change which needs to be made is that there is no longer any reason for supposing that the Chacones were different from the other Pueblos, since the same blanks have been drawn in the great cliff-dwellings on Mesa Verde, in Marsh Pass, and the large open sites of the thirteenth and fourteenth centuries. I do not share Kidder's anticipation that these cemeteries will eventually be found, as I think that when the Pueblos began crowding together in their large communities they abandoned their ancient burial practices, being more concerned with affording protection to the living than in showing respect to the dead. Lacking purposeful burials, I think it is reasonable to suppose that bodies of the dead were carried outside the walls of the pueblo to be disposed of by natural agencies—decomposition, sun, wind, and rain—and it was only occasionally that bodies of prominent people were buried in rooms, a practice which was unknown before A.D. 1000. Regardless of whether this supposition is right or wrong, the fact remains that burials accompanied by pottery or other offerings became increasingly rare after A.D. 1000, and cultural interpretations and reconstructions by archaeologists became correspondingly less dependable. Here, again, I believe that the cause of the crowding and of the change in burial customs can be traced directly to the upheavals which resulted from the arrival of the Athabascan nomads—in Chaco Canyon in the eleventh, and in the Mesa Verde and Marsh Pass districts during the twelfth and thirteenth centuries.

ENTIRELY ASIDE from the dearth of archaeological knowledge for the centuries following A.D. 1400, which in itself is sufficient reason for an archaeologist to be wary of trespassing in this field, it seems to me that, in spite of having been in contact with Spaniards for three hundred and with Americans for one hundred years, there has been surprisingly little change amongst the Pueblos during the last five hundred years. Since A.D. 1400, the location of the three main Pueblo concentrations in the Hopi towns, the Zuni villages, and the upper Rio Grande pueblos, has shown no significant change.

A few shifts have occurred, as when a band of Tanoan (Tewas) left the Rio Grande Valley and moved west to the Hopi towns where they founded Hano, on First Mesa, in A.D. 1696. (In fact, it was a Tanoan woman, Nampeyo, who strongly influenced Hopi pottery making in 1897 when she copied the designs on the pots which Dr. Fewkes was excavating from the ruins of Sikyatki, a seventeenth century pueblo on the side of the mesa below Hano.) Another shift took place in A.D. 1838 when, in the face of persistent Comanche raids from the east, the surviving remnant of Pecos Pueblo gave up the fight and joined their kindred in Jemez, west of the Rio Grande. These movements, while certainly important to the people concerned, had little more than temporary local effects on the development of the culture and history of the Pueblos. Their architecture, both as regards living quarters and kivas, is practically the same as it was at A.D. 1400, and their ceremonies and social organization give the appearance of having come down to the present day without much, if any, change from the remote past. Some of the people undoubtedly became true converts to Catholicism. Others played both ends against the middle and were good Christians when it suited them, but otherwise remained good pagans. It is typical of the Pueblo character that with Franciscan missionaries living in the midst of their communities, they have retained their ancient customs and ceremonies to the extent that, even today, their old rites still survive, as in the Shalako Festival at Zuni, the Snake Dance at Walpi, and the strange mixture of pagan and Christian ritual in the Corn Dance at Santo Domingo in the Rio Grande Valley.

From all of this, I think it is clear that although the wanderings of Cabeza de Vaca, the journey of Marcos de Niza, and the expedition of Coronado were important events in the *Spanish* history of the Southwest, they had little or no effect on the cultural or social development of the various Indian tribes with whom the Spaniards came in contact. We know the names and pedigrees of the Spanish conquistadores, and have been told where they went, what they wore, what they said, and what they did, but there is surprisingly little information about what the Indians were making and doing during the sixteenth, seventeenth, and eighteenth centuries. To one concerned with local history, the Spanish invasion—or conquest, as it is often called—was chiefly of interest because of the insight it gives into the character of the two peoples. On the one hand, we are told of the trust and generosity which the Indians of Sonora extended to Marcos de Niza; of the supplies and provisions obtained by Coronado at Culiacan; and of the drum and fife band which welcomed Alvarado on his first visit to Pecos— and incidentally, where did the Pecans get their drums? None have ever been found in any prehistoric site in the Southwest. On the other hand, we read in Castañeda, the historian of the Coronado Expedition, of food that was seized by the Spaniards; of the ultimatum followed by the storming of Hawikuh; of the Pueblo people at Bernalillo turned out of house and home to provide quarters for Coronado's army; of the confiscation of their clothes; the violation of promises; holding hostages in chains; and the burning alive of two hundred captives who had surrendered under a guarantee of pardon.

Confronted by men in armor who were equipped with swords, halberds, harquebuses, and cannon, and who were mounted on creatures they had never seen before, the Pueblos met the attacks of their more powerful opponents with interesting strategy. At Hawikuh, the Zunis put up a stiff fight and almost succeeded in killing Coronado, but as soon as they realized that they could not prevail against Spanish arms and armor, they withdrew to their inaccessible refuge on top of Toyollani and refused all pleas to return to their pueblos until after Coronado had left to spend the winter in the Rio Grande Valley. With the departure of the Spaniards in their search for gold, the Zunis returned to their homes, and life in their pueblos was resumed in the same way as before the invasion—from which it would seem that the policy of nonresistance did not originate with Mahatma Gandhi.

WHAT HAS BEEN SAID applies to the Pueblos on the Plateau. Below the Rim even less is known, chiefly because the Apaches had left very few people to tell their tale. Following upon the fall of Casa Grande, early in the fifteenth century, the archaeological record is a complete blank and is of no value in helping to confirm the Spanish accounts which themselves were usually confused and often inaccurate. Sometimes these accounts were written by men who were actually eyewitnesses of the events they described, but allowed a considerable time to elapse between the event and the writing of the description—as in the case of Castañeda who waited for twenty years before writing his narrative of the Coronado Expedition. Sometimes the cause of confusion was due to faulty translation—as has been charged in regard to the Ternaux version of Castañeda's narrative. And sometimes the narrator has been baldly accused, both by his contemporaries and by modern students, of having been a plain unadulterated liar.

Under such circumstances, one hesitates to put much faith in unsupported accounts, particularly when it is realized that the men who took part in these events were exploring lands which were entirely unknown to them, and their descriptions of the route they followed are often impossible to identify with modern landmarks. When Coronado led his expedition through southern Arizona in A.D. 1540, he passed no occupied pueblos after leaving Sonora until he reached Hawikuh. By that time the large White Mountain communities at Kinishba and Point of Pines had been in ruins for a hundred years or more. Casa Grande, Gila Pueblo, and the other late Salado pueblos in Tonto Basin, the Gila Basin, and along the Middle Gila had long since been sacked and their defenders massacred or dispersed, and it is consequently impossible to reconcile the conflicting statements in the Spanish accounts with definite peoples or places.

While this is true of the Spanish exploration of southern Arizona during the sixteenth century, the next hundred years brought important changes. During the early part of the seventeenth century the Jesuits were pushing northward through Sonora and by A.D. 1650 they had reached the Pimas along the border of Arizona. In 1687, Father Eusebio Kino, one of the most famous Jesuits of the Order in New Spain, founded the mission of Dolores, near Magdalena in northern Sonora, and during the next twenty-five years this served as the base for his many expeditions into southern Arizona. With the advent of Father Kino, the confusion of earlier accounts was clarified. His descriptions were clear. Many of the names he gave to various places are still in use. For the first time, we are given locations of specific tribes and also some descriptions of their ways of life.

Along the border were the Pimas, raising cotton, corn, beans, and squash by means of irrigation—which helps to identify the Pima as the descendants of those Hohokam who moved southward from the Gila Basin in the thirteenth and fourteenth century. North of the border, in what is now the Papagueria, were the Papago, also of Piman stock, living chiefly on beans which were grown by irrigation. To the northwest were the Yuman Maricopa along the lower reaches of the Gila, practicing agriculture, but without irrigation—which is all as it should be since the Yuman tribes were not related to the Hohokam. On the lower Colorado, there were Yumas and Cocopas—also Yuman, also agricultural, and also without irrigation. And to the northeast, in the valley of the San Pedro, were the Sobaipuri, a branch of the Piman Papago family, who seem to have possessed the rare faculty of knowing how to deal with the Apaches.

Father Kino first visited the Sobaipuri in September, 1692, when he reached the San Pedro where Benson now stands and followed the valley southward for about fifteen miles to the village of Quiburi, near modern Fairbank. Here, according to Kino in Bolton's *Rim of Christendom* was the "principal and great rancheria; for it has more than four hundred souls assembled together, and a fortification or earthen enclosure, since it is on the frontier of the hostile Hocomes"—from which it is interesting to learn that some three hundred years after the fall of Casa Grande, the Sobaipuri were still using compounds as a defense against the (Hocome) Apaches. There is more to this, however, than the mere mention of compounds.

Upon reading these accounts in the *Rim of Christendom*, we at once set out to retrace Bolton's tracing of Kino's expedition to the Sobaipuri villages in the San Pedro Valley. With Bolton's descriptions to guide us, we visited each of the sites that had been mentioned and made collections of sherds. We found, as Kino had said, that the villages were numerous, fairly close to one another, but not particularly large, being rarely over fifty rooms or houses in size. The surface evidence showed houses, pueblos, and compounds which appeared to be the same as those at other Salado sites of the fourteenth century in Tonto Basin and along the Middle Gila. Decorated pottery was scarce, but there was enough of it to show the same types of polished red-on-brown and black-white-and-red polychromes as those at Gila Pueblo, Casa Grande, and other late Salado ruins. The only difference which we were able to detect was that there was a marked increase in the amount of redware, which was thicker and coarser than that usually associated with Salado polychromes of the fourteenth century. At the ruins of the *presidio* at Quiburi, this crude redware was the only kind of pottery we could find, and in this case, it was associated with fragments of glass and crockery.

On the strength of this evidence, it seems fair to assume that the Sobaipuri who were living in the San Pedro compounds at the end of the seventeenth century were probably the direct descendants of the people who had occupied the valley during the fourteenth century. This would agree with the distinctions between Salado and Hohokam which have been drawn in preceding chapters, and makes it seem probable that the Sobaipuri were ex-Salado and that the Pima were ex-Hohokam. It might also be added that this would afford an explanation for the difficulty which Russell encountered in his study of the Pimas when they denied that they knew anything about "the builders of the great stone and adobe pueblos that now lie in ruins on the mesas of the Gila and Salt River Valleys." If I am right, it was the Salado-Sobaipuri who built the great pueblos and compounds, and the Hohokam-Pima neither shared in their construction nor lived in them, as at all times they preferred their own single unit family houses.

THIS, I think, is about as far as an archaeologist should venture, and the rest of the tale belongs to the ethnologists and students of modern history. It may simplify their problems if I end up this prehistoric section of the story of the Southwest with a brief summary.

X V I I I

Summing Up

IT IS ALWAYS fairly easy for an imaginative individual to coin theories which may be difficult for more serious-minded specialists to disprove. You may think it is all perfect nonsense—as I do—but you would find it hard to prove that the fabled continent of Atlantis was not the cradle of native American civilizations; that American Indians were not one of the lost tribes of Israel; or that American Indians did not duplicate some of the Old World cultures by independently inventing anything they wanted, whenever and wherever they felt like it. So, as I have launched a number of new ideas in this book, I think that this is probably a good time for me to insert the alibi which the bankers use when they have bonds to sell: "Nothing is guaranteed, but this prospectus is based on information which we believe to be reliable."

TURNING BACK to the beginning, we find a distinct possibility that men may have been in North America for a much longer time than is generally believed, or for which there is any convincing evidence. Taking everything into consideration—lowered sea level to facilitate human movements, association with extinct fauna, character of stone tools, hyper-long skulls, geographical location south of the ice-sheet, and the need for more time to develop the foundations of agriculture—it may be that the earliest men came over from Asia during the last Interglacial, at about the same time that some of the islands in the southwestern Pacific were also being populated. But regardless of the exact time when these early migrations came over from Asia, upon reaching North America they moved south, well below the southernmost limits of the ice-sheet, and as hunters and foragers, they settled in the zone lying between the coast of southern California and the Gulf Coast of Texas.

It is out of these early foragers and hunters of the Stone Age in California, Arizona, New Mexico, and Texas that the beginnings of Southwestern history must be sought—Basket Makers in the Four Corners, Foragers in southeastern Arizona, and Cave Dwellers in southwestern New Mexico and western Texas, all linked together by similarities of stone tools, perishable culture, and physical type.

At about A.D. 200, a migration of people whom I have called the Farmers reached the northern frontier of the Southwest and established contact with the Basket Makers. They settled first around Durango, in southwestern Colorado, and it was from these early Farmer colonies that the Basket Makers in southeastern Utah and northeastern Arizona acquired their knowledge of 18-row corn, pottery, housebuilding, slab-lined storage cists, and a number of other traits which heretofore have been credited to Basket Maker origins—due to the unfortunate custom of regarding the Farmers, north of the San Juan, as having belonged to the same stock and as possessing the same culture as the Basket Makers, south of the river. The Farmer's house-type points to a comparatively recent exodus from northeastern Asia, and their possession of 18-row corn suggests that their migration had moved down through the western plains. Few, if any, of the traits which the Basket Makers acquired from the Farmers were shared by the Foragers of southeastern Arizona or the Cave Dwellers of the Upper Gila and western Texas, so denying any claim that the Farmers had come up from the south.

For five centuries, from A.D. 200 to 700, the Farmers throve in the neighborhood of Durango, and their population showed a great and rapid increase, probably augmented by continuing immigration. Large villages of several hundred rooms were built, consisting of long rows of surface contiguous rectangular rooms, served by subterranean kivas with all of the appropriate accessories. The arrangement of storage, living, and ceremonial space indicates a cooperative society foreshadowing the Pueblo social organization, and the uniform style of dwelling, together with the absence of larger or more elaborate quarters, implies that there was no privileged class or inherited authority.

During this same period of five hundred years, the Basket Makers in northeastern Arizona progressed to the point where, by about A.D. 450, true fired pottery was being made and a house was built in Obelisk Cave. By A.D. 600, several houses had been built in Broken Flute and other caves in Red Rock Valley, but in each case, the houses and storage cists were built as separate individual structures; there were no ventilating systems; no signs of a kiva; and it seems that Basket Maker life at this time revolved around the family as a unit. Since several of the caves were occupied by only one family, and as none of them were large enough to shelter a large number of people, it is probable that the Basket Maker population as a whole was considerably smaller than has generally been supposed.

At about A.D. 700, the Farmers began moving out of the Durango area, some down to the La Plata Valley, others west to Mesa Verde and Montezuma Valley, and beyond, to Alkali Ridge in southeastern Utah. But neither at this nor at any later time, until after A.D. 1200, are there any indications that any group of Farmers settled south of the San Juan. As Farmers, and later when they came to be known as Mesa Verde people, their pottery and architecture were distinct and remained distinct from that of any other Southwestern culture.

As the Farmers moved down into the La Plata Valley and spread westward to the mesas bordering the north side of the San Juan at about A.D. 700, the Basket Makers abandoned their caves in northeastern Arizona and drifted southward along the eastern and western foothills of the Chuska Mountains. On the eastern side their progress is marked by the village of Shabik'eschee in Chaco Canyon, with dates which fall at about A.D. 775, and a series of unexcavated Basket Maker sites reaching from Mitten Rock down to Tohatchi. On the western flank of the Chuskas, Basket Maker sites dating in the eighth century have been found around Chinlee, the Jeddito Wash, Ganado, and on the Rio Puerco at White Mound and Whitewater. Some Basket Maker groups or families worked their way down to the Petrified Forest; some as far south as Forestdale, on the Mogollon Rim; and some as far west as Flagstaff, where their pottery has turned up in the Cinder Basin site; and traces of their influence can be seen in the form of architecture at the Baker Ranch, north of Flagstaff, and in pottery designs in the Verde Valley.

THE SOUTHERN SECTION of the Southwest, to which we turn now, had been occupied for several thousand years by Foragers in southeastern Arizona and Cave Dwellers in the Upper Gila reaching eastward into western Texas. At a time which may have begun at about A.D. 500, but which lasted until about A.D. 700, a series of new traits began to appear in an otherwise primitive Stone Age culture—first, corn of an 8-row variety, followed successively by kidney beans, a circular tipi-type of house, undercut storage pits, polished red and brown pottery, slip, mineral paint and rectilinear designs on decorated pottery, and pottery baked in an oxidizing atmosphere—no one of which had been known in the Southwest before the arrival of this migration. Whereas the physical type of the Foragers and Cave Dwellers had been long-headed, in conformity with the basic underlying long-headed stock which originally stretched from California to Texas, the skulls of the people who were introducing these traits were broad, low-vaulted, and deformed by artificial flattening.

I have called the people of this incoming migration the "Reds," after the color of their pottery, and they appear to have come up from Mexico along the east coast, as suggested by their distribution and the fact that many of the distinctive features of their culture have also been found in Mexico. Upon reaching the mouth of the Rio Grande, some swung eastward into Texas, to share in forming the Caddoan tribes; others followed the valley of the Rio Grande and so entered the Southwest. What appear to be the earliest indications of their arrival are the 8-row corn and kidney beans in the Bat Cave in the Upper Gila, prior to A.D. 500. Circular houses, undercut storage pits, and the agriculture which these imply, reached the Foragers in the San Pedro Valley during the 500's. As the Red migration swelled in size during the 600's, some of their groups moved in on the Foragers of southeastern Arizona, as at the Cave Creek village, the combination resulting in the formation of the Mogollon Culture. Settlements were established at the San Simon village; in the Mimbres Valley at the Harris and Cameron Creek villages; and in the San Francisco Valley, beginning in the south at the Mogollon village and spreading north up to the S. U., Starkweather, and Luna villages—all Mogollon—all founded in the early 700's.

Other Red bands moved westward along the Gila, turning northward to the Plateau as opportunity offered. Some worked their way up the San Carlos drainage and through Tonto Basin to the canyons which head under the Mogollon Rim, as at the Bluff Site, near Forestdale, in Pleasant Valley, and around Payson. Others penetrated as far west as Snaketown, and many used the Verde Valley as a means of access to the Plateau. From the San Francisco Valley in the east to the Verde Valley in the west, the Reds swarmed up every canyon and valley which led up to the Rim and so to the Plateau. Wherever they went they left their trail of polished redware, rectilinear designs, and broad deformed skulls—not a trace of which had been known in any section of the Southwest before the Reds made their first appearance, so that whenever and wherever these things are found it is a sure sign that Reds have been there.

As the Red bands fanned out around the southern border of the basin of the Little Colorado, they met Basket Makers coming down from the north. The mixture of Reds and Basket Makers, in varying proportions, has been found along the Mogollon Rim at the Bluff and Bear ruins, near Flagstaff at the Cinder Basin and Baker Ranch sites, in the Petrified Forest, on the Rio Puerco, in the Jeddito drainage, and up through Marsh Pass as Pueblo I. Their designs, mineral paint, slip, oxidized red pottery, and broad deformed skulls crossed the San Juan, reaching Alkali Ridge in the late 700's; and actually spread east as far as the southern La Plata towns before dying out. To the west, redware, slip, and broad-line rectilinear designs indicate the passage of Reds through Yuman territory up the Verde, east and west of the San Francisco Peaks to the Grand Canyon, west to Nevada, and east to Marsh Pass, to overlie Pueblo I and so give the impression of cultural continuity. As a broad generality, it may be said of all sites showing a mixture of Reds and Basket Makers that the farther south, the greater the Red component, the farther north, the heavier the Basket Maker representation; but during the eighth century, while the mixtures were occurring, no two sites were exactly the same either in regard to pottery or architecture.

ALSO IN SOUTHERN ARIZONA, and beginning early in the eighth century, another migration of an entirely different kind entered and settled in the Gila Basin. This was made up of the people known as the Hohokam, who brought with them a remarkably advanced culture based on canal irrigation. Judging by their great ball-courts, copper bells, mosaic plaques, etched shell, tripod trays, and modelled clay figurines, it seems reasonably certain that the homeland of the Hohokam was somewhere in Mexico, or possibly even farther south. From the fact that they settled in the Gila Basin, it seems probable that they reached southern Arizona by way of the west coast of Mexico, although no traces of their passage have yet been found. It has been suggested above that at the time of leaving their former home, the culture of the Hohokam was already so specialized that it required certain essential conditions for its proper functioning, such as running water, a low gradient, and flat arable land. Failing to find such conditions along the west coast, the migration continued northward until the Gila was reached, so accounting for the lack of pottery and other indications of semipermanent stations along their route. Regardless of how they came, once arrived, the Hohokam were unusually self-sufficient and self-contained. They established temporary colonies in the Verde Valley and as far east as Tonto Basin, and relations were maintained with the people around Flagstaff to the north and the Mogollon villages to the east, as shown by cross-finds of pottery. The idea of their great lodges was adopted by the Mogollon villagers in the 700's, and their ball-courts have shown up in the San Simon village, on the Middle Gila, in the Verde Valley, and around Flagstaff in the tenth and eleventh centuries. Otherwise there are no indications of any exchange of cultural traits or influence between the Hohokam and the peoples on the Plateau until after A.D. 1100, when the Salado people began to arrive in the Gila Basin. It is strange and probably significant that in a Southwest in which people were so dependent upon agriculture, the canal irrigation of the Hohokam was never adopted by the Pueblo tribes, since it implies that the conditions necessary for its successful practice were restricted to the Gila Basin.

I think there can be little doubt that the social organization of the Hohokam differed in certain respects from that of the Pueblos. They lived in single separate one-family houses, grouped in more or less compact settlements, but it would seem that the immense amount of labor involved in digging many miles of irrigation canals, in excavating their ball-courts, and in building their great lodges would necessitate some sort of central authority to plan and direct such undertakings. Maybe the great lodges were the Pentagons of those days, but if so, we shall never know whether the offices were filled by men who inherited their jobs or were selected by the proletariat.

DURING THE NINTH CENTURY the Southwest was shaking down into the patterns with which most archaeologists are familiar. North of the San Juan the Farmers were becoming the Mesa Verde people, and it is rather peculiar that from large compact villages of several hundred contiguous rooms which embodied the idea of a pueblo, they began to turn to small separate units of a few rooms and a kiva. It is possible that this trend was influenced by the people of other cultures, since it was at this time that the rest of the Southwest was going through what might be called its Small House Period. In the Marsh Pass, Chaco, Cibola, Mogollon, and Flagstaff areas, everyone was living in small one-family houses of from one to five rooms, sometimes in pit-houses, as in the Mogollon and Flagstaff districts, or with a pit-house near by, as in Marsh Pass and the Red Mesa Valley. In southwestern New Mexico, the Mimbres and Cibola Branches were beginning to attain distinction as northern influence increased in the Mogollon villages and modified the local culture. In Marsh Pass, the Kayenta Branch was beginning to form out of an ancestry that was chiefly Basket Maker, but with a strong Red strain which seems to have been largely responsible both for the excellence of Kayenta pottery and also for some rather queer ideas as to how kivas should be built. Nevertheless, although these ideas may have been unorthodox, it is worth noting that the Kayenta people were the only descendants of the Basket Makers who had sense enough to take advantage of the shelter afforded by a cave to protect their flimsy huts. They and their Basket Maker ancestors were actually the earliest Cliff Dwellers—a title which was not earned by the Mesa Verde people until the eleventh century, and never by the Chaco.

The oustanding feature of this period, from the middle 800's to the late 900's, is that all of the various peoples of the Southwest—with the possible exception of the Hohokam—were conducting their lives under a system of private enterprise in which each family built its house of a size and in a way to suit its own convenience, in a location of its own choosing, and that these decisions were not prompted by any fear of interference by neighbors or foreign enemies. Although these small house sites have been found throughout the Southwest in all cultures and can be counted in the hundreds, I do not know of a single instance which could definitely be said to indicate that the character of the building or the choice of its setting had been governed by a desire for defense. In the light of their earlier community villages and their later development of Puebloan architecture, it would not be surprising if some of the Mesa Verde people, at this time, built houses to accommodate more than one family, but with this possible exception, I think it doubtful if there were any dwellings in any section of the Southwest at A.D. 900 which could properly be claimed to be a pueblo. Furthermore, I think it is significant that at A.D. 900 there do not appear to have been any great kivas in the Kayenta, Chaco, Cibola, or Flagstaff districts. In fact, it is by no means certain that the pit-houses which were situated near the small surface houses in these areas were necessarily used for ceremonial purposes. In a climate where winter temperatures often dropped below zero, it is very strange that fireplaces are rarely to be found in the surface rooms, if they were used for year-round dwellings, and it may be that the pit-houses with their ventilating and heating systems served as winter quarters.

In other words, the independence of individual families and the apparent lack of ceremonial structures in the central sections of the Southwest during the early 900's imply an unusual degree of confidence, and suggest that one small section of humanity may have temporarily earned the most unattainable of the Four Freedoms—freedom from fear.

THE INDIVIDUAL FAMILY retained its importance as a social unit throughout the Southwest during most of the tenth century, and it is remarkable that although these families were often scattered over wide areas, each unit conformed to some one of eight different cultures which were uniform within their respective ranges, but distinct from one another. In the 700's, the Farmers north of the San Juan and the Hohokam in the Gila Basin were the only two peoples who possessed distinct and homogeneous cultures. Between these northern and southern extremes, all else was in a state of flux, with no two sites exactly alike, and there were often striking differences between adjacent and contemporaneous sites, as at White Mound and Whitewater. During the two hundred years which followed, the four peoples who made up the population of the Southwest—Farmers, Basket Makers, Reds, and Hohokam—had settled down into eight distinct groups or cultures, and by A.D. 950 there is rarely any difficulty in identifying the products of each group, even when found in sites of other cultures.

The Mesa Verde potters were turning out good black-on-white ware, but had abandoned the making of redware in any form. The architects and masons were good, particularly in heavy construction, and were the kiva-specialists of the Southwest.

In the Chaco Branch, the potters were accurate in drawing their hatched designs, but the pottery itself was only fair. The masons, however, were very good and were beginning to show flashes of the genius that later made them famous.

The Kayenta potters were among the best, if not the best, in the Southwest and excelled in their black-on-white, black-on-red, and polychrome. But the masons were no better than second rate, as they were not skillful in shaping stone and relied too much on mud to fill the interstices in their walls. No two of their architects could agree on how to build a kiva.

In the Cibola Branch, in the upper San Francisco Valley, the women were beginning to specialize in their corrugated and indented brownware, in which they were in a class by themselves. They had also started to decorate their black-on-white and black-on-red wares with balanced designs in which solid and hatched elements were opposed. The men were having trouble with chunks of lava as building material and cannot be blamed for the poor quality of their construction, and there were too many Red cells in their blood for them to be able to design and build a real kiva.

Mimbres women monopolized most of the fame of their culture with their accuracy of line and the complicated patterns on their black-on-white ware.

Although their grandmothers had been Mogollon, their mothers must have come
down from the north, as they baked their pottery in a reducing atmosphere, and
the nearest they ever came to a red was when their black-on-white bowls were
overfired. It is rather peculiar that the Cibola potters favored decorated jars and
plain brown bowls, while in the Mimbres, near by, the bowls were decorated
and the jars were brownware. Mimbres men suffered from the same handicaps
as the Cibola masons, and I doubt if they ever succeeded in building a two-story
house, and they never built what a Mesa Verde man would recognize as a kiva.

By A.D. 950, the Mogollon people were showing a marked decline in numbers, due to the fact that most of their children had chosen to marry Cibola or
Mimbres husbands or wives. The remaining Mogollon women were still turning
out polished redware and a small amount of red-on-brown decorated pottery.
Mogollon men had been persuaded to adopt the Hohokam type of house, and
at the San Simon village they had even started to build a ball-court—possibly
as an inducement for their sons to stay at home.

The Hohokam, as at all times, were paying strict attention to their own
affairs. It may be significant that their culture showed no improvement or elaboration over the years—in fact, in some ways, it declined—which suggests that
they lacked the stimulation of their old contacts in Mexico, or wherever it was
they came from.

The Salado Branch hardly qualifies as a full-fledged culture at A.D. 950, but
I include it, as someone below the Rim was making a great deal of redware which
does not fit anywhere else and it later was incorporated in the list of Salado
pottery types.

These are the eight cultures in the Southwest which had crystallized by
about A.D. 950. There were one or two crossroads, such as Flagstaff, and one or
two arteries, such as the Verde and the Puerco, where conditions were somewhat confused, but otherwise I am sure that anyone who is at all familiar with
the Southwest would have no trouble in identifying, say, a Mimbres sherd if it
should be picked up in a site of any of the other seven cultures. I am equally
sure that a Chaco site in the Red Mesa Valley would show the same homemade
pottery and the same style of architecture as in a contemporaneous Chaco site
fifty miles or more to the north or twenty-five miles to the east or west. It is for
this reason that I have emphasized above the intra-cultural uniformity and the
inter-cultural diversity of these eight groups of people.

TOWARD THE END of the tenth century, the first rumblings of the approaching
storm were heard when the vanguard of the Athabascan invasion reached the
Southwest. The people around Mount Taylor and west through the Red Mesa
Valley were among the earliest to show that they realized the gravity of this
menace when they abandoned the entire area and moved northward along the
eastern side of the Chuskas. One-family houses ceased to be built, and the people
assembled in small pueblos of twenty to thirty rooms with three or four kivas,

suggesting a gathering of the clans. It was at this time, about A.D. 1000, that Chaco Canyon received a large influx of people, and it was in the course of building the Talus Pueblos along the south side of the canyon that most of the trees within carrying distance were cut down to provide posts and beams—so starting an erosion problem which later was to add to their troubles.

As the Athabascan horde increased in numbers and poured into the area west of the Jemez Mountains, it split, and some bands who were to become the Navajo turned to the west, attracted by the prosperous and exposed settlements in Chaco Canyon and on Mesa Verde. The remainder, later to be known as Apaches, continued south to the Upper Gila, to raid the Mimbres, Cibola, and Mogollon villages.

On Mesa Verde, soon after A.D. 1000, the people began their cliff-dwelling period with the construction of Mug, Bone Awl, and Spruce Tree houses—all obviously built with an eye to defense—and the small unit-type pueblos were enlarged or combined.

Farther south, in the Mimbres, small isolated houses were replaced by large aggregations of rooms, as at the Swarts, Cameron Creek, and Mattocks sites, and the outlying farms were abandoned.

In the upper San Francisco drainage, the people concentrated in pueblos of twenty or more rooms, such as the Starkweather and Gallo pueblos, and by the middle of the eleventh century, some groups had pulled out and started their long trek to the west.

Still farther south, in the San Simon Valley, the Mogollon people stood not upon the order of their going, but promptly abandoned their villages and withdrew westward to the Sulphur Spring Valley.

For a time, during the late half of the eleventh century, the assembling of people in large communities resulted in an efflorescence of culture which culminated in the building of the great pueblos in Chaco Canyon and which reached its peak in Pueblo Bonito at about A.D. 1100. Here the people were called upon to meet the brunt of the Navajo attack, and their response was to build bigger, higher, and wider kivas, which have appropriately been called Great Sanctuaries. But their days were numbered, and soon after A.D. 1100 a large number left the canyon and established themselves at Aztec, some sixty miles to the north and nearer to their more powerful Mesa Verde neighbors. Other groups of Chaco people moved down to the Cibola villages south of the Puerco, where, in Nutria Canyon, they built their great kivas, but failed to convince the local people of their efficacy, since the Cibola-Zunis seem to have preferred their kivas square and aboveground. It took more than the Athabascans to teach anyone with Red blood in their veins how to build a kiva. What with the difficulty of defending the exposed fields in Chaco Canyon, the lowering of the water table due to erosion, and the reduction in the population as groups moved down to Cibola or up to Aztec, the great Chaco pueblos appear to have succumbed by about A.D. 1150.

Far to the south, in the Mimbres, the results were the same. The scattered clusters of one-story rooms that made up the Mimbres villages offered no effective resistance to Apache raids, and soon after A.D. 1100, the people and their culture were completely eliminated. There is a suggestion in the decoration on some Casas Grandes polychrome that Mimbres artists may have helped the local potters with their line-work, but aside from this, there is not a trace of Mimbres culture in any section of the Southwest after A.D. 1150.

Seeing what was happening to their Mimbres neighbors, the Cibola people in the upper drainage of the San Francisco did not stop to argue with the Apaches, and abandoned their villages while they were still able to walk. Some of them took the high road north to their compatriots around Zuni, others took the low road to the west through the Salt River drainage, and reached Tonto Basin by about A.D. 1150, to start the Salado Culture on its way—so leaving the entire Upper Gila and Mimbres country in the hands of the Apaches.

IN THE NORTH, by A.D. 1200, the Navajo had cleared most of northwestern New Mexico, from the Jemez Mountains west to the Chuskas, and from the San Juan south to the Zuni Mountains. From their camps in the Chuskas, the western bands raided through Red Rock Valley down to the Canyon de Chelly and over Black Mesa to Marsh Pass, where the Kayenta people sought refuge in their great cliff-dwellings or withdrew southward to the growing communities on Antelope Mesa. The northern Navajo bands started to operate against the eastern settlements of the Mesa Verde people in the Animas and La Plata valleys, as a result of which there was a rapid evacuation of this densely populated but exposed area. Most of the people moved down into the upper Rio Grande Valley to found the Tanoan pueblos, some down to Aztec, others westward to the refuge area on Mesa Verde.

By A.D. 1250, southwestern Colorado east of Mesa Verde had been cleared. Aztec fell soon after A.D. 1250, and the Navajo were ready to attack Mesa Verde itself. This was the most difficult operation the Navajo had undertaken and it probably cost them heavily. Not only was there a considerably larger population, but the Mesa Verde people had built their cliff-dwellings in inaccessible locations in the walls of canyons where surprise attacks were hard to launch and the surface of the mesa was rough and broken. But while it is probably true that the cliff-dwellings were impregnable against attack by an enemy equipped only with spears and bows and arrows, the end was inevitable. On the one hand were virile, aggressive nomads, practicing hit-and-run warfare, with no fixed establishments that could be destroyed. On the other, were a Pueblo people tied down by the necessity of protecting their families, homes, and possessions, but frequently compelled to leave the protection of their pueblos and cliff-dwellings to draw water, to obtain meat, and to sow, tend, and harvest their crops.

Under the strain of unceasing pressure and daily threat of attack, one group after another pulled out and sought safety to the west, in southeastern Utah, where they built watchtowers and fortresses with blank walls that could only be scaled with ladders, and to which archaeologists have given such suggestive names as Cut-Throat Castle. Each group which left Mesa Verde, however, made it more difficult for the remainder to defend themselves, and the end came soon after A.D. 1280. A few of the fortresses to the west may have lasted for a few years longer, but they were picked off, one by one, and it is very doubtful if there was a Mesa Verde man, woman, or child left alive at A.D. 1300, north of the San Juan.

In Marsh Pass the results were exactly the same. The exodus which had begun in the early and middle 1200's was over, and it would have been increasingly dangerous to travel the seventy-five miles from Marsh Pass to Antelope Mesa after A.D. 1250. The die-hards who chose to ride out the storm in Tsegi Canyon huddled together in Betatakin and Kiet Siel—the two largest cliff-dwellings in the Southwest, each over one hundred rooms—and saw their friends and relatives gradually killed off until the last bow was drawn in Kiet Siel in about A.D. 1290.

At A.D. 1300 on the Plateau, the settings of the modern stage were in place. All of the Pueblo people west of the Chuskas had assembled in the Hopi towns, on the southern edge of Black Mesa, in the great pueblos on Antelope Mesa, across the Polacca Wash, or in the Homolobi, Chevelon, and Four Mile pueblos along the southern border of the Colorado Plateau. Some groups, in their determination to put as much distance as possible between themselves and the Navajo, had already led the way southward over the Rim in the late 1200's, and had wound up in the Verde Valley or in Tonto Basin among the Salado compounds.

East of the Little Colorado and north of the Upper Gila, everyone had gathered together in the Zuni villages by A.D. 1300, and with the devil of the Navajo to the north and the deep blue sea of the Apache to the south, a good many of them had headed east, taking their glaze-painted pottery with them, and founded the Keresan pueblos in the upper Rio Grande Valley.

BELOW THE RIM, during the thirteenth century, the Salado people in Tonto Basin were given a short breathing spell back of the protection afforded by the White Mountain pueblos at Kinishba and Point of Pines, and the people who had holed up in the cliff-dwellings of the Sierra Ancha. Then, at about A.D. 1250, Kayenta-Hopi refugees began to stream down from the north, bringing bloodcurdling tales of Navajo atrocities. These, added to what they already knew about the Apache, were enough to accelerate the Salado movement into the Gila Basin and to send other groups down to the Middle Gila, some to the San Pedro Valley, and some all the way down into Chihuahua.

Soon after A.D. 1300 the eastern frontier began to crack. By A.D. 1350, the Sierra Ancha cliff-dwellings had caved in. Kinishba had probably fallen, although some of the garrison at Point of Pines may still have held out for a few years.

The Salado compounds along the Middle Gila had been overrun. The compound pueblos and cliff-dwellings in Tonto Basin had been abandoned or destroyed by A.D. 1375, if not before; and by A.D. 1400, Gila Pueblo, Casa Grande, and all other Salado strongholds in the Gila Basin had fallen to the Apaches.

As one Salado group after another was destroyed or dispersed, the survivors, if any, found or fought their way down to the Salado-Sobaipuri villages in the San Pedro Valley, the heterogeneous settlements south of Animas in the extreme southwestern corner of New Mexico, or the Casas Grandes in northwestern Chihuahua. The Animas settlements were probably eliminated soon after A.D. 1400 if not earlier; the Casas Grandes people were almost certainly annihilated by A.D. 1450; but for reasons for which it is difficult to advance a satisfactory explanation, the Salado-Sobaipuri fought off their enemies and were still successfully holding their own when Father Kino visited the San Pedro Valley in A.D. 1692.

WHEN ONE LOOKS over the entire Southwest at A.D. 1450, one sees the end results of what happened to five different peoples who played their parts on this stage. Since A.D. 1450 there have been no important shifts in their locations, and with the exception of the Athabascans, no significant changes in their cultures. It seems that a balance had been struck.

The Navajo today hold the region which they held in A.D. 1450, and the principal change in their status since that time is that when they found they could no longer profitably prey upon the Pueblos, they turned to the arts of peace and learned to fend for themselves. From their former victims they learned weaving and sandpainting; from the cribbed roofs of the Mesa Verde kivas they learned to build their cribbed hogans; from the Spaniards they acquired horses, sheep, and silversmithing; and from the Post Exchange at Fort Sumner their women obtained the velvet bodices, full skirts, and pointed-toed high-laced shoes which were being worn by Army wives in 1863 when the Navajo were interned at Bosque Redondo, and which are still the fashion on the Navajo Reservation.

Owing to the fact that they had killed off most of the people from whom they might have learned the rudiments of civil society, the Apaches did not do so well. At the time of Father Kino's visit to the Sobaipuri in A.D. 1692, Bolton credits the Apache with being "devoted somewhat to agriculture," but this leaves a good deal to one's imagination. They build a grass-thatched wickiup which bears a striking resemblance to the sort of house which the Reds brought up from Mexico and which is also found among the Caddoan Wichita in Texas, Oklahoma, and Kansas; but whether the Apache brought their wickiups over with them from Asia, picked them up in the western Plains as they came down from Canada, or borrowed the idea from the Reds, I do not know. If it was a Red acquisition, the possibility arises that the Athabascans came down from the north even earlier than I have suggested, but this would not be very surprising.

For the Pueblos there is little more to be said. The tale of what these people made and did has been told, and it only remains to ask oneself if this record has any significance over and above the tedious descriptions of pottery and house types which have made up so much of the evidence. To answer this question, one would first have to try to decide what sort of people we have been dealing with, and this is not as easy as it seems.

With the five Pueblo stages of the Pecos Classification in mind, I think that most of us would probably start with the generality that the local social organization was "Puebloan," but as La Rochefoucauld once said: "All generalizations are dangerous, even this one," and in this case most of us would almost certainly be wrong.

Judging by the long rows of contiguous rooms and what appear to have been kivas in their early villages, it looks as if the Farmers may have known some kind of communal life before they reached the Southwest, and it might therefore be said that they brought a sort of Puebloan social organization with them when they settled down in southwestern Colorado. But while this may have been true of the Farmers up to about A.D. 900, it could hardly be said that there was anything to suggest what has come to be known as a pueblo in the pit-houses of the eighth century in the Chaco, Puerco, Flagstaff, San Francisco, and Mimbres areas; in the one and two-room houses of the ninth century at the Grand Canyon, and along the Mogollon Rim; or in the one-family unit houses of the tenth century in the Red Mesa Valley and on Mesa Verde. Aside from the customs and conventions which always act as a restraining influence wherever two or more are gathered together, these pit-houses, one-room houses, and unit-types point to a way of life in which each family exercised its own initiative. Not only was there nothing Puebloan about these one-family houses, it is even more significant that after several hundred years of communal life, the Farmers north of the San Juan appear to have suddenly and completely changed their habits during the 900's, when they broke apart into small one-family units of about the same size as those in all other sections of the Southwest. As a result, I think it very doubtful if at A.D. 1000 it would have been possible to find a house anywhere in the Southwest of more than one story, or one which was large enough to hold more than one family.

From this one is justified in supposing that up to about A.D. 1000, the peoples on the Plateau who later were reshuffled into the modern Pueblo tribes were free to decide when, where, and how their houses should be built; how much and what kind of pottery and other things to make; and when and if to pull up stakes and move somewhere else. There is nothing to indicate, at this or any later time, that some individuals were granted favors not shared by all others, and there is no evidence that power, position, or wealth was inherited.

By A.D. 1000, it is apparent that something was taking place which brought about a marked change in this free and easy way of life. Beginning with the people of the Chaco Branch during the ninth century, the single family units which had been scattered through the Red Mesa Valley and along the eastern foothills of the Chuskas were gradually abandoned. At the same, and also for the first time, people assembled in Chaco Canyon in large numbers, building small pueblos of twenty to thirty rooms with three to five kivas, which suggest that families were gathering together into clans. By the end of the eleventh century, the tendency to congregate in large and still larger pueblos led to the building of great structures, such as Pueblo Bonito, Chetro Ketl, and Pueblo del Arroyo, with as many as five hundred rooms and the added protection of defense walls which theretofore had been unknown anywhere in the Southwest.

On Mesa Verde, during the eleventh century, the trend was in the same direction, taking the form of larger and combined unit-types, and it was also during the 1000's that the people on Mesa Verde began building their first cliff-dwellings.

To the south and west, the same conditions prevailed. From scattered groups of pit-houses and surface houses containing only one or two rooms, the people of the Kayenta Branch were beginning to assemble in small pueblos and cliff-dwellings. Ladder House and Turkey House in Tsegi Canyon, the White House and Antelope House in the Canyon de Chelly, the Tusayan Ruin on the south rim of the Grand Canyon, Wupatki and Medicine Fort in the Flagstaff district, all have yielded beams which show that they were under construction in the 1000's.

During the four centuries from A.D. 1000 to 1400 on the Plateau, the trend was steadily toward larger concentrations, until at 1400 all of the Pueblo people had assembled in the three centers where they are to be found today—the Hopi towns, the Zuni villages, and the Rio Grande pueblos. As of today, each of these pueblos is ruled by a governor, a war chief, and a council, who, in most cases, are elected annually, and it may be that some such form of political organization originated in the eleventh and twelfth centuries when clans first began to combine into pueblos and each clan was represented on the council.

Summing up the archaeological evidence as it has been presented and interpreted in this book, I think it can safely be said that the peoples of the Plateau cultures were industrious, peaceable, and self-sufficing. They showed no disposition to expand, to subjugate other people, or to submit to the domination of any individual, clique, or dynasty. They were agriculturalists of unusual ability, and by developing deep-rooted drought-resistant varieties of corn they succeeded in maintaining themselves in an environment which by our standards was extremely unfavorable for farming. It seems possible, if not probable, that it may have been their system of matrilineal descent which, prior to A.D. 1000, exerted a conservative and stabilizing influence on the family as a unit and resulted in what appears to have been a slow and peaceful cultural progression. After A.D. 1000, as the pressure of nomadic enemies increased, it may be that it was again the bond which is implicit in maternal ancestry that resulted in the building of clan-pueblos in which related families sought to protect themselves and each other. From this stage, as the menace grew, it was a natural step for the clans to combine and assemble in great communal pueblos, some of which, such as Oraibi, Acoma, and Pecos, have come through to recent times without much change since the 1300's.

For those who may wish to go more deeply into the details of the social and political life of the Pueblo tribes, there is a large and ever-growing library. For present purposes, however, to help us in deciding what sort of people we have been dealing with, I think that this brief outline should be sufficient.

We have witnessed a changing order. From a beginning two thousand years ago, we have seen scattered bands of foragers slowly acquiring the arts of agriculture, pottery making, housebuilding, weaving, and other crafts. This technological advance was accompanied by the development of a social organization which resulted in a society governed by a council, made up of clan representatives, elected by the people themselves. There were no dynasties, no hereditary power, no privileged castes or cliques, no class distinctions, no slave labor, no great state or religious buildings or monuments.

I emphasize these points because when one looks back over the last thousand years of their history, during which they were fighting off the Navajo and learning how to live in the same world with Europeans, there must have been many occasions when it would have been natural for these people to have turned to a strong man for leadership. At such times, when people are scared, it is easy to cede authority to a dominating personality, but it is not always so easy to persuade a budding dictator to relinquish his control when the emergency has passed. Once this point has been reached, the procedure is much the same; relatives and friends become the nobility, but it is hardly worth while being a noble unless the sovereign provides some palaces to be noble in. Medicine men become priests—only to discover that they need temples and monasteries. Soldiers need barracks and fortresses, but one cannot be a noble, a priest, or a soldier, and at the same time also be a pick-and-shovel-man, so the sovereign sends off his army to defend the empire by raiding the neighbors and bringing home slaves. Up go the palaces, temples, monasteries, and fortresses, and before you realize what has happened, you have something which future historians will describe as a "civilization."

It has happened time and time again. So often, that around the Mediterranean and the Middle Americas it seems to have become a habit, and it comes as a surprise to find that the Pueblos did not follow the customary pattern, but chose to work out their destiny by retaining control of their society through a system of popular representation.

This is just a rough outline of the character of the people with whom we have been dealing, but it is enough to make one wonder if our present attitude toward the study of history may not be somewhat off balance as a result of the emphasis which has been placed on the material remains of a culture rather than on the spiritual or social qualities of the people themselves. This may be due partly to archaeologists who have invariably concentrated their first investigations on the largest and most imposing ruins, but I think it is also partly due to those of our modern historians who can only see the past in terms of the rise and fall of the supermen or ruling cliques that left these great monuments behind them. It all sounds rather discouraging until you ask yourself if you really hope that the next cycle will lift us back to the good old days when the right people could get something for nothing from the wrong people. Or you may wonder who declined—the right people who ordered the great monuments to be built, or the wrong people who, as Morley said in his *Ancient Maya*, "were the actual builders of the great ceremonial centers, the lofty pyramid-temples, the vast colonnades, the palaces, monasteries, ball courts, dance platforms, terraces, and raised stone highways which connected the principal cities." From which it seems that a historian, balancing a theory in his head, and a pyramid builder, balancing a rock on his head, might not regard the rise and fall of empires from the same point of view.

It seems that more problems are being posed than settled, but this is quite as it should be. It is all too easy to forget that this thing which we call civilization began less than ten thousand years ago, and although we have made some progress, it is most earnestly to be hoped that we shall never settle all of our problems. It is the stimulus resulting from unrestrained discussion and disagreement that is one of our most priceless human possessions, and the thing to be feared above all else is complacency. After writing this book, I strongly suspect that I shall not have to complain of complacency in the years that lie ahead.

Bibliography

AMSDEN, C. A.
  1936   *An Analysis of Hohokam Pottery Design.* Medallion Papers XXIII. Gila Pueblo. Globe.
ANTEVS, E. (Sayles)
  1941   *The Cochise Culture.* Medallion Papers XXIX. Gila Pueblo. Globe.
BEALS, R. L. (Brainerd and Smith)
  1945   *Archaeological Studies in Northeast Arizona.* Publications in American Archaeology and Ethnology. Vol. 44. No. 1. University of California. Berkeley.
BOLTON, H. E.
  1936   *Rim of Christendom.* The Macmillan Co., New York.
  1949   *Coronado.* McGraw-Hill Book Co. and the University of New Mexico Press. Albuquerque.
BRADFIELD, W.
  1929   *Cameron Creek Village.* School of American Research. Santa Fe.
BRAINERD, G. W. (Beals & Smith)
  1945   *Archaeological Studies in Northeast Arizona.* Publications in American Archaeology and Ethnology. Vol. 44. No. 1. University of California. Berkeley.
BREW, J. O.
  1946   *Archaeology of Alkali Ridge, Southeastern Utah.* Papers of the Peabody Museum of American Archaeology and Ethnology. Vol. XXI. Harvard University. Cambridge.
BRUES, A. M.
  1946   *The San Simon Branch.* Excavations at Cave Creek and in the San Simon Valley. Skeletal Material. Medallion Papers XXXV. Gila Pueblo. Globe.
CAMPBELL, E. W. & W. H.
  1935   *The Pinto Basin Site.* Southwest Museum Papers. No. 9. Los Angeles.
CAREY, H. A.
  1931   *An Analysis of the Northwestern Chihuahua Culture.* American Anthropologist. N. S. Vol. 33. Menasha.

CARTER, G. F.
>1945   *Plant Geography and Culture History in the American Southwest.* Publications in Anthropology No. 5. Viking Fund. New York.

COLLINS, G. N.
>1921   *(In) Basket-Maker Caves of Northeastern Arizona.* Papers of the Peabody Museum of American Archaeology and Ethnology. Vol. VIII. No. 2. Harvard University. Cambridge.

>1922   *(In) A Basket Maker Cave in Kane County, Utah.* Indian Notes and Monographs. Museum of the American Indian. New York.

COLTON, H. S.
>1939   *Prehistoric Culture Units and their Relationships in Northern Arizona.* Bulletin 17. Museum of Northern Arizona. Flagstaff.

>1939 a *The Reducing Atmosphere and Oxidizing Atmosphere in Prehistoric Southwestern Ceramics.* American Antiquity. Vol. IV. No. 3.

>1946   *The Sinagua: A summary of the Archaeology of the Region of Flagstaff, Arizona.* Northern Arizona Society of Science and Art. Flagstaff.

COSGROVE, C. B.
>1946   *Caves of the Upper Gila and Hueco Areas.* Papers of the Peabody Museum of American Archaeology and Ethnology. Vol. XXIV. No. 2. Harvard University. Cambridge.

COSGROVE, H. S. & C. B.
>1932   *The Swarts Ruin.* Papers of the Peabody Museum of American Archaeology and Ethnology. Vol. XV. No. 1. Harvard University. Cambridge.

CUMMINGS, B.
>1940   *Kinishba.* Hohokam Museums Association and the University of Arizona. Tucson.

CUSHING, F. H.
>1886   *A Study of Pueblo Pottery as Illustrative of Zuni Culture Growth.* 4th Annual Report. Bureau of American Ethnology. Smithsonian Institution. Washington, D.C.

DIXON, R. B.
>1923   *The Racial History of Man.* Charles Scribner's Sons. New York.

FEWKES, J. W.
>1912   *Casa Grande, Arizona.* 28th Annual Report of the Bureau of American Ethnology. Smithsonian Institution. Washington, D.C.

FULTON, W. S.
>1938   *Archaeological Notes on Texas Canyon, Arizona.* Contributions. Vol. 12. No. 3. Museum of the American Indian. New York.

FULTON, W. S. (Tuthill)
>1940   *An Archaeological Site near Gleeson, Arizona.* Publication No. 1. The Amerind Foundation. Dragoon.

BIBLIOGRAPHY

GETTY, H. T.
1939   *(In) Modified Basket Maker Sites, Ackmen-Lowry Area, South-western Colorado.* Anthropological Series. Vol. XXIII. No. 3. Field Museum of Natural History. Chicago.

GLADWIN, H. S.
1928   *Excavations at Casa Grande.* Southwest Museum Papers No. 2. Los Angeles.

GLADWIN, H. S. (Haury, Sayles & Gladwin)
1937*a*   *Excavations at Snaketown. I. Material Culture.* Medallion Papers XXV. Gila Pueblo. Globe.

GLADWIN, H. S.
1937*b*   *Excavations at Snaketown. I. Comparisons and Theories.* Medallion Papers XXVI. Gila Pueblo. Globe.

1940*a*   *Methods and Instruments for use in Measuring Tree-rings.* Medallion Papers XXVII. Gila Pueblo. Globe.

1940*b*   *Tree-ring Analysis. Methods of Correlation.* Medallion Papers XXVIII. Gila Pueblo. Globe.

1942   *Excavations at Snaketown. III. Revisions.* Medallion Papers XXX. Gila Pueblo. Globe.

1943   *A Review and Analysis of the Flagstaff Culture.* Medallion Papers XXXI. Gila Pueblo. Globe.

1944   *Tree-ring Analysis: Problems of Dating. The Medicine Valley Sites.* Medallion Papers XXXII. Gila Pueblo. Globe.

1945   *The Chaco Branch: Excavations at White Mound and in the Red Mesa Valley.* Medallion Papers XXXIII. Gila Pueblo. Globe.

1946   *Tree-ring Analysis: Problems of Dating. The Tusayan Ruin.* Medallion Papers XXXVI. Gila Pueblo. Globe.

1947   *Tree-ring Analysis: Tree-rings and Droughts.* Medallion Papers XXXVII. Gila Pueblo. Globe.

1948   *Excavations at Snaketown. IV. Reviews and Conclusions.* Medallion Papers XXXVIII. Gila Pueblo. Globe.

GLADWIN, N. (Gladwin, Haury & Sayles)
1937   *Excavations at Snaketown. I. Material Culture.* Medallion Papers XXV. Gila Pueblo. Globe.

GLADWIN, W. & H. S.
1928*a*   *A Method for the Designation of Ruins in the Southwest.* Medallion Papers I. Gila Pueblo. Globe.

1928*b*   *The Use of Potsherds in an Archaeological Survey.* Medallion Papers II. Gila Pueblo. Globe.

1929*a*   *The Red-on-buff Culture of the Gila Basin.* Medallion Papers III. Gila Pueblo. Globe.

1929*b*   *The Red-on-buff Culture of the Papagueria.* Medallion Papers IV. Gila Pueblo. Globe.

366

1930*a*   *The Western Range of the Red-on-buff Culture.* Medallion Papers V. Gila Pueblo. Globe.

1930*b*   *An Archaeological Survey of Verde Valley.* Medallion Papers VI. Gila Pueblo. Globe.

1930*c*   *A Method for the Designation of Southwestern Pottery Types.* Medallion Papers VII. Gila Pueblo. Globe.

1930*d*   *Some Southwestern Pottery Types. Series I.* Medallion Papers VIII. Gila Pueblo. Globe.

1931   *Some Southwestern Pottery Types. Series II.* Medallion Papers X. Gila Pueblo. Globe.

1933   *Some Southwestern Pottery Types. Series III.* Medallion Papers XIII. Gila Pueblo. Globe.

1934   *A Method for the Designation of Cultures and their Variations.* Medallion Papers XV. Gila Pueblo. Globe.

1935   *The Eastern Range of the Red-on-buff Culture.* Medallion Papers XVI. Gila Pueblo. Globe.

GUERNSEY, S. J. (Kidder)

1919   *Archaeological Explorations in Northeastern Arizona.* Bulletin 65. Bureau of American Ethnology. Smithsonian Institution. Washington, D.C.

1921   *Basket-Maker Caves of Northeastern Arizona.* Papers of the Peabody Museum of American Archaeology and Ethnology. Vol. VIII. No. 2. Harvard University. Cambridge.

1922   *(In) A Basket Maker Cave in Kane County, Utah.* Indian Notes and Monographs. Museum of the American Indian. New York.

GUERNSEY, S. J.

1931   *Explorations in Northeastern Arizona.* Papers of the Peabody Museum of American Archaeology and Ethnology. Vol. XII. No. 1. Harvard University. Cambridge.

HARRINGTON, M. R.

1933   *Gypsum Cave, Nevada.* Southwest Museum Papers. No. 8. Los Angeles.

HAURY, E. W.

1931   *Kivas of the Tusayan Ruin: Grand Canyon Arizona.* Medallion Papers IX. Gila Pueblo. Globe.

1932   *Roosevelt: 9: 6. A Hohokam Site of the Colonial Period.* Medallion Papers XI. Gila Pueblo. Globe.

1934   *The Canyon Creek Ruin and the Cliff Dwellings of the Sierra Ancha.* Medallion Papers XIV. Gila Pueblo. Globe.

1936*a*   *Some Southwestern Pottery Types. Series IV.* Medallion Papers XIX. Gila Pueblo. Globe.

1936*b*   *The Mogollon Culture of Southwestern New Mexico.* Medallion Papers XX. Gila Pueblo. Globe.

HAURY, E. W. (Gladwin, Sayles & Gladwin)

1937   *Excavations at Snaketown I. Material Culture.* Medallion Papers XXV. Gila Pueblo. Globe.

HAURY, E. W.

1940*b*   *Excavations in the Forestdale Valley, East-Central Arizona.* Social Science Bulletin No. 12. University of Arizona. Tucson.

1945   *The Excavations of Los Muertos and the Neighboring Ruins in Salt River Valley.* Papers of the Peabody Museum of American Archaeology and Ethnology. Vol. XXIV. No. 1. Harvard University. Cambridge.

HAURY, E. W. (Sayles)

1947   *An Early Pit House Village of the Mogollon Culture.* Social Science Bulletin No. 16. University of Arizona. Tucson.

HAWLEY, F. M.

1934   *The Significance of the Dated Pre-History of Chetro Ketl.* Bulletin: University of New Mexico. Albuquerque.

HOOTON, E. A.

1930   *The Indians of Pecos Pueblo.* Papers of the Phillips Academy Southwestern Expedition. New Haven.

1933   *Notes on Five Texas Crania.* Bulletin: Texas Archaeological and Paleontological Society. Vol. 5. Abilene.

1941   *(In) The Cochise Culture.* Medallion Papers XXIX. Gila Pueblo. Globe.

HOUGH, W.

1907   *Antiquities of the Upper Gila and Salt River Valleys in Arizona and New Mexico.* Bulletin 35. Bureau of American Ethnology. Smithsonian Institution. Washington, D.C.

1919   *Exploration of a Pit House Village at Luna, New Mexico.* Proceedings, U. S. National Museum, Vol. 55. Washington, D.C.

JOCHELSON, W.

1908   *The Koryak. Jesup North Pacific Expedition.* Vol. VI. American Museum of Natural History. New York.

JUDD, N. M.

1924   *Two Chaco Canyon Pit Houses. Archaeological Investigations at Pueblo Bonito.* Smithsonian Report for 1922. Smithsonian Institution. Washington, D.C.

KIDDER, A. V. (Guernsey)

1919   *Archaeological Explorations in Northeastern Arizona.* Bulletin 65. Bureau of American Ethnology. Smithsonian Institution. Washington, D.C.

1921   *Basket-Maker Caves of Northeastern Arizona.* Papers of the Peabody Museum of American Archaeology and Ethnology. Vol. VIII. No. 2. Harvard University. Cambridge.

1922   *(In) A Basket Maker Cave in Kane County, Utah.* Indian Notes and Monographs. Museum of The American Indian. New York.

KIDDER, A. V.

1924   *An Introduction to the Study of Southwestern Archaeology.* Papers of the Phillips Academy. Southwestern Expedition. New Haven.

1936   *The Pottery of Pecos.* Vol. II. Papers of the Phillips Academy Southwestern Expedition. New Haven.

KLUCKHOHN, C. (Reiter et al)

1939   *Preliminary report on the 1937 Excavations BC 50-51, Chaco Canyon, New Mexico.* Anthropological Series. Bulletin: 345. University of New Mexico. Albuquerque.

KLUCKHOHN, C. (Leighton)

1946   *The Navaho.* Harvard University Press. Cambridge.

KROEBER, A. L.

1916   *Zuni Potsherds.* Anthropological Papers. Vol. XVIII. Pt. 1. American Museum of Natural History. New York.

1923   *Anthropology.* Harcourt Brace & Co. New York.

LANCASTER, J. A. (Watson)

1943   *Excavation of Mesa Verde pit houses.* American Antiquity. Vol. 9. No. 2.

LEIGHTON, D. (Kluckhohn)

1946   *The Navaho.* Harvard University Press. Cambridge.

LEIGHTON, M. M.

1936   *Geological Aspects of the Findings of Primitive Man, near Abilene, Texas.* Medallion Papers XXIV. Gila Pueblo. Globe.

MANGELSDORF, P. C. (Smith)

1949   *New Archaeological Evidence on Evolution in Maize.* Botanical Museum Leaflets. Vol. 13. No. 8. Harvard University. Cambridge.

MARTIN, G. C.

1929   *Notes on some Coast Campsites and other remains.* Bulletin: Texas Archaeological and Paleontological Society. Vol. 1. Abilene.

MARTIN, P. S. (Rinaldo)

1939   *Modified Basket Maker Sites, Ackmen-Lowry Area, Southwestern Colorado.* Anthropological Series. Vol. 23. No. 3. Field Museum of Natural History. Chicago.

1940   *The S. U. Site; Excavations at a Mogollon Village, Western New Mexico.* Anthropological Series. Vol. 32. No. 1. Field Museum of Natural History. Chicago.

MARTIN, P. S.

1943   *The S. U. Site; Excavations at a Mogollon Village, Western New Mexico.* Anthropological Series. Vol. 32. No. 2. Field Museum of Natural History. Chicago.

MARTIN, P. S. (Rinaldo)

1947 *The S. U. Site; Excavations at a Mogollon Village, Western New Mexico.* Anthropological Series. Vol. 32. No. 3. Field Museum of Natural History. Chicago.

MARTIN, P. S. (Antevs & Rinaldo)

1949 *Cochise and Mogollon Sites.* Fieldiana: Anthropology. Vol. 38. No. 1. Chicago Natural History Museum.

MERA, N. P.

1934 *Observations on the Archaeology of the Petrified Forest National Monument.* Technical Series. Bulletin No. 7. Laboratory of Anthropology. Santa Fe.

MINDELEFF, C.

1896 *Casa Grande Ruin.* 13th Annual Report of the Bureau of American Ethnology. Smithsonian Institution. Washington, D.C.

1897 *The Repair of Casa Grande Ruin.* 15th Annual Report of the Bureau of Ethnology. Smithsonian Institution. Washington, D.C.

MORRIS, E. H.

1919 *Preliminary Account of the Antiquities of the Region between the Mancos and La Plata Rivers in southwestern Colorado.* 33rd Annual Report. Bureau of American Ethnology. Smithsonian Institution. Washington, D.C.

1921 *The House of the Great Kiva at the Aztec Ruin.* Anthropological Papers. Vol. 26. Pt. 2. American Museum of Natural History. New York.

1927 *The Beginnings of pottery making in the San Juan.* Anthropological Papers. Vol. 28. Pt. 2. American Museum of Natural History. New York.

1938 *The Aztec Ruin.* Anthropological Papers. Vol. XXVI. American Museum of Natural History. New York.

1936 *Archaeological Background of Dates in Early Arizona Chronology.* Tree-Ring Bulletin. Vol. 2. No. 4.

1939 *Archaeological Studies in the La Plata District.* Publication No. 519. Carnegie Institution of Washington, Washington, D.C.

1949 *Basketmaker II Dwellings near Durango, Colorado.* Tree-Ring Bulletin. Vol. 15. No. 4. Tucson.

MORRIS, E. H. (Burgh, R. F.)

1954 *Basketmaker II Sites near Durango, Colorado.* Publication 604. Carnegie Institution of Washington, D.C.

MORSS, N.

1931 *Notes on the Archaeology of the Kaibito and Rainbow Plateaus in Arizona.* Papers of the Peabody Museum of American Archaeology and Ethnology. Vol. XII. No. 2. Harvard University. Cambridge.

NESBITT, P. H.
  1938   *Starkweather Ruin*. Publications in Anthropology. Bulletin No. 6.
          Logan Museum. Beloit.

NUSBAUM, J. L.
  1922   *A Basket Maker Cave in Kane County, Utah*. Indian Notes and
          Monographs. Museum of the American Indian. New York.

OETTEKING, B.
  1930   *Skeletal Remains from Texas*. Indian Notes. Vol. 7. No. 3. Museum
          of the American Indian. New York.

PRUDDEN, J. M.
  1897   *An Elder Brother to the Cliff-Dweller*. Harpers Monthly Magazine.
          June, 1897.

RINALDO, J. B. (Martin)
  1939   *Modified Basket Maker Sites, Ackmen-Lowry Area, Southwestern
          Colorado*. Anthropological Series. Vol. 23. No. 3. Field Museum of
          Natural History. Chicago.
  1940   *The S. U. Site; Excavations at a Mogollon Village, Western New
          Mexico*. Anthropological Series. Vol. 32. No. 1. Field Museum of
          Natural History. Chicago.
  1947   *The S. U. Site; Excavations at a Mogollon Village, Western New
          Mexico*. Anthropological Series. Vol. 32. No. 3. Field Museum of
          Natural History. Chicago.

ROBERTS, F. H. H., Jr.
  1929a   *Recent Archaeological Developments in the vicinity of El Paso, Texas*.
          Smithsonian Miscellaneous Collections. Vol. 81. No. 7. Smithsonian
          Institution. Washington, D.C.
  1929b   *Shabik'eshchee Village*. Bulletin 92. Bureau of American Ethnology.
          Smithsonian Institution. Washington, D.C.
  1930   *Early Pueblo Ruins in the Piedra District, Southwestern Colorado*.
          Bulletin 96. Bureau of American Ethnology. Smithsonian Institution.
          Washington, D.C.
  1931   *The Ruins of Kiatuthlanna, Eastern Arizona*. Bulletin 100. Bureau of
          American Ethnology. Smithsonian Institution. Washington, D.C.
  1932   *The Village of the Great Kivas on the Zuni Reservation, New Mexico*.
          Bulletin 111. Bureau of American Ethnology. Smithsonian Institution.
          Washington, D.C.
  1939   *Archaeological Remains in the Whitewater District, Eastern Arizona.
          Part I*. Bulletin 121. Bureau of American Ethnology. Smithsonian In-
          stitution. Washington, D.C.
  1940a   *Developments in the Problem of the North American Paleo-Indian*.
          Smithsonian Miscellaneous Collections. Vol. 100. Smithsonian Institu-
          tion. Washington, D.C.

1940*b*   *Archaeological Remains in the Whitewater District, Eastern Arizona. Part II.* Bulletin 126. Bureau of American Ethnology. Smithsonian Institution. Washington, D.C.

ROGERS, D. B.

1929   *Prehistoric Man of the Santa Barbara Coast.* Santa Barbara Museum of Natural History. Santa Barbara.

ROGERS, M. J.

1939   *Early Lithic Industries of the Lower Basin of the Colorado River and Adjacent Areas.* San Diego Museum Papers. No. 3. San Diego.

1945   *An Outline of Yuman Prehistory.* Southwestern Journal of Anthropology. Vol. 1. Albuquerque.

RUSSELL, F.

1908   *The Pima Indians.* 26th Annual Report of the Bureau of American Ethnology. Smithsonian Institution. Washington, D.C.

SAUER, C.

1936   *American Agricultural Origins.* (In) Essays in Anthropology. University of California Press. Berkeley.

SAYLES, E. B.

1935   *An Archaeological Survey of Texas.* Medallion Papers XVII. Gila Pueblo. Globe.

1936*a*   *Some Southwestern Pottery Types.* Series V. Medallion Papers XXI. Gila Pueblo. Globe.

1936*b*   *An Archaeological Survey of Chihuahua, Mexico.* Medallion Papers XXII. Gila Pueblo. Globe.

SAYLES, E. B. (Gladwin, Haury & Gladwin)

1937   *Excavations at Snaketown I. Material Culture.* Medallion Papers XXV. Gila Pueblo. Globe.

SAYLES, E. B. (Antevs)

1941   *The Cochise Culture.* Medallion Papers XXIX. Gila Pueblo. Globe.

SAYLES, E. B.

1945   *The San Simon Branch. Excavations at Cave Creek and in the San Simon Valley. Material Culture.* Medallion Papers XXXIV. Gila Pueblo. Globe.

SAYLES, E. B. (Haury)

1947   *An Early Pit House Village of the Mogollon Culture.* Social Science Bulletin No. 16. University of Arizona. Tucson.

SCHULMAN, E.

1949*b*   *An Extension of the Durango Chronology.* Tree-Ring Bulletin. Vol. 16. No. 2. Tucson.

SELTZER, C. C.

1944   *Racial prehistory in the Southwest and the Hawikuh Zunis.* Papers of the Peabody Museum of American Archaeology and Ethnology. Vol. 23. No. 1. Harvard University. Cambridge.

SHEPARD, A. O. (Kidder)

1936   *The Pottery of Pecos. Vol. II.* Papers of the Phillips Academy Southwestern Expedition. New Haven.

SHEPARD, A. O.

1939   *(In) Archaeological Studies in the La Plata District.* Publication No. 519. Carnegie Institution of Washington. Washington, D.C.

SMITH, W. (Beals & Brainerd)

1945   *Archaeological Studies in Northeast Arizona.* Publications in American Archaeology and Ethnology. Vol. 44. No. 1. University of California. Berkeley.

SPIER, L.

1917   *An Outline for a Chronology of Zuni Ruins.* Anthropological Papers. Vol. XVIII. Pt. III. American Museum of Natural History. New York.

STALLINGS, W. S., JR.

1937   *Southwestern Dated Ruins. I.* Tree-Ring Bulletin. Vol. 4. No. 2.

1941   *A Basketmaker II Date from Cave du Pont, Utah.* Tree-Ring Bulletin. Vol. 8. No. 1. Tucson.

TUTHILL, C. (Fulton)

1940   *An Archaeological Site near Gleeson, Arizona.* Publication No. 1. The Amerind Foundation. Dragoon.

VAILLANT, G. C.

1932   *Some Resemblances in the Ceramics of Central and North America.* Medallion Papers XII. Gila Pueblo. Globe.

WATSON, D. W. (Lancaster)

1943   *Excavation of Mesa Verde pit houses.* American Antiquity. Vol. 9. No. 2.

WILLOUGHBY, C. C.

1935   *Antiquities of the New England Indians.* Peabody Museum of American Archaeology and Ethnology. Harvard University. Cambridge.

WINSHIP, G. P.

1896   *The Coronado Expedition. 1540-1542.* 14th Annual Report of the Bureau of Ethnology. Smithsonian Institution. Washington, D.C.

WOODBURY, G.

1936   *(In) The Mogollon Culture of Southwestern New Mexico.* Medallion Papers XX. Gila Pueblo. Globe.

WOODBURY, G. & E.

1935   *Pre-Historic Skeletal Remains from the Texas Coast.* Medallion Papers XVIII. Gila Pueblo. Globe.